Michael Langford

35mm
HANDBOOK

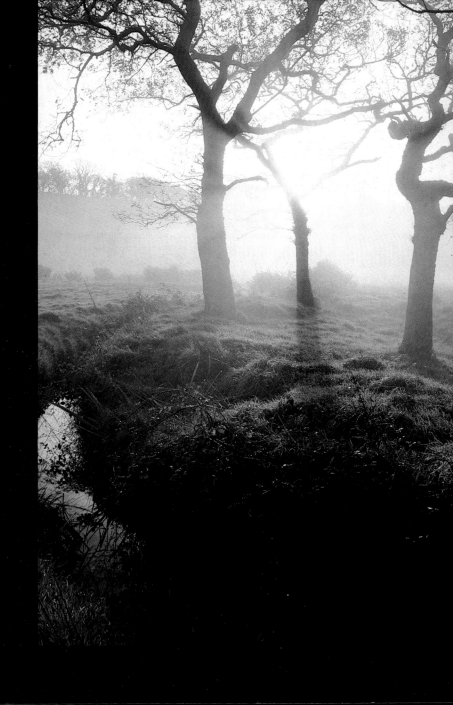

Michael Langford's
35mm
HANDBOOK

Alfred A. Knopf, New York, 2002

Contents

Michael Langford's 35mm Handbook was
conceived, edited, and designed by
Dorling Kindersley Limited,
9 Henrietta Street, London WC2E 8PS

Project editor Jonathan Hilton
Art editor Neville.Graham
Editor Judith More
Designer Nick Harris
Managing editor Alan Buckingham
Art director Stuart Jackman

Third Edition
Published June 1, 1993
Reprinted Five Times
Seventh Printing, December 2002

Project editor Jonathan Hilton
Art editor Phil Kay

This is a Borzoi Book
Published by Alfred A. Knopf, Inc.

Library of Congress Cataloging in
Publication Data

Langford, Michael John, 1933-
  Michael Langford's 35mm handbook
  - 3rd ed.

  Includes index
  1. 35mm cameras - Handbooks, manuals,
  etc. 2. Photography-Handbooks, manuals,
  etc. I. Title. II. Title: Thirty five mm handbook.

  TR262.L377 1993 771.3'2 - dc20 92-54920

ISBN 0-679-74634-X

Filmsetting by
Chambers Wallace Limited, London
Reproduction by
F. E. Burman Limited, London
Printed and bound in Spain by
Artes Gráficas Toledo S.A.U.
D.L. TO: 1139 - 2002

TACKLING SPECIAL PROJECTS

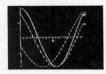

FLASH

ACCESSORIES

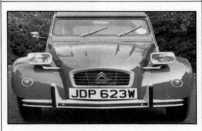

SPECIAL EFFECTS

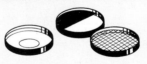

REFERENCE CHARTS

Introduction

This book is a concise, practical guide for anyone with a 35 mm single lens reflex or compact camera, or thinking of buying one. The contents concentrate on advice and tips to improve your camera expertise, expand your range of picture taking, and help you obtain greater enjoyment from this fascinating subject. Use this book as a "pocket wisdom" – broader and less biased than an instruction manual, a source of teaching and reference, but most of all as a collection of commonsense ideas that you can pick out easily and quickly.

Cameras are under-utilized

One of the problems with photography is that people simply do not use their cameras enough. Modern equipment allows results under such wide-ranging conditions, it deserves much greater use. No one would agree that owning a car and driving it only three or four times a year is getting good use from it. Yet this is the average number of times most family cameras are utilized. The less you use something the less sure you become about its controls and possibilities, and so it becomes more effort. The opposite is also true – experience makes you less preoccupied with the mechanics of the camera, and more able to look through it and relate to the scene and the final picture.

Give yourself the chance to experiment with the full range of controls offered by your camera. For example, slow shutter speeds and time exposures are a way of introducing movement and abstraction

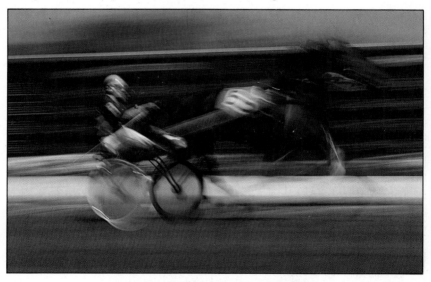

Interpretative approach The type of picture above can be taken with a quite basic camera, provided it will give a shutter speed of 1/30 or longer. Streaks and blurs, caused by moving the camera to follow the action while shooting, add greatly to the atmosphere.

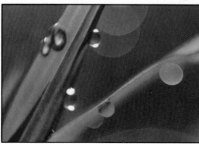

Close-ups Larger-than-life images and restricted focus (left) are possible with a simple close-up lens.

Night conditions Modern equipment allows you to photograph whatever the eye can see, as in this time exposure shot (facing page).

6

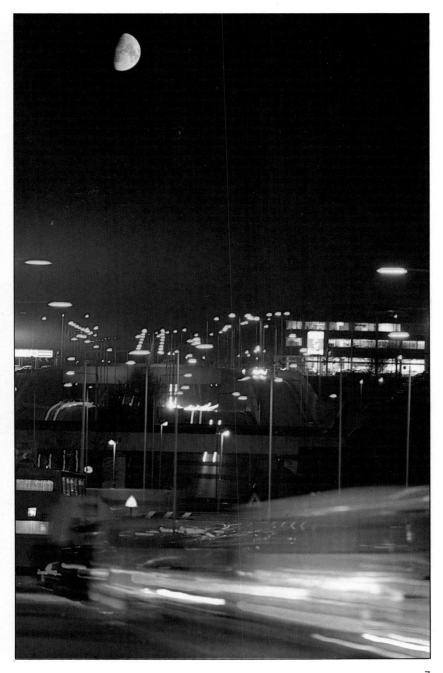

into photographs. A macro facility lens or extension tube opens up an entire world of close-up subject matter.

The quality of light
One of the great plus factors in taking photographs is that you notice and enjoy more the visual effects of light. Light becomes more than just something to see by – it noticeably transforms textures, colors, depth, and the emphasis of one thing over another. These are things you must consider closely if you are aiming for exceptional photographs. Sometimes it will mean revisiting a spot at different times of the day or under different weather conditions. Sometimes you can add or substitute lighting of your own. These are all personal choices, subject to the way the scene looks to you at the time. Many of the subject and picture problem topics in this book show

examples where lighting has made all the difference to the final result.

In time, your growing awareness of lighting – its direction, quality, and contrast – not only improves your photography but also seems to enrich ordinary, everyday observation. It is possible to obtain great enjoyment from the diverse moods of light simply for its own sake.

Picture composition
Some people cannot be bothered about composition. After all, it sounds complicated, and seems to be concerned with rules that have more to do with painting than photography. And yet basically you compose each and every time you look through the camera and aim it to include some elements and leave out others.

Composition as such is not mentioned often in this book. But it shows in practical

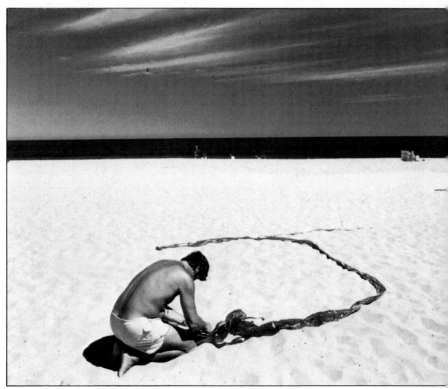

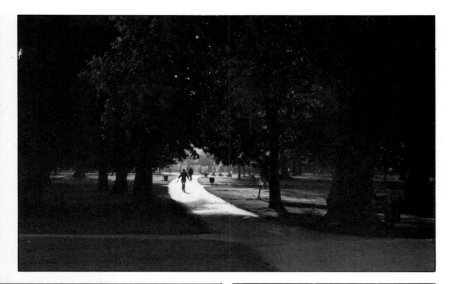

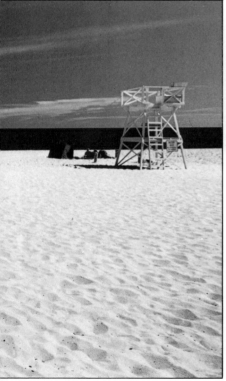

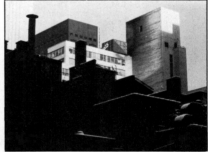

Beach scene Harsh lighting and an extremely clear atmosphere give the picture on the left strong graphic qualities. The effect is one of openness and space. Every item here counts, contributing to a balanced composition. The blue sky was darkened with a polarizing filter to help emphasize the clouds. Their long shapes compliment the sweep of sand, picked out by side-lighting.

Low-key effects The picture, top, uses large areas of shadow to help give brilliance to the sunlit path. Backlighting throws figures and other objects into silhouette. For this effect measure exposure from the lightest areas only.

Urban landscape Low evening light and cast shadows reduce the roofs and buildings (above) to simplified shapes.

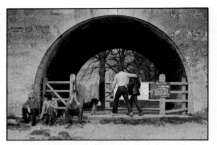

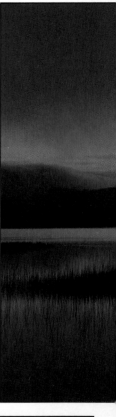

Enclosing structure Sometimes you can structure a picture by picking a strong simple shape, like the arch on the left. It helps to draw together various interesting but unrelated figures.

Overall pattern In contrast, this telephoto shot (left) succeeds by forming a tapestry of colors, texture, and pattern.

Reflective foregrounds Both landscapes (below and right) make use of a water foreground to reflect colored light. The night shot below shows distant street lights spread out like flares across the sea. The scene on the right was taken just after sunset as sea mist rolled into gloomy valleys. A few moments later color had gone and mist blocked the entire view.

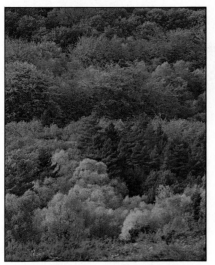

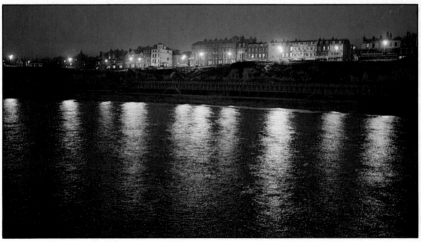

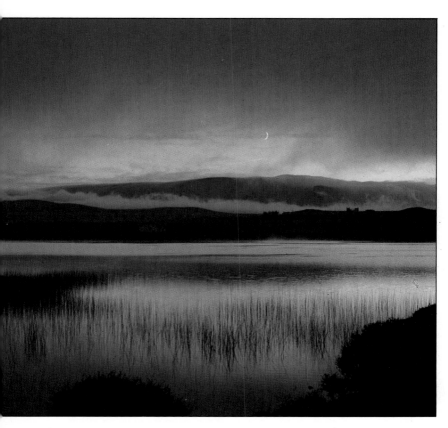

ways how to use foregrounds and backgrounds, avoid distracting elements, emphasize the main feature, and add a sense of drama, movement or humor. In other words, it helps you to show things in the strongest, most interesting way possible. You could call this photographic composition, or just suggestions that give better, more direct images. The point is that they seem to work and can be applied to a wide range of subjects, from portraits to landscapes and natural history to architecture. In fact, structuring of pictures can become one of the most rewarding aspects of photography.

Color or black and white

Most people prefer to shoot in color. Color gives more information and helps to add atmosphere. The orangey glow of indoor light, the blue tint of snow, strident color mixtures or harmonious blends can all be used constructively. Black and white on the other hand can be a welcome change. It has deceptive simplicity and is growing as an advanced area of photography – something you now graduate to as an enthusiast, after mastering color. This book, therefore, pays due regard to black and white, especially considering the recent introduction of instant picture 35 mm films.

The fact remains that over 95 per cent of all films sold are color types. You need to know how to use them with greatest control when a photograph has to be factual and accurate, or at other times how to produce interpretative and atmospheric effects. One of the challenges of photography is to

Family subjects One of the most important subjects for photography is your own family. The shot shown right, with its accent on relationships, is the kind of natural document you must not miss. Pick a simple setting, work close, and be patient.

Extending your range Often, photography combines well with other interests, such as natural history. A shot such as the swan (facing page) is not difficult with a telephoto. It forms a timeless picture that can sell and do well in competitions.

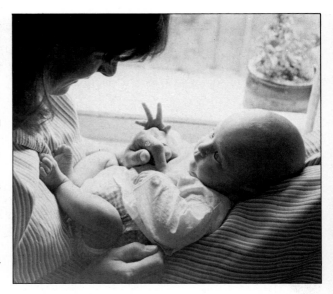

know when to relax accuracy and make good use of false color effects. These can be achieved in many ways and at minimal cost – through the use of mismatched film and light source, or simple lens filter attachments, for example.

Choice of subjects

Surveys have shown that the most popular and generally rated most rewarding subjects for photography are people – especially younger members of the immediate family. The subject section of this book therefore starts with this area before moving on to other topics popular with the vast majority of camera users – travel, sport, animals, still-life, nudes, and natural history, for example. You will find thirteen such subject topics, each giving a breakdown in terms of types of approach, equipment, problems to avoid, and practical tips. Perhaps you see photography mostly as a way of recording your family over the years. But if you have hobbies other than photography, these too can be fruitful subjects for your camera. More specialized areas of photography demand extra special knowledge, and the results might well have commercial value. One hobby can therefore

help offset the cost of the other. You will find advice on selling your photographs in the back reference section. The important thing is to try a wide range of subjects, especially as a beginner. Certainly all the subjects featured here should be within your scope. Leave specialization until later when you find one area most absorbing.

Planning your equipment needs

Photographic equipment itself is a mixed blessing. Cameras and their accessories are such ingenious, attractive items of technology that there is always the temptation to collect them for their own sake. Without going this far, extra items do allow you to extend and, above all, personalize your camera outfit. The SLR in particular is designed to form the nucleus of a system, which includes lenses and attachments, supports, flash gear, and much more. One of the functions of this book is to show and compare these items impartially. You find that some simple accessories such as an extension tube or polarizing filter can have many uses, whereas other complex pieces are strictly for special tasks.

Much the same applies to special effects attachments – devices to tint images

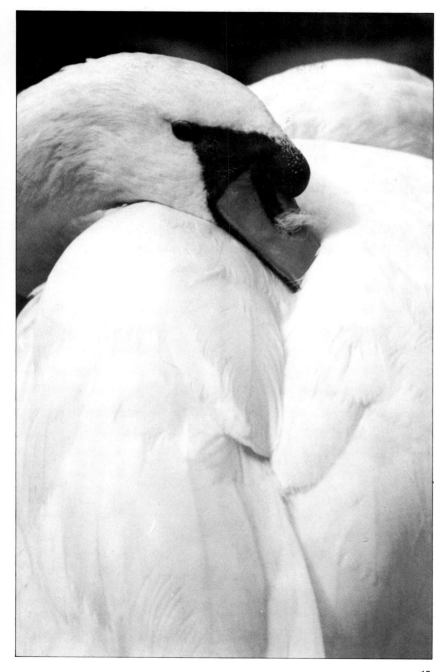

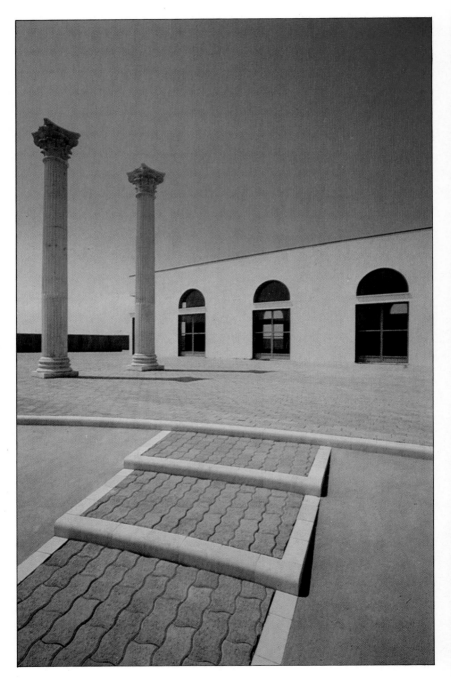

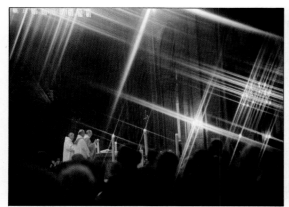

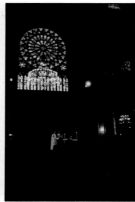

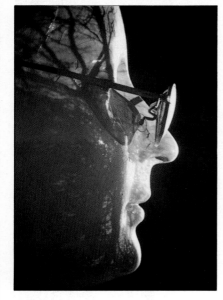

selectively, split, spread, and diffuse them, or create rainbow effects around bright lights. One or two of these are worthwhile, but many are too assertive for more than very occasional use. Most of the special effects in this book are surprisingly simple – it is the ideas behind them that count.

How to use this book

This handbook is intended to offer concentrated practical advice in a compact form. It is divided into eight sections, each identified for quick reference by a color or tint at the page edges. The first section is concerned with the different types of compact and SLR cameras. It looks at what the main types offer and how their features can help your photography. For the beginner this section will teach you all the basics you require. More experienced photographers will find that it brings them up to date on modern camera advances. Make use too of the "Hints and tips" boxes spread throughout the text. They distil extra advice, and can be used as a quick checklist.

Section two takes you over the range of films available for 35 mm cameras. It discusses the points that make one film a better choice than another for particular subject conditions. It also helps you identify faults if your results are not correct.

The next sections are concerned with picture shooting problems. Section three picks out more than twenty common situations that can cause problems – either

Unusual effects The picture facing page is tinted by a pink graduated half-filter covering the lower part of the lens. It works best with pictures like this with a central division. Both pictures at the top of the page were shot using existing light. One version, taken with a starburst filter, has flared the lights into the shadow areas – adding drama and reducing contrast. To produce the macabre profile above, a slide of trees was projected on a man's face in a darkened room. A small lamp gave some additional rim lighting.

15

The importance of viewpoint Of all the factors affecting successful photographs, choice of viewpoint is the most important. This picture uses an unusual viewpoint to frame the birds within the structure of the basket. Lighting also helps to contrast the bird shapes against the angular wickerwork background, so that curves and lines work in together without confusion.

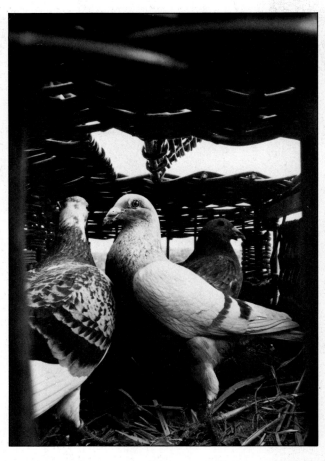

technically or from a picture-structuring point of view. These include shooting at night or against the light, avoiding inaccurate colors, and working in confined spaces to name but a few. Section four solves problems in the context of different subjects – people, places, events, and many more. Use these topics as a quick reminder guide before tackling such subjects.

Sections five and six take your equipment further, into the areas of flash and other accessories such as lenses. Here, equipment is described in practical detail so that you can see what is involved and what the market offers. Special effects, section seven, is a mixture of accessories

and techniques designed to challenge your ability to produce striking pictures and to help to sharpen your technical skills.

The final reference section helps to fill in more detail. Rather than congest the main text with lists of brands and figures, they all appear here.

In all, this is a book to answer questions and encourage you to do more. It should increase the quantity and quality of your pictures so you make fuller use of your equipment and skills. Exploiting a resource such as a camera is not only enjoyable and creative, it accumulates memories, too. These tend to grow more precious with the passing of time.

CAMERAS

This first section of the book introduces the 35 mm camera and its main controls. A look at the features needed in any 35 mm camera leads on to the differences between the compact and the single lens reflex (SLR) – the two most popular camera designs today. You will see how models range from the totally automatic to types that bristle with controls all requiring user attention. Each camera type has its advantages and limitations, and choice is not simply a matter of price.

The first control discussed in detail is the viewfinder. The next, and related, control is lens focusing, from fixed focus to cameras that have the latest electronic focusing aids. This introduces the important consideration of just how much of your picture you want sharp at any one time.

A similar factor applies to your choice of shutter speed, and this, together with lens aperture, determines the amount of exposure to light the film receives. Depending on the type of camera you use, exposure can be either fully automatic or completely manual with several semi-automatic options, too.

Lastly, and bearing in mind that cameras are tools for picture making, there are suggested checks and working methods designed to give you the highest success rate with your photographs.

How cameras work

All cameras have certain basic features. These include the lens, film, and shutter. But it is the viewfinding device that separates 35 mm cameras into two basic easily recognizable types.

The first type has a viewfinder close to, but quite separate from, the taking lens. These cameras are commonly referred to as "compacts". The second type has a mirror that allows you to look through the actual camera lens, up to the moment of shooting. These are known as "single lens reflex" (SLR) cameras.

Camera versatility

Manufacturers design both 35 mm compacts and SLRs in models ranging from those offering an extensive choice of lens and shutter controls, to others with only a few settings, ready for simple "point-and-shoot" photography. In general, the more controls offered the greater the versatility of the camera, but to use this added flexibility you must understand more technical aspects of photography.

Cameras requiring fewest settings are either economy models, which have their controls fixed for "typical" light conditions, or cameras where adjustments are performed by sophisticated circuits, which are capable of a high average success rate under most subject conditions. These fully-automatic cameras usually have a manual override facility for difficult situations.

---

35 MM v OTHER FORMATS

1 In relation to cameras for other picture sizes, the 35 mm format gives the best compromise between image quality and equipment that is versatile and light in weight.
2 In terms of cost per frame, 35 mm film is cheaper than all other formats – either smaller or larger.
3 35 mm film is made in the greatest variety of types. Lengths range from 12-exposure cassettes to bulk film for 750-exposure special film backs.
4 35 mm film is standard for audio-visual shows, and is universally accepted for illustrations in magazines and books.
5 Darkroom work is easy. The widest range of user processing and enlargement equipment is made.

Five basic features
Every camera must have a *lens* to collect and focus the light reflecting back from the subject, and a light-sensitive *film surface* to record it. If the lens-film distance is variable, then you have a choice of focus settings for close or distant subjects. A *viewfinder* is essential as it allows you to aim the camera and shows accurately the limits of your image. The *shutter* controls the precise moment you take the picture – most cameras give a choice of timed settings to help control exposure. Finally, an adjustable lens *aperture* alters image brightness, linking with the shutter to help control exposure.

Lens The lens forms an image – like a magnifying glass projects a tiny picture of a scene on to shaded paper. All images are formed upside down.

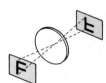

Film 35 mm film is housed within the camera so that it will only receive light through the lens. Film is wound into a light-tight cassette at loading and unloading.

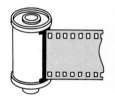

Viewfinder The viewfinder may be a direct optical sight (right), giving a separate view of the scene, or a reflex system using a mirror found in SLR designs.

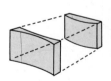

Shutter In a compact, the shutter is a series of blades that pivot open within or near the lens (right). An SLR has a moving, blind-type shutter just in front of the film.

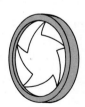

Aperture The lens aperture or diaphragm is set between the glass elements of the lens. Here, it can open or close in order to brighten or dim the whole image evenly.

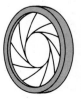

COMPACTS AND SLRs – THE BASIC DIFFERENCES

The diagrams below pick out the basic differences between the two most popular kinds of 35 mm camera design. Single lens reflex cameras offer the most accurate picture composition, and allow you to change lenses. But internally they are more complex and bulky than the average compact. Features such as the lens diaphragm, shutter release, and film wind-on mechanism are omitted here because they are basically the same for both types of design. (See also pp. 20–2 and pp. 23–5.)

Compact layout Compact cameras have a separate optical viewfinder, recognizable by its window on the front of the body near the lens. Your subject appears clear and sharp, even when the camera lens is not focused. The picture is recorded when the shutter fires.

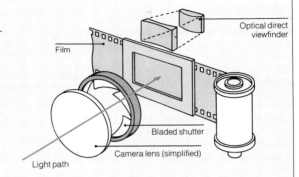

Optical direct viewfinder

Film

Bladed shutter

Camera lens (simplified)

Light path

SLR (viewing) SLR cameras have a mirror between the lens and film. This reflects the image so that it appears the right way up on a translucent focusing screen. You then compose and focus by referring to the screen image seen through an eyepiece behind the camera. The characteristic pentaprism glass block reflects the image and corrects the reversed left-to-right view produced by the reflex mirror.

SLR (shooting) Pressing the release button causes the mirror to lift, allowing the image to reach the back of the camera. The blind shutter then opens and exposes the film. Distances from lens to film and lens to screen (via the mirror) are identical. An image, if sharply focused on the screen, will also be sharp when exposed on the film.

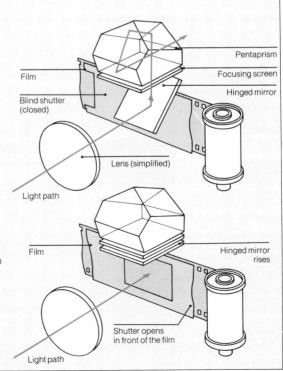

Pentaprism

Focusing screen

Hinged mirror

Film

Blind shutter (closed)

Lens (simplified)

Light path

Film

Hinged mirror rises

Shutter opens in front of the film

Light path

19

Compact cameras

The main feature of this particular camera design is, as the name implies, its inconspicuous size. Yet, despite this, it still takes pictures filling the full 24 x 36 mm size of the 35 mm frame. A compact camera is a complete package, often with everything built in – flash, exposure meter, autofocusing, and motordrive.

Range and scope

Originally, compacts were only very simple cameras, designed basically for beginners. Due to advances in miniaturized circuitry, however, compacts now range from low-cost basic cameras to advanced models offering every type of automation (see p. 22). Compacts are ideal if you want a minimum of controls to adjust and yet expect a high success rate in a wide range of subject conditions. They are excellent for subjects beyond about 4 ft (1.5 m) and in scenes where you want generous sharp detail rather than objects singled out through the use of localized focus, previewed before shooting (see pp. 33–8).

The direct vision viewfinder of the compact is often clearer to use than the viewfinder of an SLR (see pp. 23–5), especially in dim subject lighting. And if you have eyesight problems, many compacts (even low-cost models) offer an autofocus facility. The viewfinder design is also suited to action photography – moving subjects can

Comparative sizes

The cameras on the right are in scale to each other and show the size difference between a typical 35 mm compact and SLR model. The compact also contains built-in flash. Dimensions for the SLR relate to body only – the overall size depends on the lens you choose to fit. This greatly influences the weight of the camera as well. SLR cameras are basically heavier than compacts.

Compact Width 5¼ ins (133 mm); height 2⅝ ins (68 mm); depth 2⅛ ins (56 mm).

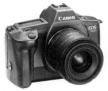

SLR Width 5¾ ins (148 mm); height 4¼ ins (108 mm); depth 2⅝ ins (68 mm).

TYPICAL LOW-COST MODEL

The camera shown on the right incorporates many features found in a modestly priced, beginner's, fixed-focus 35 mm compact. These features include built-in flash and a built-in exposure meter that automatically programs aperture and shutter speed settings. After loading the camera (see pp. 46-7) you must set the film speed on a scale. (Many modern cameras read film speed directly from the cassette in the film compartment, see p. 51.) Setting the film speed alters the sensitivity range of the light sensor. The lens is fixed to focus subjects about 12 ft (3 m) away, but it also gives tolerably sharp results from about 6ft (1.5m) to the horizon ("infinity"). Other cameras offer you a choice of subject distance focus settings. The longest shutter speed available is 1/125 sec. When the meter programs widest lens aperture (at this shutter setting), because of dim light, a signal warns you to switch on the flash. The built-in flash illuminates subjects adequately up to about 13 ft (4 m) from the camera.

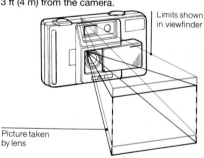

Limits shown in viewfinder

Picture taken by lens

Parallax error The viewfinder shows the scene superimposed with bright corner marks or a complete rectangular frame line. These represent the limits of your picture area when subjects are distant. The viewfinder window, however, is slightly above the camera lens – enough viewpoint difference to create errors with pictures taken of close-up subjects. This viewpoint difference is known as *parallax error*, and gives pic-

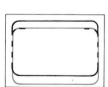

tures with less image at the top and more at the bottom than you composed in the viewfinder. To help correct this, two additional lines on the viewfinder screen (above) show the offset limits when working at the camera's closest focusing setting.

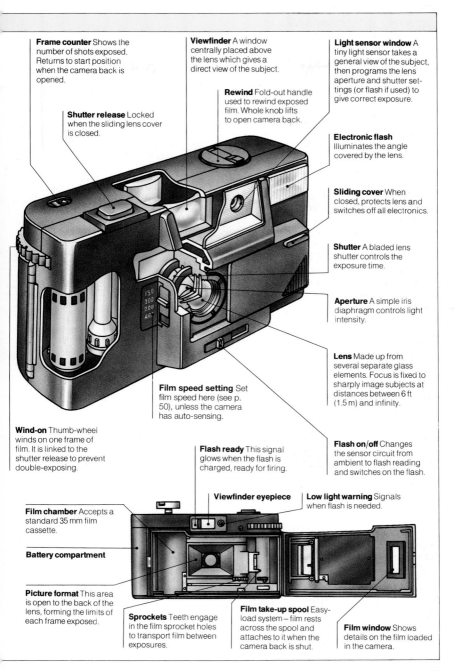

Frame counter Shows the number of shots exposed. Returns to start position when the camera back is opened.

Viewfinder A window centrally placed above the lens which gives a direct view of the subject.

Light sensor window A tiny light sensor takes a general view of the subject, then programs the lens aperture and shutter settings (or flash if used) to give correct exposure.

Rewind Fold-out handle used to rewind exposed film. Whole knob lifts to open camera back.

Shutter release Locked when the sliding lens cover is closed.

Electronic flash Illuminates the angle covered by the lens.

Sliding cover When closed, protects lens and switches off all electronics.

Shutter A bladed lens shutter controls the exposure time.

Aperture A simple iris diaphragm controls light intensity.

Lens Made up from several separate glass elements. Focus is fixed to sharply image subjects at distances between 6 ft (1.5 m) and infinity.

Film speed setting Set film speed here (see p. 50), unless the camera has auto-sensing.

Wind-on Thumb-wheel winds on one frame of film. It is linked to the shutter release to prevent double-exposing.

Flash ready This signal glows when the flash is charged, ready for firing.

Flash on/off Changes the sensor circuit from ambient to flash reading and switches on the flash.

Viewfinder eyepiece

Low light warning Signals when flash is needed.

Film chamber Accepts a standard 35 mm film cassette.

Battery compartment

Picture format This area is open to the back of the lens, forming the limits of each frame exposed.

Sprockets Teeth engage in the film sprocket holes to transport film between exposures.

Film take-up spool Easy-load system – film rests across the spool and attaches to it when the camera back is shut.

Film window Shows details on the film loaded in the camera.

ADVANCED COMPACT

Advanced models offer automatic features and will tackle a wide range of subject lighting and distances. Instead of a wind-on lever, a motor advances the film. The lens automatically adjusts the focus for different subject distances, and you can adjust focal length to alter the amount of subject included in the picture. The lens may also have a macro (close-up) setting.

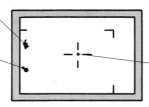

Shutter release Depress halfway to trigger and lock lens autofocusing.Depress fully to take picture.

Autofocusing Two windows compute and set focus for any subject center frame, down to 12 ins (0.3 m) (see p. 32).

Internal electronics Film speed is sensed from cassette. Motor transports film after each exposure, rewinds it after last frame.

Lens Wider aperture and shutter speed range allows photography under many different lighting conditions.

Zoom control Changes focal length, continuously or in steps, to alter apparent subject size from same shooting position.

Red symbol Pulses when flash is needed. Steady when flash is switched on and ready to use.

Green symbol Steady when the subject is within autofocus range and sharp, flashes when it is too close.

Measurement zone The camera automatically focuses on detail in marked central area. Position main subject here.

be seen before they enter the marked-out picture zone. Compacts, however, allow you a less wide range of lens focal lengths than SLR cameras. This, and viewfinder inaccuracies when working close-up, limit the compact's use with subjects such as natural history (see pp. 134-5).

Advanced models

The more expensive the compact camera, the more automatic features it tends to offer. These extend the camera's success rate to a wider range of subject types and lighting conditions, yet require you to make virtually no adjustments. Autofocus, auto wind-on, auto film speed setting, and autoexposure, with settings made from an extended range of shutter speeds and apertures, make these cameras truly "point-and-shoot". The system warns you when conditions will not allow technically good results, locking the shutter release or switching on the flash.

No matter how non-technical you may be, you should still consider using a camera that offers a few manual controls. "Fail-safe" devices, which prevent you from shooting at shutter speeds resulting in blur, or force you to use flash, for example, tend to give stereotyped results. Later, as you learn more about photography, you may regret that these features prevent you taking more interpretative images.

see pp. 134-5

● Make sure your fingers do not obstruct the lens, light-sensing or autofocus window.
● An automatic compact is ideally suited to situations where you have little time for fine adjustments.
● Cameras with built-in flash tend to produce "red eye" effect (see p. 151). Some are better designed to overcome this than others. It is a helpful feature, too, if the camera allows you to switch off the flash unit and use existing light only whenever you choose.

see p. 151

HINTS AND TIPS

Single lens reflex cameras

Single lens reflex (SLR) cameras have a very distinctive shape. First, they do not have the separate front viewfinder window found on compact cameras (see pp. 20-2). Their second main distinguishing feature is the centrally placed dome, which houses a glass pentaprism. This pentaprism allows you to see the image formed by the lens when you look through the eyepiece at the back of the camera. Seeing the actual image formed by the lens is important both in terms of extremely accurate viewfinding and focusing, as well as allowing you to preview the precise effect of the vast range of accessories available.

Basic models

These SLRs are manually controlled, which makes them slower to use than automatic models. However, they do not rely on battery power, so you can use them when the battery is flat. All SLRs have interchangeable lenses and built-in light metering. And since each manufacturer's lenses fit nearly all their camera bodies, image quality can be as good as with an advanced model.

Like all SLRs, basic models allow you to check subject sharpness visually, and since there is no parallax error you can frame and

1 Viewing and focusing

2 Mirror rises, aperture reduces

3 Shutter opens to expose the film

4 Camera returns to viewing mode

How the picture is taken SLRs differ in detail, but they all use the same mechanical sequence to take pictures. With the mirror at 45° you can compose and focus the image on the screen. The lens aperture is fully open, giving the brightest possible image. Pressing the release causes the mirror to rise, reduces the aperture to the one selected for correct exposure, and fires the shutter blind. The mirror then immediately returns and the aperture opens wide again, allowing you to resume viewing.

RANGE OF MODEL TYPES AVAILABLE	
Typical body features	**Comments**
Basic (manual)	
Offers up to ten shutter speeds. You must focus and adjust the shutter or aperture manually until the meter signals correct exposure. No built-in flash.	Budget model. Only about half the price of some advanced cameras, but accepts the same range of lenses. Good starter camera if you are prepared to learn the controls.
Fully automatic	
Minimizes user adjustments. You simply point the camera and it makes focusing and exposure settings. It may not indicate the settings made. Accepts dedicated flash (see p. 148), or has one built-in.	Medium price. Ideal camera for casual and non-technically-minded photographers. The autofocusing facility is helpful for those with poor eyesight. Quick and easy to use.
Semi-automatic	
Gives you the choice of setting all the controls manually or switching to an automatic mode.	More expensive than auto only. Very popular – you can select automatic for non-technical members of the family to use or for quick candids, and then change to manual for more considered shots.
Advanced (multimode)	
Widest range of shutter speeds. Choice of light reading methods, and semi- or fully-automatic exposure programs according to subject and shooting conditions. Autofocusing, built-in motordrive, and flash.	Most complex and expensive model. Intended for advanced amateurs and professionals who want maximum flexibility and control. Often forms the core of a comprehensive system capable of any application.

TYPICAL MANUAL SLR

Wind-on lever Thumb-operated lever transports the film and sets the shutter. Move it a few degrees – to its preset "stand-off" position – to switch on the meter.

Film ISO window Set film speed on dial, unless self-sensing.

Shutter speed control Speeds are marked in fractions of a sec, plus B setting for longer exposures.

Hot shoe Holds flash (or other accessories). Contains contacts which transfer information between flashgun and camera (see pp. 146–7).

Shutter release With locking collar. The threaded button accepts a cable release – essential for long exposures.

Film rewind knob Pulls upward to open camera back.

Aperture setting ring Scaled in f numbers. Has adjacent depth of field scale (see p. 33).

Focusing ring Scaled in feet and meters.

Frame counter Shows the number of frames exposed. Resets each time the back is opened.

Focal plane shutter Acts as a curtain just in front of film – covers film from light even when changing lenses.

Lens aperture Remains fully open until exposure made, or preview button (not shown) is pressed.

Lens This one has a regular 50 mm focal length and widest aperture of f 1.4. The whole lens unit detaches from camera and interchanges with dozens of other types (see p. 162).

The center of a basic SLR viewfinder screen will have a ring of microprisms as an aid to focusing. Some also include a split-image zone. At one side of the screen you will find some form of exposure-signaling device.

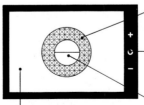

Microprism ring In this area unsharp detail has a shimmering, broken-up appearance.

Exposure signaling Controlled by meter circuit. When the center diode lights up the camera settings made will give correct exposure.

Matte screen You can see the picture go in or out of focus over the whole of this etched surface as you focus the lens.

Split-image zone Here image detail appears split and offset when unsharp (see p. 31).

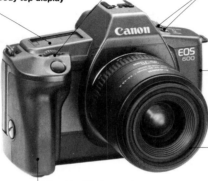

The camera, left, is a typical manual SLR. You can use it to focus on subjects as close as about 2 ft (0.6 m) – or even closer using extension tubes (see p. 170). You must first load the film and set its ISO speed (see p. 46). Look through the eyepiece and turn the focus control until your main subject appears sharp. Then, alter the shutter speed or aperture to make the exposure-meter-signal, along-side the focusing screen, indicate that correct exposure is set. After taking each picture, advance the wind-on lever. This moves the film and resets the shutter.

Pentaprism The pentaprism allows you to see the focusing screen from eye level. It also corrects the screen's laterally reversed mirror image. Without this correction you would find it difficult to relate the picture to the scene in front of you, or pan moving subjects.

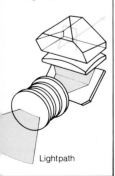

Lightpath

Advanced SLR
These SLR cameras contain the same features as basic SLR models, but they are electronically controlled and they also have extra options. With this type of camera you can choose the modes and controls that best suit your own way of working. Some features you may rarely use, however, and others only when you add special accessories.

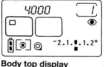

Body top display

Shutter speed Ranges from 1/2000–30 sec, permitting shooting in widely differing lighting conditions.

Exposure modes Choose from seven automatic or semi-automatic methods by which the light reading sets exposure, or set controls manually.

Choice of backs Removable camera back is interchangeable with special-purpose backs (see p. 179).

Lens 35-70 mm zoom lens fitted here, but you can select from more than 20 interchangeable lenses, all autofocusing types.

Film drive Film is wound on (at up to five frames per second) and rewound by motor.

focus close-ups accurately. The effects of changing lenses or adding lens attachments are visible on the focusing screen.

Advanced models
These cameras accept a range of interchangeable, autofocus lenses, which may also be manually focused. You can select "focus priority", whereby the shutter will not fire until the image is sharp. Detectors sense the film speed from the cassette. With these models, you can choose the way in which the light reading is made. Readings are internally computed and you may select automatic setting of the shutter and aperture, following one of a choice of programs to best suit the lens and subject. Or you can pre-set the shutter or aperture and allow the metering system to set the other control. Some models also offer "auto-bracketing", a burst of, say, three shots, each at a different exposure setting.

HINTS AND TIPS
● A basic SLR will cope with a wider range of situations than a basic compact.
● For serious work, buy an SLR that offers an aperture preview button.
● A camera model with excessive choice of modes and controls may be confusing and slow to use.
● Before commiting yourself to a particular camera system, investigate the extent and cost of its lenses and other accessories.

Camera handling and care

Your camera is a precision picture-taking instrument, and as such deserves to be handled with care. There are really only two basic requirements for trouble-free photography: the first is to hold the camera comfortably and steadily when shooting, and the second is to carry out sensible, routine maintenance.

Holding the camera still

Avoiding camera shake when shooting does not always mean supporting the camera in the same way or at the same height. Your first consideration is the viewpoint required to give the picture effect you want. Then choose the best way to keep the camera steady in this spot. Often, this will be a convenient standing height, or you may have a monopod or tripod (see p. 176). Sometimes, though, it will mean lying on the floor or balancing the camera on a table.

The degree of steadiness required for a particular shot depends on the shutter speed you select (see pp. 39–41) and the

Supporting your camera There are many techniques for holding the camera steady when shooting. Most people hand-hold the camera while standing, bracing their body. If you can, carry a monopod, tripod, or rifle grip (see p. 176). If this is not possible, you can utilize a cable release or the camera's delayed action release.

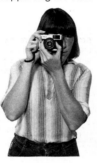

Hands and arms Press the camera against your face, giving most support with one hand. Use the fingers of the other hand to squeeze the release gently. Keep elbows tucked in.

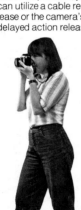

Bracing your feet Place your feet slightly apart, one foot forward. Breathe out gently when firing the shutter. If you are left handed, try using the camera upside down, but do not use flash.

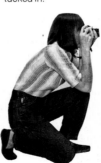

Kneeling This is much steadier than standing. Rest one elbow on your knee to give exposures up to about 1/30 or 1/15.

Side bracing Exposures of about 1 sec should be safe if you brace yourself against a wall or door frame. Position the whole camera base hard against the flat surface, pressing firmly with both hands.

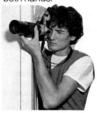

Lying down If you lie flat, taking all the weight on both elbows, you should be steady enough for exposures of about 1/15. Better still, support the camera on a pocket mini-tripod in this position. As an alternative, you can rest a long focus lens on a camera bag.

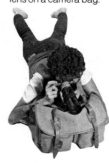

Tripod A good-quality tripod with a tilt head and a cable release allow you to use any length exposure.

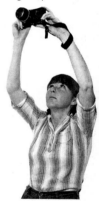

Overhead If your SLR has a removable pentaprism, you can compose and take pictures over the heads of crowds and other obstructions. Hold the camera inverted at arms' length above your head. Avoid shutter speeds slower than 1/125.

weight and type of lens. Speeds slower than 1/60 require particular care.

Avoiding damage

All mechanical parts of the camera are subject to wear, but you can cause excessive damage through unintentional mishandling. The best advice is never to force any of the controls.

You should take special care when mounting your camera on a tripod. Overtightening the screw can cause the base-plate to buckle, jamming the shutter. More routinely, never carry your camera with the body and lens unprotected. Use the ever-ready case supplied with most cameras and fit a lens cap whenever possible. Damp is especially damaging to the glass and electronic components of your camera. Avoid excessive humidity and protect the camera completely in the rain or when near the sea. Even more damaging than damp is battery neglect. Leaving old and leaking batteries in the camera can result in corrosion.

POTENTIAL PROBLEM AREAS

The areas of the camera picked out here tend to be prone to the most damage and abuse. Most of the examples apply equally to SLRs and compacts. Ironically, often the best way to protect a camera is to use it. A camera stored for long periods with the shutter tensioned, or with old batteries, or subject to damp, can end up more damaged than if used everyday.

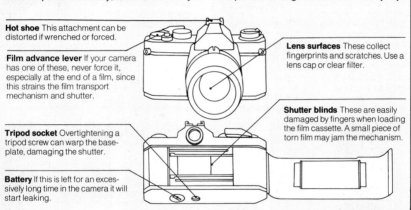

Hot shoe This attachment can be distorted if wrenched or forced.

Film advance lever If your camera has one of these, never force it, especially at the end of a film, since this strains the film transport mechanism and shutter.

Tripod socket Overtightening a tripod screw can warp the base-plate, damaging the shutter.

Battery If this is left for an excessively long time in the camera it will start leaking.

Lens surfaces These collect fingerprints and scratches. Use a lens cap or clear filter.

Shutter blinds These are easily damaged by fingers when loading the film cassette. A small piece of torn film may jam the mechanism.

Battery care Most cameras use pill-shaped batteries, or penlight cylindrical types (required for models with built-in flash or motorwind). Batteries last about a year (some types up to five years). Make sure contacts are clean, and that the battery is correctly inserted. Always replace batteries as a set. Remove batteries if the camera is to be stored for a long period.

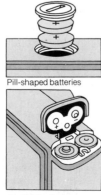

Pill-shaped batteries

Penlight batteries

● If your camera has a test button, check battery condition before every shooting session.
● One or two small specks of dust on the lens are far less serious than grease or scratches. Do not clean lens glass surfaces obsessively.
● If you must use your camera in the rain or in dusty conditions enclose it in a clear plastic bag. Make a hole in the bag just large enough for a clear UV filter attached to the lens. Seal the edges with tape.
● In your camera bag always have a blower brush, lens tissues, a small can of compressed air, and spare batteries.
● Regularly inspect your camera for any signs of wear, especially internal surfaces.

HINTS AND TIPS

Using the viewfinder

The viewfinder is the most important control on the camera. At a basic level, it is there to ensure that you include all the important subject elements. At a more advanced level you can think of it as your working area for picture making. If you are going to produce photographs that are strong in design and imaginative, begin by choosing a camera with a viewfinder that will be comfortable to work through, and not form a barrier between you and your subject.

Framing your picture accurately
To make sure you aim the camera correctly, you must see all four corners of your picture area at one time when looking through the viewfinder. With some compact cameras

you may not see the "suspended" white frame line at all unless your eye is centered and close to the eyepiece. When using an SLR you must also see clearly any exposure signals or focusing aids on the screen. If you wear glasses, it may be better to take them off and use an optical glass, eyesight-correction lens element over the eyepiece. Some advanced cameras have focusable eyepieces. They also allow you to change focusing screen (see p. 31) and, occasionally, the viewfinder itself (see p. 178), so that you can pick combinations that best suit you. When shooting with a compact, make sure you use the parallax marks, but the separate positions of viewfinder and lens may upset very precise alignments of near and distant subjects.

VIEWFINDING ERRORS AND IMPROVEMENTS

One of the most common viewfinding errors is not including important parts of the subject. The opposite problem to this is standing too far back, making everything too small and also including a mass of unwanted detail.

Provided you are using the eyepiece of the viewfinder correctly – and allowing for parallax

if necessary – it is a good idea to fill up the frame as much as possible. Look out for unimportant but assertive items in the foreground or background of your pictures. Some of these may be "hidden" out of focus when you view the scene through an SLR with the lens fully open, but they may record clearly when the

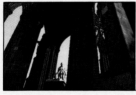
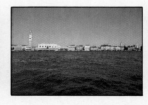
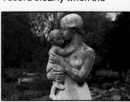

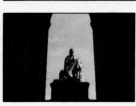
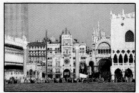
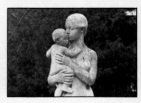

Filling the frame In the top picture of this pair the main element (the stone figure) is overwhelmed by the assertive surrounding shapes. A closer viewpoint and simpler use of one shape to frame the figure has a stronger effect, as in the version above.

Positioning the horizon It is generally a weakness to divide your picture exactly in half with the horizon (top). A high or low horizon (above), with the main element in the larger part, is often a more interesting composition.

Shifting viewpoint The top picture has an awkward background, with assertive light patches. Moving the camera to the left changes this to plain foliage (above). It also gives a different angle on the figures. A movable subject could rotate with the camera.

Information display

Most compact camera viewfinders signal such information as "flash on" and "subject in focus", as well as showing parallax correction and autofocus zone. Manual SLRs may display the aperture and shutter speed at the screen edge. Advanced SLRs show information such as exposure override settings. Data is often repeated, with information on the number of frames shown on a body top display panel (see p. 25).

Compact

SLR

aperture closes down for the actual exposure. Always look closely at the edges of the viewfinder, and make sure that you do not create any ugly shapes by cutting objects off awkwardly. This can occur easily when parts of buildings or parts of people are cropped off against the sky. Include surrounding shapes and detail that add to rather than compete with your subject.

Although some "faults" look bad in the viewfinder, they will not appear on your final picture. Specks of dust, for example, on a focusing screen or compact viewfinder window are annoying but unimportant.

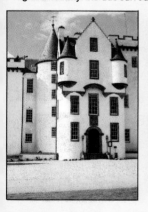

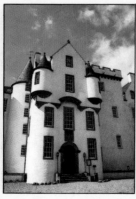

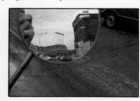

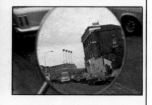

Converging vertical lines In the pair of pictures above, the left-hand version has some unattractive features – vertical lines, just slightly converging, and excessively tight cropping at the top of the frame. For the right-hand shot, the photographer exchanged the standard

50 mm lens for a 28 mm wide-angle lens, moved closer to the building, and angled the camera upward. If you have to tilt the camera, it is often better to work closer in and so make convergence a dynamic feature.

Viewfinder accuracy The top version was taken with a compact, ignoring parallax marks. Even if correctly framed the viewfinder would not show mirror contents (including the hand) as seen by the camera lens. An SLR gives complete close-up accuracy (above).

Using focus control

Your camera lens must be the correct distance from the film to produce a sharply focused image. The nearer the subject is, however, the more you have to increase this lens-to-film distance. On very basic compact cameras, the lens may be "fixed focus", meaning that it is permanently at a compromise setting to accommodate both near and far subjects. Other compacts and all SLRs have adjustable focusing. Manually adjustable cameras often allow you to focus visually through the viewfinder, with the help of various aids. Autofocus (AF) cameras have mechanisms that automatically focus for whatever part of the scene is central in the frame, as soon as you start to press the shutter release.

Advantages of focusing

A fixed-focus camera is inexpensive and easy to use. In most cases, the lens is set to record sharply everything from the far horizon down to about 6 ft (2 m) from the camera. With these cameras the lens has a small maximum aperture and short focal length lens to maximize depth of field (see pp. 33–8). But there will be times when you want important foreground parts of the photograph to be clearer than more distant detail. A background can become too assertive if it is as sharp as everything else. The background may also be inappropriate and therefore needs suppressing. Selective, or "differential", focus is an effective way of emphasizing one chosen element in a scene at the expense of another (see p. 70). Only an adjustable-focus lens gives you this control, and it also allows you to focus on subjects at closer minimum distances than a fixed lens.

Manual focusing

The most basic focusing system uses a subject distance or (on simple compact cameras) a symbol scale. Settings appear on a focusing ring around the lens, and sometimes inside the viewfinder, too. With practice and care, you can judge settings, but at closest distances there is little room for error. All single lens reflex cameras allow you to focus visually. The image seen in the viewfinder changes as you alter the lens focus settings, making focusing more positive and accurate.

Autofocusing

This feature is provided on almost all medium- and higher-priced compacts, and on most advanced SLRs. With a compact, the center part of the scene being photographed is viewed from two windows above the lens. The system uses a motor to move the camera lens backward and forward when you begin to press the shutter release. At the same time, the view from one window is scanned and compared with the other. When both views converge, a detector causes the lens to stop moving, since focus has been achieved, and allows

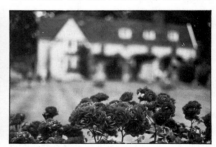

Fixed focus lens A fixed focus lens shows far away detail more sharply than objects in the immediate fore-ground. To make the roses sharp in the scene above you must photograph from fur-ther back. (The house will not become out of focus.)

Adjustable lens Using a camera with adjust-able focus allows you to concentrate atten-tion on the foreground. For the result above the lens was set to 4 ft (1.2 m) – "head-and-shoulders" on a sym-bol camera. The differ-ential focus gives a strong effect of depth.

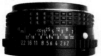

the shutter to fire. In an SLR, a small, central part of the internal "reflex" mirror, which is positioned directly behind the camera lens, splits the image of the subject on to electronic sensors positioned in the base of the camera body. These sensors halt the lens-focusing motor when they detect that the image is sharp (see p. 201). Most compact cameras and all SLRs work on a "passive" autofocus system, detecting correct focus by matching the pattern of light and dark areas in the two views.

MANUAL FOCUSING AIDS

For distant subjects you can guess the focus setting to make on a scale of distances indicated on a ring around the camera lens or, on older cameras, pick the appropriate symbol. But focusing is more precise if the picture in the viewfinder looks clear only when the lens is correctly set. Single lens reflex cameras allow you to see focusing adjustments as changes of subject detail over the whole focusing screen. For extra clarity, an arrangement of central prisms break up that part of the image on the screen if the lens is not properly set. This and the microprism ring are helpful if you wear glasses.

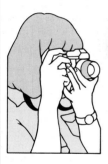
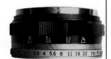

Distance scale Subject distance scales are uniform on all SLR lenses. Typical closest focusing distance is 1.5 ft (0.45 m). Lens also shows depth of field (see p. 36).

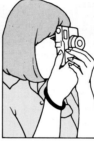

Symbol scale Some compacts show symbols, not distances. A head-and-shoulders may denote 4 ft (1.2 m), a half-length figure 6 ft (1.8 m), and a mountain, infinity (∞).

Focusing screen You can use the whole of a (standard) SLR focusing screen to see subjects at different distances from the camera coming into sharp focus as you turn the focus ring. As an additional check, align the ringed, split zone with the main subject. If the picture is out of focus, this center zone shows vertical lines offset, and detail shimmers in the surrounding microprism ring. Both effects disappear when you accurately focus. Part of these focus aids black out at small lens apertures.

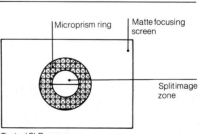

Microprism ring

Matte focusing screen

Splitimage zone

Typical SLR screen

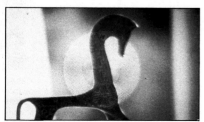

Image in focus

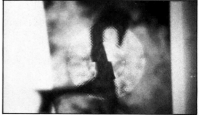

Image out of focus

LIMITATIONS OF AUTOFOCUS SYSTEMS

No autofocus system is foolproof. You must make sure that the main subject is lined up in the focus measuring area. Most, but not all, cameras allow you to lock focus at this particular point so that you can recompose the picture with an off-center subject.

Passive autofocus can be fooled by repetitive patterned or low-contrast subjects, or fail in dim lighting. Active systems may reflect back off glass if shooting through a window and give faulty settings. They cannot measure subjects more than a few meters away.

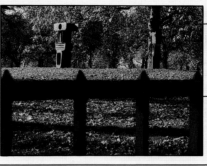

The off-center sculpture in this shot may cause problems if it is the main subject, unless it is first centered, focused, and then focus locked, and the picture recomposed.

Pronounced areas of light and shade patterning may confuse passive autofocus systems.

Infrared and ultrasonic systems would tend to focus on the fence.

However, since this may possibly fail with dimly lit subjects, some compacts use an "active" system instead. This works in the same way as a television remote control, by projecting a beam of infrared or ultrasound to reflect off the subject back to the detector window. An active system is necessary to focus automatically when shooting with flash in dim light or in darkness. Some compact cameras incorporate both passive and active systems, while autofocusing SLR cameras use special flashguns that transmit infrared or ultrasound to assist the camera's autofocus system (see p. 146).

Using autofocus

Autofocus is ideal when you have a mobile, active subject – children or animals, for example – composed in center frame. It leaves you free to concentrate on facial expressions or overall composition. If your camera has "focus priority" it will not be possible to release the shutter until the (central) subject is in focus. However, if you have an autofocusing SLR, it is valuable to be able to elect to focus manually as well. By turning the focus control yourself, you can compare the visual effects of focusing on the foreground, mid-distance, or background before deciding how to shoot.

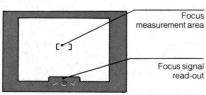

Focus measurement area

Focus signal read-out

In-focus indicator

Some form of "in-focus" signaling device is located within the viewfinder of most autofocus compacts and SLRs. Here (see above), a colored diode glows when the image in the measuring area is at maximum sharpness. If the subject is too close for the lens to focus, or conditions confuse the system, the signal flashes instead.

HINTS AND TIPS

● If your camera focuses by zone or distance scale, practice judging and pacing out distances. Learn how large a head looks in the viewfinder at set distances.
● A split-image focusing screen dividing the image horizontally helps you focus vertical lines. For horizontal subjects, twist the camera briefly.
● Take care with autofocus cameras to position the main subject correctly for focusing.
● Some low-cost autofocus cameras may be too slow to adjust for very fast action pictures.

Aperture and depth of field

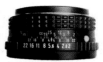

The lens aperture on your camera exercises two very important controls over picture appearance. First, it gives you variable control of image brightness. This is one method of altering exposure (the other being shutter speed – see pp. 39-41). Second, reducing the size of the aperture has a unique optical effect – it increases the range of objects at different distances from the camera that will appear sharp at one focus setting. This band of sharpness is called *depth of field*.

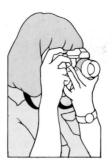

f number scale Most SLR lenses have the aperture ring marked in f numbers. Each change to the next highest number halves the amount of light entering the camera.

Aperture and exposure

Most cameras have an adjustable aperture formed by an iris diaphragm positioned between or near the glass elements making up the lens. On a compact camera, the diaphragm is often positioned directly behind the shutter blades. Automatic-exposure (AE) compacts, however, frequently have no diaphragm. Instead the shutter blades themselves open to form a circular aperture of the required diameter, under the control of the camera's light-measuring circuit, at the moment you press the shutter release.

If your camera has an aperture control ring, it is likely to be scaled in what are known as "f numbers". This is an internationally agreed number scale and runs: f2, f2.8, f4, f5.6, f8, f11, f16, f22, and so on. The widest aperture (lowest f number) offered by your particular lens is also engraved on its rim. This often appears as a ratio, for example 1:2.8.

"STOPPING DOWN" THE LENS

The f number itself is effectively the number of times aperture diameter will divide into the lens focal length. For example, at f 4 aperture diameter is one-quarter the focal length. All lenses set to the same aperture will transmit the same amount of light. The scale below is universal, but some lenses "stop down" further, to f 22 or more. A more expensive, "fast" lens may open as wide as f 1.4 or f 1.2. Sometimes, the maximum aperture departs from the regular series – f 1.2 for example is only half a setting wider than f 1.4, but it may be the fastest aperture setting that your lens can give.

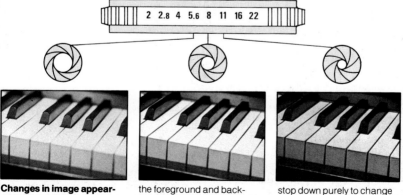

Changes in image appearance As you stop the aperture down, the image produced dims. But notice how objects in the foreground and background also grow sharper. Use the dimming effect to compensate for brightly lit subjects – or stop down purely to change depth of field (countering the change in image brightness by using a longer shutter speed).

On an SLR camera you can watch the diaphragm change as you turn the aperture control, provided that you keep the preview button depressed or remove the lens from the camera body.

A few single lens reflex cameras have the letter "A" engraved one setting beyond the smallest aperture. When you set the camera to "A", the most suitable aperture size for the prevailing levels of light reflecting back from the subject is determined. This is automatically chosen by the camera's exposure meter when you press the shutter release (see pp. 42-5).

Simple compact cameras sometimes have an aperture control scaled in weather symbols, denoting "direct sun", "cloudy sun", "overcast", and so on. If your camera has no aperture scale of any description, this may indicate that the camera's exposure is completely automatic, or that it is a simple, fixed-aperture camera with

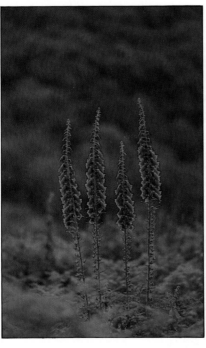

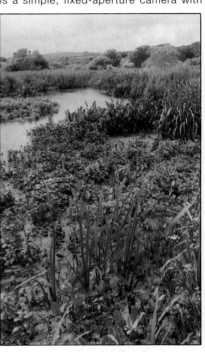

Choosing depth of field In the photographs above the lens was focused for the near middle distance. The left hand image was shot at widest aperture, limiting sharpness to the point of focus. For the landscape above right, the photographer set f 22 to make everything equally sharp.

WHAT F NUMBERS DO

Each f number shown below doubles the amount of light let in by the previous setting or "stop". As the diameter of the circle is doubled (change of two f numbers) its area increases fourfold.

f numbers

f 16	f 11	f 8	f 5.6	f 4	f 2.8	f 2
x 1	x 2	x 4	x 8	x 16	x 32	x 64

Relative light admitted

exposure being altered by changes of the shutter speed alone.

Aperture and depth of field

Aperture affects depth of field, the distance between the nearest and farthest parts of a scene that appear sharp at one focus setting. For example, a lens set at f 2.8 focused for a subject 10 ft (3 m) away may record sharply everything from about 9.5 ft (3 m) to 12 ft (3.5 m). But change to f 16 and depth of

field will extend from 6 ft (2 m) to 18 ft (5.5 m). So by choice of aperture – and care over your focus setting – you can either localize detail, picking out objects at one distance only, or make everything equally detailed from the near foreground to the far distance.

Each time you change aperture you will have to compensate for the extra brightness or darkness of the image by setting shorter or longer times on the shutter. Sometimes there is conflict between the

CONDITIONS WHICH ALTER DEPTH OF FIELD

There are three main ways to alter the depth of sharp detail in pictures. You can increase depth of field by using a smaller aperture, or by moving further away from the subject, or changing to a wide-angle lens (see pp. 162–7). Changing aperture is usually most convenient,

but if the light is dim or you have a slow film it may be easier to make one of the other two changes (both of which produce a smaller image). Even though you may later need a bigger enlargement from the film, the result will still show increased depth of field.

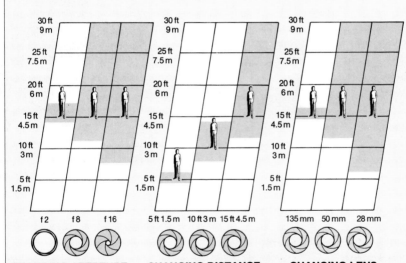

CHANGING APERTURE
The diagram above represents a sharply focused subject 15 ft (4.5 m) from a camera with a 50 mm lens. Working at f 2, depth of field extends from about 14 ft (4.2 m) to 16½ ft (5 m), a distance of 2½ ft (0.7 m). At f 8, depth of field is 11–33 ft (3.3–10 m), a total of 22 ft (6.7 m). At f 16 depth is from 8 ft (2.4 m) to infinity.

CHANGING DISTANCE
This diagram shows the result of changing subject distance with a 50 mm lens set at f 8. With a subject 5 ft (1.5 m) away, depth of field is 4½–6 ft (1.3–1.8 m), giving 1½ ft (0.4 m) in sharp focus. At 10 ft (3 m), depth becomes 7½–14 ft (2.2–4.2 m) – a total of 6½ ft (2 m). And at 15 ft (4.5 m) depth is 11–33 ft (3.3–10 m), giving 22 ft (6.7 m).

CHANGING LENS
Using different lenses, aperture is set at f 8 and subject distance is 15 ft (4.5 m). A 135 mm telephoto is in sharp focus from 14½–16 ft (4.3–4.8 m) – only 1½ ft (0.4 m). A 50 mm lens gives 11–33 ft (3.3–10 m), a sharp field of 22 ft (6.7 m). And with a 28 mm lens the sharp field is from 6 ft (1.8 m) to infinity.

Reading depth of field The depth of field scale on a typical SLR lens is located under the distance scale. The diamond indicates the distance actually focused, and f numbers left and right show you the limits of depth of field at each aperture. The depth expands from a few inches at f 2 (top) to several feet at f 16 (bottom).

brightness conditions and depth of field – such as a dark interior shot that must be sharp throughout. Here, use a fast film (see pp. 54–6), or very long exposure, or flash. For most conditions, however, you will be able to choose from a reasonably large range of f numbers.

Previewing depth of field

Lenses with focus adjustment and variable apertures usually show depth of field on a scale. Bear in mind that with an SLR you view the image with the lens at widest aperture. Setting a smaller aperture has no effect until you press the shutter release, so your picture may have more depth of field

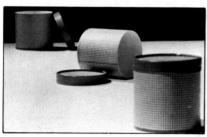

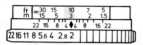

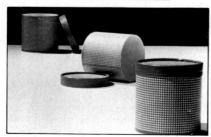

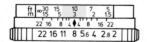

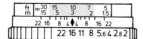

HYPERFOCAL DISTANCE

There is a method of maximizing depth of field at any aperture for distant subjects such as landscapes. If you set your focusing for infinity (∞) and then shoot at, say, f 16, depth of field extends from the horizon to about 16 ft (5 m) away (see below). This near point is the *hyperfocal distance* for your lens at f 16. If you then refocus for the hyperfocal distance (see bottom), the landscape will still be sharp at the horizon, but now the nearest sharp object is at only half the hyperfocal distance, 8 ft (2.5 m).

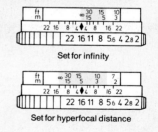

Set for infinity

Set for hyperfocal distance

Maximizing depth of field This shot (facing page) uses depth of field to give sharp detail from the far distance to within 3 ft (0.8 m) of the lens. The photographer used a wide-angle lens at f 22. He set focus so that f 22 on the depth of field scale just read infinity. (Setting the lens at its hyperfocal distance for f 22.) In bright lighting you can also set depth of field visually. Focus one-third inside the zone you want sharp (the nearest post here). Then depress the preview button and watch the depth of field expand as you reduce the aperture.

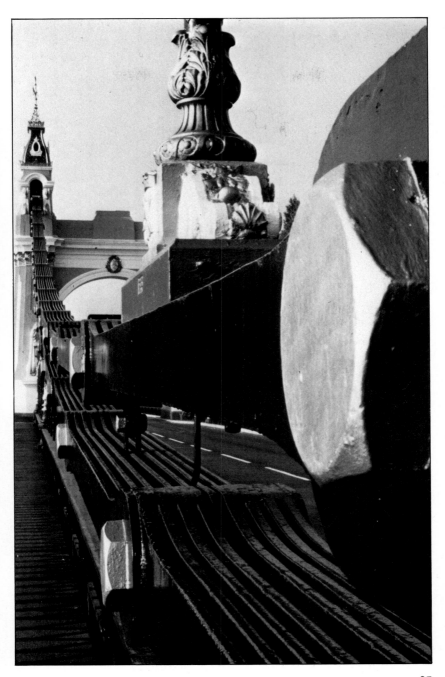

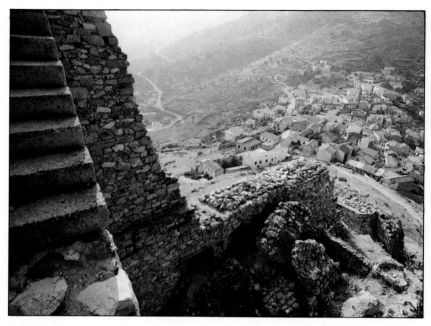

Depth of field choices
Focusing technique depends on subject and lighting. This boldly lit shot gains detail from extreme depth of field. But in flat, overcast lighting, limiting the zone of sharpness to the distant village may be the best way to imply distance.

than you expect or want. You can see this before shooting if your camera has a preview button. Pressing this changes the diaphragm to the size it will be when you take the picture and so allows you to see how sharp final results will be.

Apertures and autoexposure cameras

Autoexposure (AE) setting cameras tend to give greater depth of field with bright subjects. This is because the system selects a small lens aperture (and fast shutter) in bright light to avoid overexposure. But if you want to maintain one aperture because of the particular depth of field it gives, your camera may allow "aperture-priority" mode to be selected. The AE system will then make changes only to the shutter settings to account for different light levels, leaving the aperture unchanged (see p. 43).

Simple, fixed-aperture cameras

Some compacts have a fixed aperture – often about f5.6. By having the lens set at the factory to focus on about 12ft (3.5m), f5.6 typically gives a depth of field between 6ft (2m) and infinity, and everything in the average picture will be sharp.

HINTS AND TIPS

- Close subjects always have shallowest depth of field, but sometimes you can change your position to make important picture elements more equal in their distance from the camera.
- Depth of field normally extends farther behind where you focus than in front.
- Using an SLR, adopt the routine of checking picture composition at your chosen aperture (using the preview button) if time allows.
- It is hard to create shallow depth of field in bright light or using fast film, because of the small aperture needed to avoid overexposure. Using neutral density or polarizing filters reduces light and allows a wider aperture.
- Depth of field on an SLR focusing screen always looks slightly greater than on the final enlargement.

Using shutter control

You use your camera's shutter to control both the moment of exposure and its duration. The best choice of shutter speed setting depends on the degree of camera or subject movement – whether or not you want the subject to look blurred or frozen. The time set also affects the amount of light reaching the film, so, like the lens aperture, the shutter has an important role to play in controlling exposure.

Types and settings

There are two main types of shutter – focal plane, found mostly in SLR cameras, and bladed, used in compacts. The actual period the shutter allows light from the subject to act on the film is, in most cases, timed electronically. This makes it easier to integrate changes in shutter speed into an electronic circuit, controlled by the camera's exposure meter.

Most automatic compact cameras have no external shutter speed scale. The camera itself selects a fast speed for bright light conditions, or in response to the user choosing a wide aperture, and selects a slow speed in the opposite circumstances.

Manual setting On a manual SLR, shutter speeds (in fractions of a second) appear on a setting ring normally located on the top of the body. Times double or halve, and so easily relate to aperture changes. Sometimes, the letter "A" appears

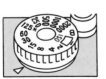

on the dial. On this setting the camera's meter determines the speed.

Electronic setting On some cameras you set the shutter speed required for your subject electronically, by pressing "up" or "down" buttons located near the top of the camera body. The speed selected appears in a data panel on the camera body (right) and usually below the picture seen inside the viewfinder, as well.

Settings shown here denote 1/15 sec at f11. When the camera is set to automatic program or aperture-priority modes (see p. 43), the exposure meter circuit determines and sets the shutter speed.

On an advanced camera, speeds may vary continuously from 1/4000 to 30 full seconds, but basic cameras are limited to 1/60, 1/125, and 1/250, or perhaps even to one speed, typically 1/125. Simplest compacts may change shutter speed when you set the film ISO speed on the camera, or alter a weather symbol scale.

Most manual SLRs have a scale of shutter speeds you set on a dial. You can select 1/2000 (1/4000 or 1/8000 on some models) down to at least 1 full second. For longer exposures you may have to use the

HOW SHUTTERS WORK

The shutter opens either just in front of the film (the plane where the image comes into focus), or consists of blades that open in the lens. Both are tensioned by the film-advance mechanism and fired by a release button. The open period is timed electronically. One speed usually works mechanically in case of battery failure.

Focal plane This type of shutter (below) is essential in an SLR as it allows you to view the image via a mirror and also to change lenses mid-film. Modern focal plane shutters have several overlapping metal blades leaving an adjustable-width slit that travels vertically. Older types use horizontally traveling fabric blinds.

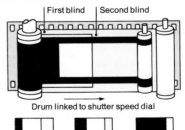

First blind | Second blind

Drum linked to shutter speed dial

1   2   3

Bladed lens shutter This type of shutter is found in or near the lens. Its set of thin, opaque blades opens from the center when a spring or magnet rotates an outer ring.

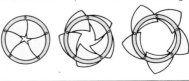

1/8 sec This photograph of a fast-moving fairground ride (below) was shot at 1/8 at f 22, using a tripod. At this slow speed, every part of the subject is blurred, and smaller elements such as some of the chains have disappeared completely.

1/60 sec This picture, taken at 1/60 at f 8, is a mixture of blurred and sharp detail. The amount of blur depends on the angle and direction of movement of the subject relative to the direction of the shutter blinds. Movement in relation to camera position is also important to the final result.

1/1000 sec A speed of 1/1000 at f 2 has frozen all the subject detail. The result now consists of silhouetted shapes. The stepped diagonals still give a dynamic image, even though all blur is lost.

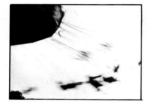

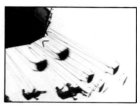

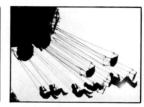

"B" setting, which holds the shutter open for as long as you keep the release depressed. Focal plane shutters have one speed (typically 1/125) colored prominently to indicate the fastest speed for flash. Some cameras signal a warning in the viewfinder when a speed slower than 1/60 has been selected. This reminds you to support the camera firmly in order to avoid camera shake, or to use flash instead.

Speeds and blur

Choosing the best shutter speed depends on how much the subject or camera will be moving, and whether you want maximum detail or a more "impressionistic" result. Lens aperture, lighting conditions, and film sensitivity will all tend to limit your choice. Generally, 1/125 is the slowest setting that will avoid camera shake when using a hand-held camera and standard type lens. Often, though, you will need a briefer setting to freeze subjects that are very fast moving, such as sports events, or very close, such as close-ups of swaying flowers. If conditions are right, use slower speeds to convey the flowing movement of a dancer or the bustle of traffic. Keep the camera still, or pan, shift or zoom to produce different types of blur (see pp. 98-9).

CHOICE OF SUITABLE SHUTTER SPEED SETTINGS	
Shutter speed	
1/1000 or less	Close action shots of auto racing and golf swings require at least 1/1000 to freeze movement. These speeds may call for strong light, a wide-aperture lens, and fast film to avoid underexposure.
1/250	Use as standard with telephoto lenses over 200 mm. Safest choice when shooting (normal lens) from a moving boat or slow-moving car. Will freeze cycle traffic and running figures, full length.
1/125	Good general purpose shutter speed for hand-held shots – set your camera to this for most outdoor candids with a normal lens. On some SLRs it is the fastest speed suitable for flash. (The flash itself gives an effective exposure of 1/500–1/10,000.)
1/30–1 sec	Regard some form of support as essential for static work. Necessary speeds for dim-light situations where a small aperture for depth of field is also required. You may need a small aperture and slow film to avoid overexposure.
Longer than 1 sec	Using the B setting you may need a locking cable release and a watch to time these shutter speeds. Suitable for fireworks, patterns from moving car lights, and night shots generally. Film may lose sensitivity and colors be distorted.

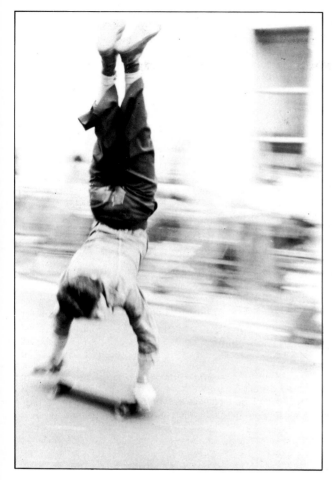

Moving the camera
For the picture left, a shutter speed of 1/15 was used with the camera panned sideways to follow the action (see diagram below). This gives a mixture of blur and sharp detail on the boy himself, and also separates him from the crowd behind. Panning at slow shutter speeds (see p. 98) allows you to convert backgrounds or foregrounds into blurred lines. This also increases the sense of movement.

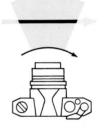

● Even slow-moving subjects may require a fast shutter setting if they are very close, moving at right-angles to your position, or taken with a telephoto lens.
● To freeze action where poor light will not allow fast shutter speeds, change to a wide-angle lens, or move back from the action, or adopt a more head-on camera position.
● To allow slow shutter speeds to be set in bright light conditions, or with fast film, without unwanted depth of field or overexposure, use a neutral density (gray) filter.
● If your camera has aperture-priority metering only, use fast film and set the widest aperture to get the briefest shutter speeds At-tach an ND filter and select the smallest aperture for slowest exposures.
● In some manual cameras, the meter switches off when you select shutter speeds of 1 sec or longer as well as the B setting.
● The compact camera's direct vision viewfinder is ideal for slow speeds and long exposures – unlike an SLR, you can still see the subject while exposing the film.
● Even when you are using fast shutter speeds, make a habit of squeezing, not jabbing, the shutter release button to avoid the possibility of blurred pictures.

HINTS AND TIPS

Using exposure controls

Exposure is a term used to describe the amount of light falling on the film. Determining "correct" exposure means assessing the brightness of a scene, relating this information to the sensitivity of the film, and then setting some combination of aperture and shutter that ensures that the film receives neither too little nor too much light. These exposure controls alter the brightness of your picture – its lightness or darkness. All but the simplest cameras contain a meter that measures the light from the subject. Automatic models then make all aperture and shutter adjustments for you.

Determining correct exposure

A low-cost compact camera may have no meter to measure subject brightness. If it has adjustable settings, follow the suggestions of the film or camera maker. Otherwise, limit yourself to brightly lit subjects.

The majority of modern cameras contain a tiny cell to measure the light. Your film's light sensitivity (ISO speed) is detected from the cassette or must be set on an external scale (see p. 39). You then point the

camera at the subject and the light meter calculates an aperture and shutter speed combination for correct exposure. With a manual camera (or one set to manual), you may alter the shutter speed or aperture until a "correct exposure" diode lights in the viewfinder. 'Dim lighting, for example, with least-sensitive film will need a slow speed

Choosing the right setting The meter (or data sheet) will indicate shutter and aperture settings for correct exposure. Each shutter speed and f number either doubles or halves the light reaching the film – so you can alter one as long as you compensate exposure with the other. Each of the exposure pairs (right) will produce the same exposure. You can pick 1/30 at f 16 for maximum depth of field, or 1/250 at f 5.6 to stop fast action.

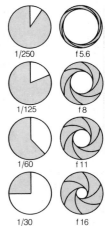

1/250   f 5.6

1/125   f 8

1/60   f 11

1/30   f 16

BRACKETING EXPOSURE

Correct exposure, as indicated by the camera meter, may not produce the effect you want. You may, for example, want a lighter or darker result to suit the mood of your subject. It is then a good idea to bracket exposures – taking, say, three versions, one exposed according to the meter, one underexposed, and one overexposed. On some advanced cameras you can select "autobracketing". The camera then produces a burst of three shots at different exposure settings when you press the shutter button.

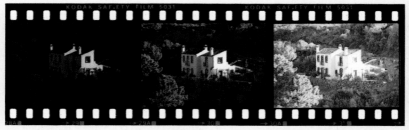

Underexposure 1/125 at f 11 gives dense shadows. Only brightly lit parts show detail. On prints, dark areas often appear flat greenish-gray.

Correct exposure 1/125 at f 5.6 has produced the best compromise between detail in light and dark areas. The subject was harshly lit.

Overexposure This slide was given 1/125 at f 2.8, two stops more than correct exposure. The dark areas show detail but bright areas are bleached.

EXPOSURE CONTROL ASSESSMENT	
Type of system	**Comments**
Automatic exposure (AE) program Depending on scene brightness, this system adjusts shutter and aperture following a preset program. No indication of the settings made may be given (see p. 202).	Typical range is from 1/2000 at f 16 to 1 sec at f 1.4 Warning light at 1/60 or longer. Effortless, but you cannot select combinations outside the program. Some models offer manual control option.
Aperture priority (semi-automatic) You preselect the f number and the meter then selects the shutter speed required to suit the brightness of the scene.	Consistent depth of field, but can give blur. Shutter speeds selected usually shown in the viewfinder. You can' use this system in reverse by turning the aperture control until the required speed is shown.
Shutter priority (semi-automatic) You preselect the shutter speed and the meter then selects the f number required.	Control over blur, but depth of field varies. Best chosen when camera is on the move or when you want a particular degree of blur or sharp detail.
Manual You can change either the shutter speed or aperture controls until "correct exposure" is signaled in the viewfinder.	Slowest system to use but lowest cost. It offers you direct control over both depth of field and the effects of movement.

and wide aperture. A bright scene with fast film may need the fastest shutter and smallest aperture. Usually, however, settings fall between these extremes. With adjustable cameras, the choice of settings allows you to vary depth of field (see pp. 33-8) and subject blur (see pp. 39-41).

Automatic exposure

Fully autoexposure (AE) cameras work through a program ranging from widest aperture and slowest shutter speed to

Where the camera measures light Cell location on a compact is usually close to the viewfinder. SLRs use through-the-lens (TTL) systems, typically with sensor cells reading the focusing screen image. Others use cells in the base, measuring light passed through a semi-silvered reflex mirror and reflected off a patterned shutter blind. During exposure, the cell reads light off the film and so it is able to adjust long exposures if lighting alters, or correct the duration of flash.

External

Pentaprism

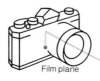

Film plane

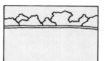

Overall External meters measure the overall scene, giving all parts equal weight. They may also include areas outside the frame, too.

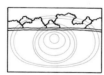

Center weighted Most TTL meters read predominantly from the center and lower parts of the frame, and less from the top and frame corners.

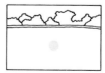

Spot Some TTL meters give you the option of reading from only a small area of the scene, marked on the focusing screen.

How much picture is measured Most compact cameras have a meter giving an overall reading. This can lead to inaccurate exposures if large, but relatively unimportant, areas of dark or bright subject matter are included in the scene (see p. 44). So-called "center-weighted" systems are in general use in SLR cameras. Spot metering, an option on some advanced cameras, allows you to measure exposure for any chosen, most important, part of the picture. When taking a center-weighted or spot reading with an AE camera, center the most important detail in the viewfinder. Then apply the exposure lock to retain this light reading if you want to recompose the picture with the key element positioned off-center.

PROBLEMS WHEN MEASURING EXPOSURE

Given average subject conditions, exposure reading with a typical center-weighted camera meter gives a high percentage of successful pictures. "Average conditions" mean that the scene contains roughly equal areas of light and dark detail and is lit mainly from behind the camera. But some scenes will fool the meter if you only take a standard reading. The scene may, for example, have extreme contrast or small but important areas much darker or brighter than the general surroundings. The best general advice then is to decide which

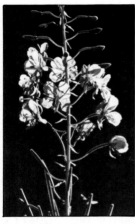

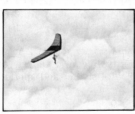

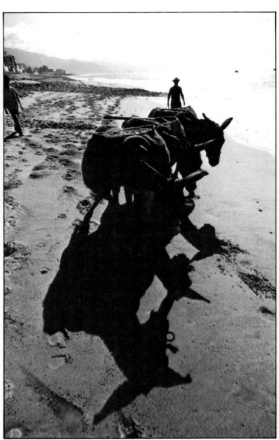

Excessive background influence Both the subjects above will cause problems with an overall or center-weighted reading. The flower's dark background (top) will affect the reading, so that plant detail will overexpose. Take your reading so that the petals fill the frame, then set the exposure lock or make settings manually. In the shot above, the background of sky will make the meter underexpose. Measure from ground detail that matches the glider in tone. If your camera has spot reading, align the zone with important subject areas.

Backlighting Backlit subjects can cause several problems. Sometimes light spills directly into the lens, affecting the meter and resulting in overexposure. To avoid this, use a lens hood or shade the camera. Backlighting creates extreme differences in brightness between subject and background. If you cannot read your main subject, take a general reading and modify your setting. When the surroundings are much brighter than the subject increase exposure by 1–2 stops, and for darker surroundings reduce camera settings.

part you want to record as midway between dark and light. Temporarily fill the whole frame with this part (or a convenient substitute that matches its tone) and take your reading. Apply the exposure lock if necessary, and then recompose the picture before shooting.

Dusk and night shots
In dimly lit settings, like the bridge scene below, your meter may fail to respond. Set a much higher ISO rating until it reads, then extend exposure in ratio with the false and correct ISO. For night traffic shots (bottom), take a similar general reading, then bracket exposures. A long exposure records traffic lights as trails.

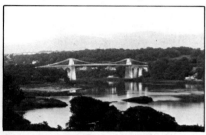

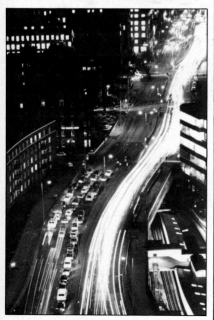

smallest aperture and fastest shutter speed. Modern systems are so versatile that they can produce correctly exposed images even when lighting conditions are rapidly fluctuating, such as when clouds are being blown across the sky and suddenly obscure the sun, or when your subject is moving from full shade to full sun. They are also excellent for fast, candid photography (see pp. 124-5), when there may be insufficient time to make reasoned decisions about how the shutter speed and aperture controls should be set, as well as for general use by those who are new to photography.

The most sophisticated autoexposure systems are capable of detecting the speed of moving subjects and can also sense when a telephoto lens is being used. In both of these circumstances, the program adjusts itself to maintain as brief a shutter speed as possible in order to avoid the possibility of blurred images.

Instead of automatic exposure measurement and setting, some cameras have semi-automatic systems, or offer these as alternative modes to fully "programmed" operation. As shown on page 43, each allows you to prioritize either aperture or shutter speed, by selecting "aperture-priority" or "shutter-priority" modes.

A totally manual system allows you individual choice of shutter and aperture settings. Inevitably, however, it is slower to use and requires greater knowledge of how the controls affect picture results.

As shown on page 43

HINTS AND TIPS

● As a general guide to exposure, divide your film's ISO figure into one second. Use this shutter speed at f 16 for frontally lit subjects that are lit by direct sunlight.
● To see how a scene looks if underexposed, view it through an SLR at smallest aperture with the preview button pressed.
● If measuring exposure with an SLR, keep your eye close to the eyepiece or light can enter and affect the sensor.
● Most SLRs offer an exposure-compensation control. This overrides the exposure meter to over- or under-expose the picture by set increments, as needed for bracketing or when the subject is backlit.

Film loading and unloading

Film loading and unloading errors account for some of the most common mistakes in 35 mm photography. Cassettes of 35 mm film are rather awkward to handle, and it is not difficult to jam the film if the cassette does not sit squarely in the film chamber. This is especially easy to do when you are working in a hurry or if you only occasionally use the camera.

Common errors

The method of using film is practically unchanged since the first 35 mm cameras of the 1920s. 35 mm perforated film is drawn out of its cassette through a slot with a velvet light trap. It then passes along guides at the back of the camera and winds on to an open take-up spool. After you have taken the last exposure, it is vital not to open the camera back until all the film has been rewound back into its light-tight cassette. Only then can you safely unload the cassette of film.

A very common loading mistake is not making sure that the film is properly attached to the take-up spool. With many camera models, it is also possible for the cassette to sit out-of-square within its compartment with the result that, after a few frames, the film jams. On manual cameras, forcing the film wind-on lever for this, or any other reason, can rip the film in half, or tear the perforations so that you cannot advance it any further – or rewind it.

FILM HANDLING WITH A MANUAL CAMERA

The sequences below are typical for both compacts and SLRs, but may differ in detail according to the camera model. First, always read your instruction manual, and load and unload the camera out of direct sunlight or harsh, bright artificial light. When you are out in the open, crouch over the camera to provide some shade. If you forget to wind on after loading, your first two or three shots will be made on fogged film. Most cameras have

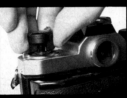

Loading 1 Open the back of the empty camera by pulling up on the rewind knob. The frame counter will return to its start position as the back opens.

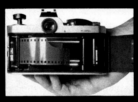

2 Place a cassette of film in the left-hand compartment. The film slot of the cassette must be facing the take-up spool, with the paler side of the film toward the lens.

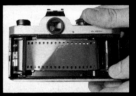

3 Secure the cassette by pressing home the rewind knob. Draw out enough film to insert the end into the slot in the take-up spool. You can rotate this spool with your thumb.

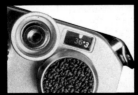

Unloading 1 After taking the last exposure on your film, the wind-on lever will jam or only partly advance. Do not force it to try to obtain an extra shot.

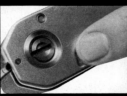

2 Press and hold in the film release stud located in the camera base. Some models have a release button near the camera top. Both release the film sprockets.

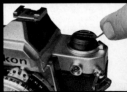

3 Fold out the handle from the rewind knob. Wind the handle in the direction of the marked arrow. You will feel the slight tension of the rewinding film.

If this happens you will have to remove the film in the dark and send it for processing.

Automatic loading and rewind

Most motorized cameras provide some form of semi-automatic film loading and rewind. Usually, all you need do is insert the film and line up the end with a mark positioned somewhere near the take-up spool. Then close the camera and simply depress the shutter release, to advance the film, until "1" appears on the frame counter. After the last exposure, the camera senses the end of the film, and signals that it must be rewound. Some cameras automatically rewind the film and then signal that the cassette is ready for removal.

- In a manual camera, you can tell whether a finished film is already rewound or not by gently turning the rewind knob in the direction of the arrow (do not touch the rewind button). If you feel resistance, the camera contains threaded film.
- If you forget to rewind and open the camera, immediately reclose it and rewind. Several of your last pictures will be ruined, but most of the others may be saved.
- If a film tears, or becomes detached from its cassette, open the camera in total darkness or use a changing bag (see p. 177). Transfer the coil of loose film to a light-proof container. Seal this and send it for processing, with a note giving the film type and length.

a frame counter that will advance even if the film is not winding on – perhaps because it has become detached from the take-up spool or has torn perforations. To make sure your film is winding on properly, all you need do is watch the rewind knob. After the first few exposures have taken up the slack, you should see it turn slightly every time you advance the film. Motor-wind cameras have an indicator to tell you that the film is advancing.

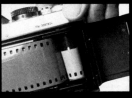

4 Gently advance the film (you may have to fire the shutter) until both rows of perforations engage with the film transport sprockets. Make certain that the film is straight.

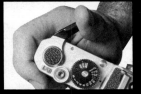

5 Close the back. Press the shutter and advance the film until the frame counter registers "1". If you wish, take up any slack by turning the rewind knob clockwise.

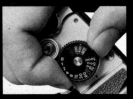

6 Set your film's speed (unless your camera reads DX-coding). Clip the box end to the camera back as a reminder of the type and length of film loaded.

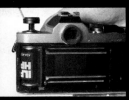

4 When the film has completely disengaged, the tension is released and the handle turns freely. Find a shaded place before opening the camera back to retrieve the film.

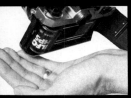

5 With the rewind knob raised, tip the film cassette into your palm. If the film end still protrudes, bend it to avoid confusing it with an unexposed film cassette.

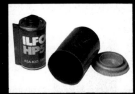

6 Store your exposed cassette of film in its original container until it can be processed. Keep the film container away from extremes of heat or cold.

Good camera habits

With practice, you can soon develop working habits which not only save time but also money by minimizing wasted film. These habits will help preserve your camera in good working order. Photographic equipment should be treated with care, but this does not mean that you should not use it for fear of damaging it in some way. The examples below are based on what can go wrong and systems of working that can result in more technically successful photographs.

Deciding priorities
For every subject make a decision about which factors are most important. If depth of field is a priority, for example, be prepared to use a shutter speed that requires a camera support. If frozen action and freedom from camera shake are essential, you may have to sacrifice depth of field.

Exposure measurement
Decide which exposure measurement system gives you the best results generally. Keep to this method for all but exceptional subjects. With these, shoot bracketed exposures to make sure of a good result.

Film stock
When you are shooting a lot of film in a short time, keep exposed cassettes in one pocket or camera case compartment, and unexposed cassettes in another. This avoids the possibility of confusion. Remove unexposed film stock from their cardboard cartons to save time.

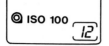

Loading procedure
Each time you load a new film into the camera, briefly inspect the back of the camera for any grit or dust. Also, make sure that the ISO film speed setting (set automatically or by hand) is correct.

Lens cleaning
At all times avoid touching the glass surfaces of your camera lens. Clean it when necessary using an anti-static brush, jet of compressed air, lens tissue, or camel hair brush. In extreme cases, wipe the glass with a clean cotton cloth moistened with denatured alcohol.

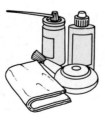

Obstructions
Even with an SLR camera, obstructions very close to the lens may not be visible in the viewfinder when shooting at full aperture. When you are focusing, the tip of the little finger of your focusing hand can easily appear in the picture. If you are using a compact camera, make sure there is not a finger, strap, or lock of hair just in front of the lens or any window. You won't see such an obstruction through the viewfinder, but it may result in a wrongly exposed or unsharp image.

Partly-exposed film
A partly exposed film can be removed from the camera at any time. You may want to do this to change from black and white to color, for example. Note the number of exposures you have already made and then rewind the film. When you later return this film to the camera, cap the lens and fire off the same number of exposures, plus at least one more for any difference in film threading.

Using two bodies
If you are taking a lot of of pictures quickly, it is much easier to work with two SLR camera bodies. You are less likely to run out of film at the wrong moment. You can also take the same shots in both black and white and color, or on negative as well as slide film. If you have two different focal length lenses in use, you will waste no time by having to change lenses.

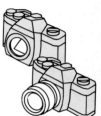

Storage hazards
Do not place your camera near a strong magnetic field – on a television set or close to hi-fi speakers, for example. This may upset its electronic metering. Also, do not store the camera near a source of chemical fumes if you have left film inside it. Color balance may be affected.

X-rays
Always empty your camera before submitting it to X-ray inspection. Even films in a lead-foil envelope are not really safe. Carry them in a separate bag and request a hand search or non-X ray inspection. Exposed fast film is more vulnerable to fogging than unexposed or slow material.

Rewind discipline
Develop the habit of rewinding immediately after you have taken the last exposure – even if there is no time just then to remove the cassette. If ever you are in doubt about whether a film has fully rewound, give plenty of additional turns of the rewind handle.

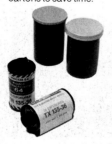

FILM

Many photographers have experience of only one or two films, either because they do not want to risk using other types or are simply bewildered by the huge range available for the 35 mm camera. Even if you finally settle with a limited range of favorite films, it is best to reach this number by experimenting with different types.

First, this section looks at the practical possibilities of different black and white and color films, for prints or slides. It discusses what each type is best for and where it would be the wrong choice. Sensitivity to light, response to colors, and special characteristics are compared as they affect your picture results.

You will also find in this section a visual guide to the types of things that can go wrong. This concentrates on errors due to subject conditions, mistaken camera settings, and mechanical problems with the film or camera itself. The examples given will help you decide whether any unexpected results are due to your mishandling or faulty material and equipment, or bad printing or processing by the laboratory. The section goes on to show you how to use the additional services offered by some laboratories to increase the speed of your film, or change its characteristics in other ways.

How films differ

You can choose from a wide range of films to use with your 35 mm camera. The first decisions to make are whether you want color or black and white, negative or slide. Most film types come in a variety of speeds (from slow to fast, depending on their sensitivity to light) and lengths (giving different numbers of exposures). Both of these factors affect price – cost per frame increases with film speed and the shortness of the roll. More unusual films are also available – these include films with an extreme contrast response, sensitivity to infrared light, as well as films allowing instant processing.

Film specifications

Most manufacturers make color and black and white films, either under their own or store brand names. A few manufacturers, such as Kodak or Agfa, make the more specialized types, and these are less widely available. In general, differences between

Cassettes 35 mm cassettes are of uniform size and can accommodate from 12–36 full-frame exposure lengths of film. As shown below, film is wound on a single spool, and then enclosed in a light-tight metal or plastic sleeve with end caps. The sleeve has a slot (light-trapped by black velvet), through which the film is drawn while in the camera. You rewind the film into the cassette before removal for processing. Most plastic and some metal cassettes can be refilled (see p. 64).

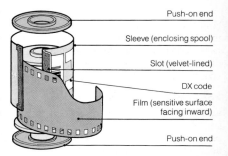

Push-on end

Sleeve (enclosing spool)

Slot (velvet-lined)

DX code

Film (sensitive surface facing inward)

Push-on end

BLACK AND WHITE FILMS

Nearly all black and white films are panchromatic (responsive to all colors, in shades of gray) and designed to give negatives for printing. They can be divided into slow, medium, and fast types. As the x20 enlargements show (below), grain is coarsest in the faster-speed films. You can gauge the size of the original images from the contact print below.

Slow film Films less sensitive than ISO 100 are relatively slow, fine-grained, and slightly more contrasty than the other types here. Use films such as Pan F, at ISO 32, for general purposes where a high degree of magnification will be required. Tech pan (ISO 25) is still higher resolution, but must be accurately exposed. Slow film will reveal maximum image detail, but you will need bright light levels or slow shutter speeds.

Medium film Films in this category range from about ISO 125 to ISO 400 and represent a good compromise between finer grain but slower types, and the more sensitive but grainier faster types. The ISO 125 grain structure (shown below) is unobtrusive for most subjects up to a full-frame enlargement size of about 8 x 10 in (20 x 25 cm). More photographs are taken on this type of film than on any other.

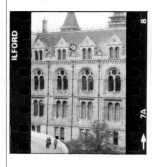

Kodak
technical
pan film
ESTAR-AH Base
36 EXPOSURES
TP 135-36

ILFORD
PAN F 135
DX 36

Kodak
Plus-X pan
125 film DX
24 EXP.
PX 135-24

ILFORD
Plus
400
DX 135 36

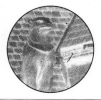

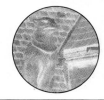

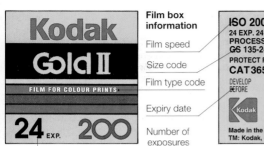

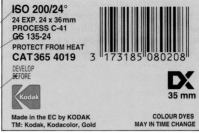

Film box information	
Film speed	Kodak Gold II
Size code	
Film type code	
Expiry date	
Number of exposures	

ISO 200/24°
24 EXP. 24 x 36mm
PROCESS C-41
GS 135-24
PROTECT FROM HEAT
CAT 365 4019
DEVELOP BEFORE

Made in the EC by KODAK
TM: Kodak, Kodacolor, Gold

DX 35 mm
COLOUR DYES
MAY IN TIME CHANGE

brands are less obvious in black and white than in color films (see p. 52). Every 35 mm film comes in a standard size cassette, packed in a box showing its size, length, speed and expiry date

At one time, film speed was shown in ASA or DIN, now standardized as ISO. The figure following ISO doubles for each doubling of film sensitivity. On simple or older cameras you have to set the ISO or ASA scale for the film loaded. Most modern cameras, however, automatically read film speed off a DX-coded pattern of squares on the cassette. If the cassette has no coding, the camera defaults to ISO 100. For subjects in dim light or if rapidly moving, you will need film of ISO 400 or higher, although the faster the film the more obvious the grain pattern of the image, especially on large prints. Simpler cameras often have a restricted ISO scale and you may not be able to set very slow or fast films.

Fast film Films of up to ISO 1600 or 3200 are also available. Some of these can be push processed by the laboratory (see p. 62) to achieve an effective speed of ISO 12,800. The granular appearance of the print breaks up fine detail, but with some subjects you can use this to your advantage. Fast films are invaluable for combining dim light and moving subjects, especially if you also want to work with a small lens aperture.

Special film Several special black and white films are made (see p. 191). The type below uses color negative chemistry to produce black and white images in dye rather than silver. This means you can send it to any laboratory for processing instead of locating the few that still process monochrome films. Nominally rated at ISO 400, it can be exposed between ISO 125 and 1600 and still produce usable negatives.

Black and white slides Special 35mm film forms black and white slides instead of negatives for printing. The enlarged detail below has been taken from the film, not a paper print. The Agfa film requires special "reversal" processing by the makers. The Polapan film is reversal processed by the user in a special processor (see p. 204). These films are slow and fine grained, and they are ideal in lectures or slide shows.

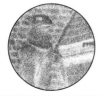 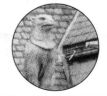

Color film

You have the widest choice of film when working in color. Apart from negative and slide differences, color films also differ in their speed and suitability for use in daylight or tungsten light. Dye variations also exist between different brands.

With slides, the original film is returned, each frame mounted ready for projection. Color negatives are only intermediates for the final paper print, and show the subject in negative tones and complementary colors, as well as having an overall yellow-pink appearance. This warm tint helps reduce contrast and improves color accuracy when enlargements are produced. It is possible, however, to have slides and black and white prints made from these color

Negatives or slides?

Films for color negatives and for slides differ in their structure and, therefore, the processing required to produce a film image.

Daylight-balanced film Slide films designed for daylight or flash will record scenes lit by tungsten (domestic or photolamp) sources with a warm orange cast. Use a blue lens filter to compensate and, preferably, for negative film too.

Correct   Incorrect

Tungsten-balanced film A few slide films are balanced for tungsten photolamp lighting. Pictures taken on this type of film with daylight or flash will have a strong blue color cast, unless you use an orange correction filter over the camera lens.

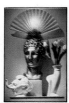

Correct   Incorrect

NEGATIVE AND SLIDE FILMS

COLOR NEGATIVE FILM
Although color negative films are sold under many different brand names, they are all made by only a handful of manufacturers. The vast majority of films are either ISO 100 or 400. The faster films are much more expensive but most can be push processed (see p. 62) to twice their ISO speed rating. For the grain comparisons here (far right) a small image area (ringed in the full-frame print near right) has been enlarged x10.

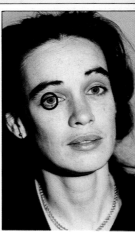

COLOR SLIDE FILM
Slide films are made in a wide range of speeds. Because there is (usually) no printing stage, slide films are balanced for daylight illumination or for tungsten. For these comparisons enlargement was x20.

Slow film Films slower than ISO 100 are very fine grained, but need ample light. Kodachrome 25 has exceptionally fine resolution. Slow films must be exposed with greater accuracy than faster types.

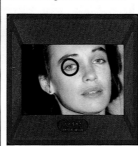

negatives, and color prints made from slides. Sometimes, though, quality will suffer due to these mis-matched processes.

Color balance and speed
Most color films are designed to give correct colors with daylight or flash. Other types of subject lighting – fluorescent or tungsten, for example – often produce greenish or orange results. Matching light source to film type is critical with slides. You may need correcting filters (see p. 82) over the lens. Color negative films are more tolerant, since colors can be corrected during the printing stage, but it is still best to use a suitable filter for light sources other than daylight or flash. As you can see from the examples below, the faster the film speed the more grainy the results – although this is less marked than in black and white materials. Most films incorporate the film speed in the product name.

Slow film Films of about ISO 100 produce images with very little apparent grain. Slow speed film is adequate for all well-lit situations as well as for flash. Subject colors are generally rich.

Medium film ISO 200 is a good film for dull conditions. Films of ISO 400 have just perceptibly more grain. They are still a good compromise between slower, finer-grain and faster, coarser-grain types.

Fast film Films of ISO 1000 and above give more muted colors and reduced resolution. However, they are excellent in poor existing light, and tolerate errors of lighting color more readily than slower types.

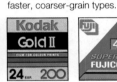

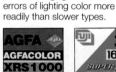

Medium film ISO 100-400 slide films offer a popular compromise between sensitivity and grain. They are useful for general lighting conditions. Ektachrome 160 is balanced for tungsten light.

Fast film Films of ISO 1000 and over show noticeable grain, although this can be attractive. Useful for sports photography or similar, in poor light. Designed for push processing with minimal loss of quality.

Special film Infrared Ektachrome is a false-color film for aerial work, but good for special effects. Polachrome gives immediate results using a special processor. Slides are darker than regular film.

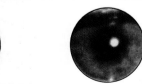

Choosing the right film

No one film type suits all kinds of photography. But changing film too often means that you never become familiar with any one type. Always choose the best film for the end result you want (prints or slides), taking into account the lighting and type of subject. Even then, unless you use all the film for one scene, your film may have to meet the needs of many different situations.

Types of result

The first decision you must make is whether you want color or black and white, prints or slides. Black and white films can give a simplified, graphic result – the subject being shown in a refreshingly interpretative form. For large prints, black and white is cheaper than color, and for certain publications, such as many newspapers, only black and white pictures can be used.

In order to cover yourself for every type of result, it is best to shoot on color negative film. From this, prints and slides, in color and black and white, can all be made. But for the highest quality color slides, and pictures for color reproduction (for books and magazines, for example), you should shoot on color slide film.

It is possible to reduce costs when you need color prints by shooting on color slide film – especially when you have taken several bracketed exposures, or you are trying many versions of a difficult technique. Then, instead of paying to have prints made from every negative, all you need do is

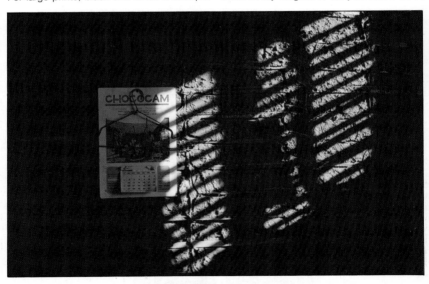

Contrasty subjects
Films vary in their ability to record light extremes in a scene. Slides need greater exposure accuracy than negative films. The picture above was shot on Kodachrome 25, reading exposure from sunlit wall areas, and taking several bracketed versions.

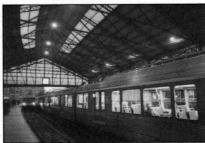

Mixed lighting Mixed light sources are more obvious in a color photograph than they appear to the eye. The picture, left, was shot on daylight-type fast film. Although more tolerant than slow film, mercury vapor station lights appear green, and tungsten train lights yellow.

MATCHING FILM AND SUBJECT

Type of subject or situation	Suggested choice of film
Sports and action. Candids of animals and children	A fast film with good latitude. Dye image film for black and white. Color film of ISO 400 or above, but avoid extreme ISO speeds.
Formal portraits, nudes, and babies	To preserve delicate subject qualities use slow or medium-speed film. For a very different effect, use a grainy black and white film of more than ISO 1000.
Active subjects in dim light, using fast shutter speeds and/or small lens apertures	Try films of ISO 1600 or faster, but avoid push processing them if lighting is also contrasty. Accept grainy image appearance and poorer tone appearance.
Mixed lighting. Color shots in rooms partly lit by daylight, partly by tungsten lamps	Use color negative rather than slide film. (Areas of the print can then be locally corrected during enlarging.) You can also use daylight slide film and add flash, or tungsten type film and try to curtain off most of the daylight.
Subjects shot under varied lighting conditions, using a camera with fixed (or limited) exposure settings	Load film according to lighting intensity. For example, ISO 100 for a sunlit beach; ISO 400 for an evening landscape; ISO 1600 for a domestic interior at night (without flash).

Unmatched color
You do not always have to match color film to lighting. The picture below was shot on tungsten film. The tungsten lamps on the Christmas tree are fairly neutral, while the more powerful flood-lights on the buildings have a bluish cast. In the shot, right, daylight color film has made the tungsten-lit fountains record as orange. This warm look can be more effective than the coldness of the correct result (see p. 82).

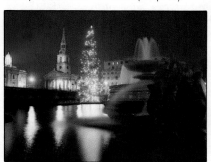

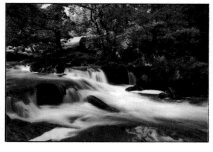

Speed for subject Try to relate the speed of your film to subject conditions, and take into account any interpretation you want to give. For example, the picture right was shot on ISO 25 film. A small (f 16) aperture made it possible to give a 1 sec shutter speed without overexposing. The long exposure time transformed fast-moving water into flowing, mist-like shapes. Always carry a fast film too for dim light, flash failure, or subjects that need fast shutter speeds. If necessary, you can use this film with a gray neutral density filter (see p.173) to give slow exposures.

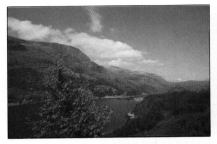

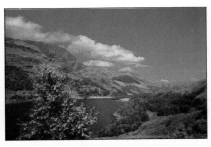

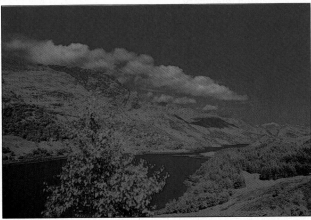

Using false color film
You can use false color infrared Ektachrome slide film for fantasy effects. It works best with subjects like sunlit growing vegetation which reflects infrared strongly (see also p. 188). The picture on the top right was taken on I-R Ektachrome through the recommended deep yellow filter. For the richer result shown right, a deep green filter was used. The same scene taken on regular Ektachrome film is shown above.

select pictures for enlarging from the easily judged, and relatively low-cost slides.

Color balance and speed

For most pictures you will need daylight-balanced film, but for a series of slides of interiors in tungsten light, or studio shots with photolamps, use tungsten-balanced film. Choice of film speed depends on lighting levels and whether or not the subject is moving. Always aim for as many exposure setting options as possible, so avoid combinations of bright light and fast film as much as dim light and slow film. A fast film is a good choice when moving subjects in dim light are too distant to freeze with flash. Slow film is ideal where subject detail and texture must be recorded faithfully. Finally, there are your own brand preferences – whether you prefer the colder tints produced by Ektachrome or the slightly richer colors of Fuji films.

● Film choice for some basic cameras is limited by the speed range of their exposure meters.
● Do not mix brands when shooting a subject in color. Alternating between, say, Ektachrome and Kodachrome in the same series, exaggerates their color differences. Similarly, prints made on Kodak, Fuji, or Agfa color papers should not be mixed.
● To shoot the same subject on two types of film, use an extra body and the same lens. But bear in mind that shooting in color requires a different visual approach to shooting with black and white film.
● Fast films can cost up to 50 per cent more than slow ones. Color negative and black and white films are, however, similar in price.
● As a precaution against flash failure or difficult lighting conditions, it is a good idea always to have one fast "pushable" film in your camera case. This should be at least ISO 400.

Identifying film faults

Sometimes, your film results returned from processing have strange and unexpected features. It is important to identify these faults, first in order to rule out equipment failure, and second so that you can avoid making the same mistake. Errors can be caused by difficult subject or lighting conditions. More often, though, they are due to lens and camera setting faults, or connected with film and film loading. Occasionally the fault lies with the processing laboratory.

Film error or print error?
If you receive prints, you must first decide if any errors present occurred during the printing stage. Compare carefully the original film images with the resulting prints. Take special note of any dark or light areas, parts out of focus, or detail cropped off the the image. Look to see how much detail you can see in the shadows and highlights on the film in relation to the same areas on the

print. If your film image seems free from any error, return it for reprinting.

What to look for
Handle the film carefully. Hold it by its two edges, pressed gently between thumb and finger. Do not touch the emulsion (less shiny) surface. Gaps between pictures, and the perforated edges, can give as many clues as the images themselves. Slight overall tints in negatives can be ignored. The orange/yellow mask in color negatives varies from brand to brand and some black and white negatives also have a pale blue tinge. The following four pages show a selection of faults, along with suggested causes and prevention. (For errors involving flash, see p. 151.) All photographers make mistakes sometimes, but while you should track down the causes, you should also look out for "faults" that are interesting in themselves. Some of these may lead you on to more interpretative pictures.

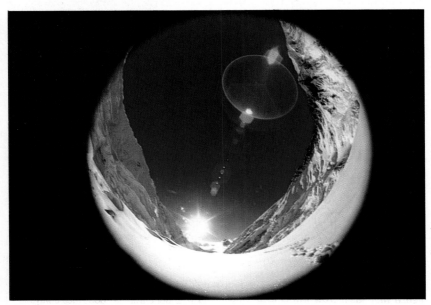

Turning faults to advantage Always look for ways of exploiting technical faults. This mountain landscape, taken with a fisheye lens, shows a series of light patches across the sky – the result of flare. They add a strange and dramatic element to an already unusual photograph. You must carefully control this effect through the choice of viewpoint, placing the sun well off center in the frame.

FAULTS – SUBJECT CONDITIONS AND CAMERA SETTINGS

The kind of faults shown below are most often caused by influences such as lighting conditions, and the careless handling of lens and exposure controls. They are common to all camera types, although problems such as obstruction of the lens and unintentional filtering are more common with compacts because you are not looking through the actual picture-taking lens.

The most important errors to recognize are over- and underexposure. At first these look very different on each type of film, but they do

OVEREXPOSURE

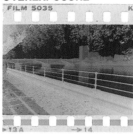
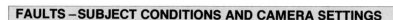

Cause The images here received too much light. This was caused by a shutter setting too slow or lens aperture too large. If the whole film is faulty, perhaps you set the camera's meter incorrectly, or your batteries may be running down.
Identification Overexposure mostly affects lighter parts of

the subject. Image detail here becomes difficult to see – either because it is bleached (slides) or very dense (negatives). Color negatives print highlight areas flat and with pale, degraded hues. Prints from overexposed black and white negatives show light subjects as featureless white paper or flat gray

tone. Enlargements often have exaggerated grain and appear less sharp than normal.
Remedy A few laboratories offer chemical reduction of black and white negatives, but grain still remains exaggerated. You can improve results by asking for development to be "held back" (see p. 62).

UNDEREXPOSURE

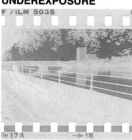
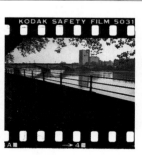
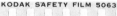
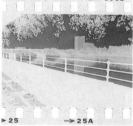

Cause The three images above have not received sufficient light – shutter speed was too short or lens aperture too small for the subject conditions and film. If only some frames are underexposed, your meter reading technique is probably faulty. If, however, the entire film is affected, your meter may

need attention or you may have set the wrong ISO speed.
Identification Each frame differs in appearance because processed negatives (left and right) look lighter the less light they receive, but slides (center) become darker. In all cases, subject shadows suffer most. Details are largely missing –

areas of clear film on negatives or dense tone on slides.
Remedy A few laboratories offer chemical reduction for dense slides. Underexposed color negatives may give an acceptable print on black and white paper. A whole film that is underexposed can be given push processing (see p. 62).

have certain features in common. The other faults here are illustrated on a mixture of films – the same symptoms will appear in different colors and reversed tones on other materials. In all cases, the best policy is to avoid making the same mistake next time, because little can usually be done to salvage good pictures at this stage. Exposure errors can sometimes be corrected if sent for skilful (and expensive) hand printing. Keep all your overexposed slides for possible use in photographic montages.

CAMERA SHAKE

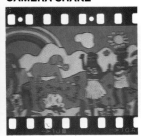

Cause Moving the camera during exposure, giving minute but equal streaking of every picture detail. Often caused by selecting too long an exposure time.
Prevention Practice bracing yourself for hand-held shooting (see pp. 26–7). Make more use of firm supports, especially with telephoto lenses.

RAINDROPS

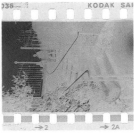

Cause Droplets of water on the lens or lens filter resulting in blurred patches of image detail.
Prevention In rain always use a lens hood. Cover the lens surface with an easy-to-clean clear glass UV filter.

FLARE

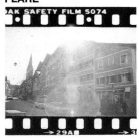

Cause Harsh, direct light shining into the lens. Gives an overall lowering of contrast or forms a series of aperture-shaped patches across the picture.
Prevention Use an effective lens hood, or shade the lens with your hand. Change camera position.

OBSTRUCTION

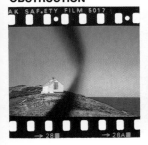

Cause Fingers, camera strap or similar just in front of the lens. Corners of the image can be vignetted by a lens hood or filters that are too deep. More common on compact cameras.
Prevention Make sure you keep things away from the lens, and that lens attachments are of the right size.

OVERALL COLOR

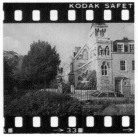

Cause Accidentally leaving a color filter over the lens producing an overall color cast.
Prevention Remove any color or special effects filters as soon as you have finished using them.

STREAKS

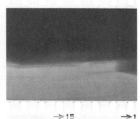

Cause Moving the film with the shutter open occurs when a slow speed is combined with a motor drive, or by winding on during a prolonged exposure.
Prevention Make sure the shutter has closed before winding on or rewinding the film.

FAULTS –FILM AND FILM LOADING

Faults illustrated below and on the facing page are due to mishaps with the film itself. They show how careless loading and handling result in totally ruined photographs. Bear in mind that the same error gives different looking results on negative and slide films. Fogging film to light, for example, makes slides turn clear and negatives turn black.

If you suspect that your camera has a light leak or it is physically damaging the film, match the fault to its source by replacing a few frames of the processed film in the camera

FILM NOT TRANSPORTING

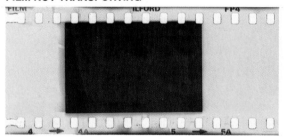

FILM END

Cause The film has become detached from the take-up spool shortly after loading. As the film remained stationary, all the pictures were taken on top of each other, giving one totally overexposed frame. Often, a nearby perforation is torn by the sprocket wheel.
Prevention This is a simple loading error anyone can make, especially if you are in a hurry when loading the camera. The best method of prevention is always to wind sufficient film on to the take-up spool, and, if using a manual camera, to make sure that the rewind knob turns as you wind the film on after each exposure.

Cause Part of the last frame missing, damaged, or fogged. This occurs when you squeeze in an extra frame. But during processing the laboratory needs the last inch to clip or tape films together, thereby spoiling your bonus picture.
Prevention Nothing can be done to prevent this.

FILM UNEXPOSED

DOUBLE EXPOSURE

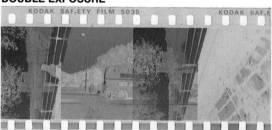

Cause A color negative film that looks like this has not been exposed. Perhaps you sent an unused film for processing, or the camera shutter is jammed, or you forgot to remove the lens cap on a compact camera.
Prevention If it is the shutter, look through the camera back while firing the shutter.

Cause If the whole film shows overlapping images and frame lines as shown above, it was probably put through the camera twice. This happens if you load an already exposed film in mistake for a new one. It can also occur if you change film in mid roll. In this case, you may have replaced the part-exposed film and wound it to the number of the last un-exposed frame, forgetting to cover the lens.
Prevention Either mark used cassettes or wind in the film leader on all exposed cassettes. If you make mid-roll changes cover the lens and leave 1–2 frames blank in case of error.

back. Locate the film where it was originally exposed, its duller, emulsion, surface toward the lens and the image upside down.

Other faults, not shown here, include various kinds of colored patches and abrasions. Colored spots and water marks are signs of bad processing. Long scratches running the length of the film are most often caused by rough handling during or after processing. Scratches are also caused by grit, either lodged inside the camera back or caught in the velvet slot of the film cassette.

FOGGED FILM

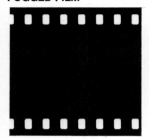

TORN FILM

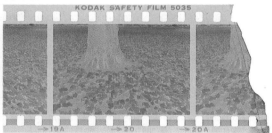

Cause This negative film has been heavily fogged. Possibly the camera back opened with the film inside unprotected. Storing film near chemical fumes or exposing it to X rays can also produce this result.
Prevention Make sure the camera back is secure and store film away from chemicals.

Cause Modern film is extremely tough and it is unusual for it to tear in half. This is almost always caused by forcing the camera's wind-on mechanism – perhaps at the end of a film or when the film has jammed for some reason. It can also be caused by a faulty motor drive unit. Tearing is more common in very cold conditions when film does become brittle.
Prevention Never force the film. If it jams open the camera in total darkness and release the film. Carefully coil the torn lengths of film into a light-tight container and send it for processing.

FRAME DEBRIS

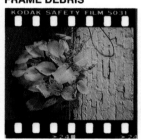

BANDS OF FOG

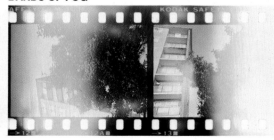

Cause Sharply defined curved lines, specks, or an irregular picture edge can be caused by debris in the camera. Typically, a hair caught in front of the film casts a shadow on every shot.
Prevention Open the empty camera, holding the shutter open on "B". Thoroughly clean the space between lens and film.

Cause The slide film above has several bands of fog, decreasing in severity, across the width of the film. This effect can be caused by opening the camera back very briefly in the light at the end of a film (perhaps because you forgot to rewind). Similar looking fog marks occur if the camera back leaks light along its hinge or catch. Degree of fogging depends on brightness of the light, length of exposure, and speed of the film.
Prevention Make sure that you always rewind the film completely before opening the back. If you suspect your camera does leak light, take it to a professional repair shop.

Manipulating film speed

The ISO rating given to your film assumes that it receives the standard, recommended processing. Sometimes, shooting conditions, such as dim lighting, force you to use a film as if it had a higher rating. Similarly, you can use film as if it had a lower speed. In both cases you must tell the laboratory to give it special processing to compensate. These speed manipulations are useful when lighting is difficult, but they do produce side effects.

Uprating and downrating film

Uprating film speed (underexposing) and extending development means that the film performs as if faster, more grainy and more contrasty. Uprating is useful when you need a faster shutter speed or smaller aperture in poor light, or to extend the effective range of your flash. You can also uprate to brighten contrast in a scene. Downrating (overexposing) and holding back development gives the opposite effects. It is useful with contrasty subjects such as interiors with bright window light.

You must treat all pictures on a film the same way when you manipulate the speed rating. You must, therefore, plan what you are doing and adjust the camera's meter to the appropriate new setting. The amount by which you can change the ISO setting and still obtain acceptable results depends on the film type. Greatest manipulation is possible with black and white film, least with color negative film. In general, fast film has wider limits than slow film, and it is usually possible to take uprating further than downrating.

Adjusting the camera

To manipulate film speed, use a camera that allows ISO speed to be manually set, or has an exposure-compensation control. To uprate film, turn the setting to twice the film's ISO figure, or set exposure compensation to -1. This will expose the film as if it were one stop faster (ISO 800 instead of 400, for example). If you set three times the normal ISO, or -1.5, the increase is 1½ stops. Adjusting in the opposite direction downrates film – settings shown below for example will expose ISO 400 film as if it were ISO 200.

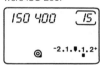

Electronic display

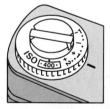

Manual set dial

THE EFFECTS O

Uprated films must have extra development, or "pushing". Downrated films need the opposite treatment and this is called "holding back". You can most easily do this if you process your own films. Alternatively, use a laboratory offering such a service. Avoid confusion by marking the film end or cassette with its revised ISO rating immediately you remove it from the camera. There are limits to the degree film speed can be changed before contrast and colors become unacceptable. With black and white film this is about a x4 uprating, and for color negatives about x2. Downrating limits are about x½ ISO for black and white and only half a stop for color. With variable speed black and white film you can have a mixture of frames exposed at ratings between ISO 125 and 1600. The film is then developed for the time suggested for the fastest setting used.

● Do not uprate slow and medium film when you could use normally processed fast film instead.
● E-6 process films (Ektachrome) tend to give warmer colors pushed beyond 1½ stops and colder colors if held back beyond 1 stop.
● Use compensation processing to help correct exposure mistakes if you or the camera misread film speed.
● If in doubt about processing, make a "clip test". Cut the first few frames and have it processed. Then adjust processing for the rest of the film according to the test results.
● Color negative film that receives heavily compensated processing may produce acceptable looking negatives, but these prove impossible to print.
● Many cities have professional laboratories that offer a wider range of compensated processing than the average laboratory.

HINTS AND TIPS

OMPENSATION PROCESSING

NORMALLY RATED AND CORRECTLY PROCESSED

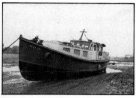

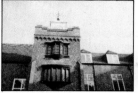

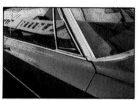

Black and white negative The print above was made from a correctly exposed and processed negative. It was printed on normal paper, designed to match the negative's contrast characteristics.

Color negative This print was made from a normally rated and processed negative. Printed on regular negative/positive color paper, color balance is consistent from highlights to shadows.

Color slide This image shows Ektachrome slide film exposed at the published ISO rating and given normal processing. Subtle shades of color can be picked out in the bright chrome and dark paintwork.

UPRATED AND PUSH PROCESSED

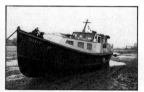

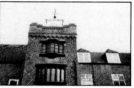

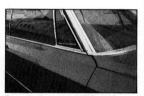

Rated x4 normal ISO Under-exposure and extended development (above) has brightened image contrast, improving the dull lighting. However, this improvement is at the expense of shadow detail – the hull is now dark and featureless.

Rated x2 normal ISO and push processed This print is brighter than the print top, but delicate color is lost in light areas such as the sky. Shadows are less colorful, too, and colors generally have a coarsened appearance.

Rated x2 normal ISO and push processed Contrast is increased. The chrome trim looks bleached, and shadows have become magenta. Graduations of color are now missing – the slide begins to take on the appearance of a copy.

DOWNRATED AND HELD BACK

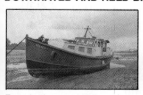

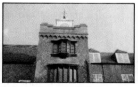

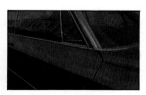

Rated x¼ normal ISO, followed by held-back processing This treatment gives a flat negative that produces a low-contrast black and white print. Shadows have ample detail, but the general effect is gray and lifeless. However, it improves results when the subject is harshly lit.

Rated x½ normal ISO, followed by held-back processing The negative produced by this effect has flatter color. The resulting print colors are richer in the highlight and shadow areas, but show different casts such as the blue sky and pink shadows in the version above, for example.

Rated x¼ normal ISO, followed by held-back processing This type of treatment gives unacceptable results. The white parts of the image have grayed-over and show a distinct color cast. Furthermore, other areas of the slide are almost colorless, dark, and flat.

Film economy and care

Films are delicate and expensive, so do not let them deteriorate through bad storage or handling. You can cut your costs by methods such as loading your own cassettes using a daylight bulk film loader. But most important of all, you must protect your finished negatives and slides – they become more important with the passing of time.

Cutting your costs

The most direct way to reduce costs is to buy a can of bulk 35 mm film and load your own cassettes. You will soon make up the cost of the loader (see right) as 100 ft (30 m) of film will produce about 19 half-price, 36-exposure cassettes. One problem, if your camera uses DX-coding (see p. 51), is that each cassette should have the correct checker-board pattern as blank cassettes are set at ISO 100 by such cameras. Other disadvantages are that you may damage film by careless handling when loading, and fewer types are available in bulk rolls.

Storage and handling

Film emulsions are sensitive to gasses and X rays, as well as light. Keep new films away from motor exhausts, solvents, paints, and pesticides. At airports, do not allow your unprocessed film to be X rayed. Avoid high

(see p. 51)

USING A FILM LOADER

A loader holds a bulk length of film in a circular light-tight chamber. The film end protrudes through a light trap so that you can attach it to the spool of a cassette. (Either buy a special cassette or re-use an ordinary type – if suitable.) Closing the light-tight lid opens the internal film chamber, and then you can wind the film into your cassette. A counter indicates the number of exposures.

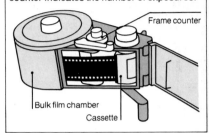

Frame counter

Bulk film chamber

Cassette

temperatures and excessive humidity as in these conditions the film's gelatin coating may start to decompose. Ideally, store your film in the main compartment of an ordinary refrigerator, or in a cool box on location. Protect processed film in paper sleeves, albums, or glass-fronted slide mounts. You must also take care when projecting your processed slides – prolonged projection may bleach the image.

STORAGE CONDITIONS AND FILM LIFE				
Film type	**Storage temperature**			
	Below 75°F (24°C)	Below 60°F (16°C)	Below 50°F (10°C)	Below 0°F to −9°F (−18°C to −23°C)
Unprocessed in original pack *Safe storage time*	Up to 2 months	Up to 6 months	Up to 12 months	Expiry date extended several years
Warm-up time (from refrigerator)* *Cassette*	—	¾ hour	1 hour	1½ hours
Can	—	2 hours	3 hours	5 hours
Processed (dye) images (life extended by)	—	x3	x8	x100

*Period required between removal from storage and opening of pack (to avoid condensation).
Notes Infrared films should be stored between 0°F and −9°F (−18°C and −23°C). Amateur film expiry dates are based on storage in or out of the camera at room temperature – 75°F (24°C). Professional color films are designed to be stored at below 55°F (13°C).

HINTS AND TIPS
● Bulk loaders are notorious for marking film unless kept scrupulously clean. Use a blower brush.
● Exposed, unprocessed film is more sensitive to light or chemical fogging.
● The effects of X-rays have a cumulative effect on unprocessed film. Many exposures at baggage checks may cause fogging to occur.

SOLVING PICTURE PROBLEMS

This, the largest section of the book, concentrates specifically on problem solving. It brings together equipment and materials, techniques and ideas, to help you meet particular picture-taking challenges that could arise.

The problems are not specific to any one subject and are more often linked to actual shooting conditions. In the same way, there is seldom just one solution, but rather a range of answers depending on the kind of effect you prefer. In some cases special equipment may be necessary. More often, though, knowledge of a few simple routines leads to successful results.

This section also deals with problems of lighting – indoors and out, natural or artificial. Sometimes the concern is mostly technical, such as shooting at night, copying drawings, or taking accurate color pictures with a mixture of different light sources. Other lighting problems here are more concerned with the visual effect and feeling you want to convey in the photograph – how to give a sense of movement, drama, or brilliance, for example. Sometimes you will find that answers overlap, but the topics as a whole have been selected to span the widest possible range of practical photographic situations.

Utilizing the picture shape

The possibility of working within an upright or horizontal picture shape is one of the most useful tools at your disposal. Choice will depend partly on the shape of your subject and its surroundings, and partly on the type of feeling you want to convey. Always try to fill up the whole frame with elements that contribute in some way to the main theme. Picture shape need not be fixed at the standard 35 mm format – you can plan shots to be cropped squarer or more rectangular.

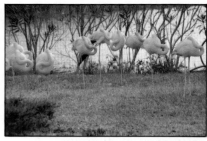

Picture shapes and proportions
Tall buildings in a city environment or open landscapes may automatically suggest vertical or horizontal framing. But provided there is room to vary your distance, or you can change lens focal length, you can show any subject within either shape. Try framing a scene both ways – horizontal pictures tend to strengthen horizontal lines and sense of sideways movement, while vertical shots have the opposite effect. The more extreme the proportions of subject elements within the frame the more your eyes are forced to scan in a particular way. A square shape is generally the most static. Experiment with proportions – especially with prints, which you can easily trim.

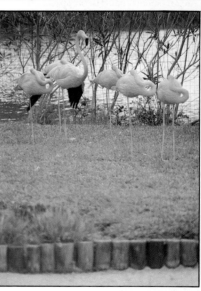

Using the space
In general, coming closer to the subject fills up and strengthens your composition.

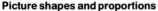

Vertical or horizontal
Simply by turning the camera, the same scene is shown with strengthened horizontal lines (top) or with more vertical flow (above).

Exaggerated proportions The beach scene (left) is improved by trimming the print at the line shown. This creates more interesting, unequal bands of blue, and encourages the eye to scan the picture.

CROPPING TO IMPROVE THE IMAGE

There is an adage in photography that the tighter you crop your pictures the better they become. You can learn much by placing two L-shaped pieces of white cardboard over your prints. When overlapped they form a four-sided frame of variable size and proportions – use this to see how much surplus content you can remove with advantage from most pictures. If your processing laboratory provides contact prints, use L shapes to indicate how enlargements should be cropped.

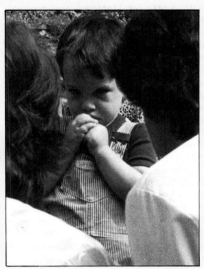

Cropping for emphasis In this candid shot, the essence of the picture is the small child's relationship with the two adults. Enlarging and cropping tightly (far right) removes distracting elements, producing a much stronger picture composition.

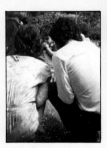

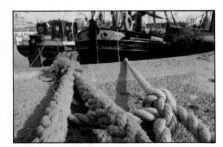

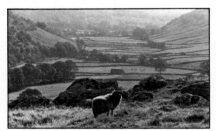

Framing and setting The pictures above use a generously framed foreground and background, respectively to provide the important

general scene. Each setting directs you to a center of interest. In the color scene ropes align powerfully with the bottom of the shot.

If for some reason you cannot work sufficiently close, use foreground vegetation or a doorway as a natural cropping device to focus attention. Sometimes, though, the general setting is equally as important as the main subject. You can, for example, keep the subject small and include foreground or background details in such a way that the eye is guided toward them. If the surroundings are featureless and empty – concrete, grassland, or flat sea, for example – giving them generous space will suggest a subject's smallness and isolation,

● You can alter the proportions of a slide by using opaque material in the slide mount to crop the image.
● When shooting a portrait (in profile) leave more space in front of the face than behind. Otherwise the picture will seem cramped.
● A zoom lens helps you fill the frame when you cannot easily change your position.
● If your pictures display a variety of shapes and proportions, they help to give lively album layouts. Uniform pictures are useful for comparisons.

Using foreground and background

A good picture can be ruined by irrelevant detail cluttering up the foreground or background. You should choose a setting which complements your main subject in tone, pattern or color. Surroundings are often a way of giving extra information – perhaps suggesting where the subject lives. You can also create strange or humorous pictures through juxtaposing unlikely subjects and surroundings. The best way of dealing with problem foregrounds and backgrounds is to examine them carefully, then control their influence through viewpoint, lighting, and depth of field.

The effects of changing viewpoint
The quickest way of filling an empty space, or excluding or covering unwanted details, is to change camera viewpoint by altering its height, shifting it to the left or right, or moving closer to or further away from the subject. Raising your viewpoint and angling the camera downward emphasizes foreground parts of the scene. Outdoors, this will set your subject against more ground than sky, and you may have brought foreground foliage into the frame. Paths or steps between you and the subject fill more

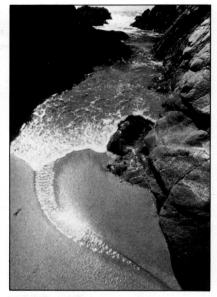

Exploiting a strong foreground For the picture above the photographer tilted the camera downward and used a wide-angle lens in order to include plenty of foreground detail. Reflected light forms a sparkling link through the whole composition.

CREATING A NEW FOREGROUND

Often the foregrounds of architectural or landscape shots are marred by parked automobiles or street signs, or a seascape is ruined by a littered foreshore. An easy way to overcome problems of this kind is to bring your camera down almost to ground level. From here small objects – grass, shingle, a ridge of snow – will cover up large areas of the previous foreground and mid-distance view. On bare ground, place wood or foliage near the lens to suggest natural growth. Professionals often carry around branches to help fill an empty sky or hide litter. Set them up near the camera and record them out-of-focus.

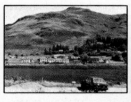

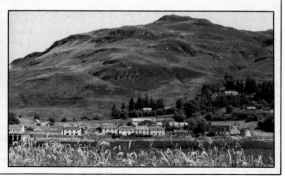

How to improve a landscape
The eye-level shot (above) shows a foreground parking lot. For the version right, the photographer placed the camera 3 ins (7.6 cm) from the ground.

Framing Sometimes an open foreground shape will relate to something in the background. Two parts of the pier (right) still look isolated, but this viewpoint creates a patterned structure.

Assertive surroundings Backgrounds can be too assertive. Surroundings in the shot below complement the flower in tone and shape. In the shot below right, flower and leaf shapes become confused.

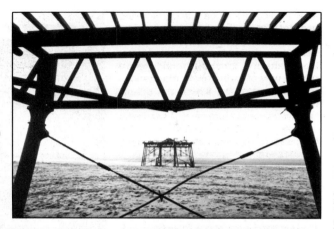

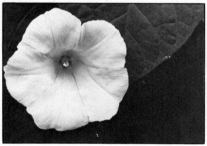
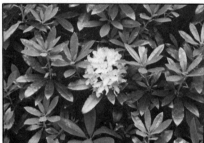

foreground space. A lower viewpoint gives the opposite effect.

Shifting to the left or right alters the foreground parts of the picture in one direction, and the background items in the other. Moving closer crops some foreground details, and makes them look larger in relation to items in the background. (Your control of scale increases if you can alter lens focal length, see pp. 162–3).

Other controls

When there is no choice of viewpoint you will have to control background and foreground in other ways. Try shooting at a wide aperture to create shallow depth of field and reduce assertive detail. For sports and action subjects you can pan the camera (see pp. 40–1). Another solution is to arrange or wait for a change in lighting which makes near or far areas much lighter or darker than the rest of the picture.

HINTS AND TIPS

● Photographing through doorways, windows, or into mirrors gives you a simple, controllable foreground.
● You can fill a foreground with part of a silhouetted human shape. Use a companion, or even yourself if you have a delayed action release.
● To soften or blur any chosen part of the foreground or background use a UV filter and smear parts of it with petroleum jelly. (See also bifocal attachments, p. 184.)
● Take into account which way the sun moves. A bright, assertive background may be subdued into shadow at a different time of day.
● To include a much greater area of background, use a wide-angle lens, not a telephoto.
● Awkward, distracting backgrounds are often a problem when taking candid shots in the street. Duck down at the moment of shooting in order to show people framed against the sky.

Isolating the main subject

Many photographers try to include too much information – the main subject becoming muddled and confused within many less important elements. What seemed strong through the viewfinder often seems slightly diminished in size and importance on the final print or slide. Your eye discriminates, separating one element from its surroundings – something a camera lens cannot do. To overcome this problem, you must use techniques such as viewpoint, contrast, blur, and focus to isolate the main subject.

Contrast

The easiest way to concentrate attention on something is to contrast it visually with its surroundings. Changing viewpoint can radically alter the background and foreground as shown in the final image (see pp. 68-9). A shadowed wall or a sheet of cardboard will be sufficient to isolate a tightly framed head shot or small-scale plant study. For larger, more complex subjects, shoot against sky, grass or pavings.

Often, your timing is vital. You can, for example, wait until a moving object coincides with the right part of its setting, or a shifting patch of light spotlights the area you want to record. Exposure, too, can be an important control, ensuring that you emphasize only the most important features of a scene while suppressing the rest.

Complementary colors between the subject and its surroundings produce the strongest contrast, as do stark tone differences in black and white. When

CHOOSING THE BEST SETTING

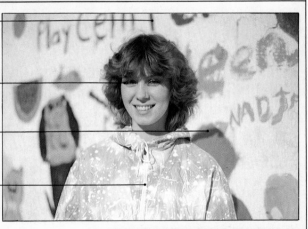

The broken-up colored patches and lettering are much too assertive. They detract from the face and merge with the pattern on the coat.

Harsh frontal lighting has caused the girl to squint. The eyes have no "catch lights" or vitality.

Cast shadow on the background creates a distracting shape.

The dead central framing of the figure is monotonous and dull.

Although the picture, right, is reproduced here smaller than the one above, it has a much bolder appeal. Setting and lighting are simpler, more organized, and harmonious. Changing to a background evenly patterned with parallel horizontal lines contrasts with the girl's vivacious face and coat. The background colors and tone isolate her more pastel, multicolored garment. Positioning the girl in the shade has avoided any cast shadows and helped to add "catch lights" in the eyes. Also, the more off-center framing produces a less static effect.

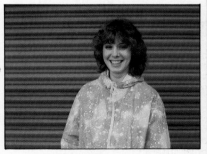

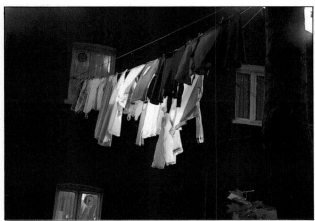

Isolating the subject through lighting It is easier to isolate your subject when its surroundings are all darker or lighter in tone. But read exposure carefully. For the picture left exposure was calculated from close to the back-lit clothes. This excluded the heavily shadowed background. A center-weighted reading from the shooting position would be too influenced by the house.

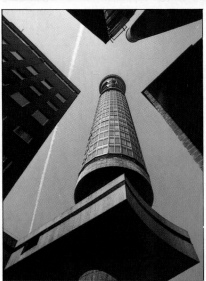

working in black and white, pick surrounding tones that are lighter or darker than the subject, particularly where they meet its edges. It is possible, during printing, to alter the tonal balance between a subject and its surroundings by changing the exposure time of the paper.

Framing

The way the main subject fits within the picture area helps to determine its importance. Precise cropping is easier with an SLR than a compact. Cropping off bits of surrounding objects creates frames and lines, which lead in to the main element. Another way of emphasizing a subject is to position it at the apex of converging perspective lines. Try to make the subject and its surroundings as unequal in area as possible. Sometimes this may mean framing the subject so that it is a relatively small splash of contrasting color or tone.

Isolating the subject by framing Shapes in pictures are created by the way objects are cropped by the frame, as well as the objects themselves. This low-angle shot of buildings was tightly composed so that the corners of nearby buildings formed a dynamic pattern.

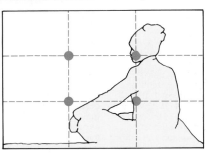

Intersection of thirds As an initial guide to positioning your main subject, imagine each side is divided into thirds. Each line forms a possible location for important structural lines. And the four intersections are strong positions for your center of interest.

71

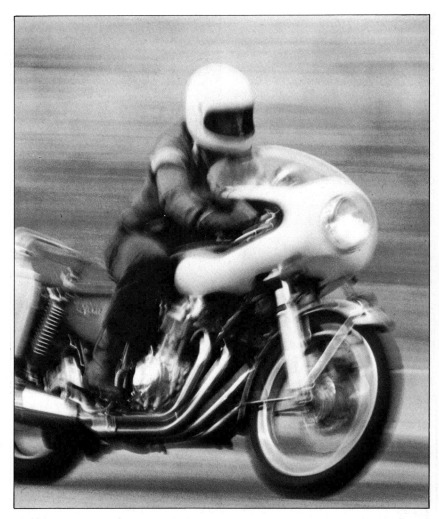

Isolation through sharpness and blur

One method of isolating your chosen subject is to lose all its surroundings in blur. If the subject is moving you can set a speed of 1/15 and pan (see pp. 39–41), as in the example above. For static subjects, use shallow depth of field.

● Try not to eliminate all the background. Plain backgrounds can be boring.
● When using shallow depth of field, check the effect (SLR) with the preview button.
● When isolating your subject using blur, take plenty of exposures to ensure a good result.
● A flashgun, used off-camera at night, will isolate subjects.
● To isolate a small, fixed subject from close surroundings, give a time exposure with the camera on a tripod. Use a small aperture, slow film, and a neutral density filter. For part or all of the exposure, drape a colored paper behind the subject. Keep paper moving continuously.

HINTS AND TIPS

Working in confined spaces

When photographing in a confined space you will frequently find it difficult to include the whole scene. Often with room interiors, large groups, or shots of the exteriors of buildings you just cannot move back far enough to show the whole scene. Usually the easiest solution is to change to a wide-angle lens (see pp. 166–7), although this can result in distortion. But even if your camera has only got a standard lens there are still ways of overcoming this problem.

Coping with lack of space

First, exploit every possible way to gain some extra distance. Try photographing through an open doorway or window. Or use a right-angle viewfinder eyepiece (see p. 178), and press the camera hard against a wall or corner. When a room has a large wall mirror, point the camera toward it from an oblique, high viewpoint. Fill your picture with the reflection, or include the mirror to show hidden parts of the scene. The 38 mm lens on most compact cameras will get in more than an SLR fitted with a standard lens. If you change to a wide-angle lens, try to avoid extreme types. And keep close objects out of the picture corners where distortion most easily occurs.

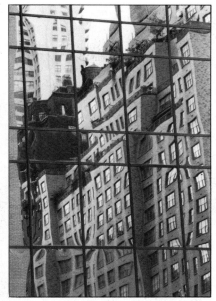

Distorted reflections Mirrors help you to include more of the subject in cramped conditions. As well as solving problems of space, some mirrors produce a distorted caricature of the scene, like the reflective glass of the building shown above.

OVERLAPPED PICTURES

If you only have access to a standard lens, one way of photographing in a confined space is to take several shots to cover the whole scene, then join up prints later. For maximum accuracy, compose every picture so that it will overlap the content of the next by at least 30 per cent (below). When you shoot, keep the camera in one spot, and just pivot it slightly for each exposure. And finally, avoid lighting fluctuations or subject movements. When you get the prints back, tape them down as a mosaic and trim off areas which overlap. If you shot the same view with a wide-angle, some distortion would result (below).

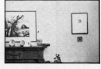

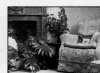

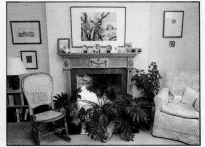

Photographing distant subjects

A common problem in photography is not being able to get close enough to your main subject. A telephoto lens will help you fill the frame, but will generally flatten perspective. If, however, you only have a standard lens there are several ways you can keep the subject small in the frame yet still make it a strong main picture feature.

Using your surroundings

Try using the surroundings in the picture in ways that build up to the main element. Pick a viewpoint, for example, so that con-verging lines lead toward the subject, or relevant shapes in front or behind form a natural frame, covering empty areas. With distant action zoom your lens during a slow exposure to turn all but the central area into streaks. Special effects attachments (see pp. 184–6) can emphasize the central area, too. Sometimes natural lighting will pick out the subject dramatically as the lightest (or darkest) element in the picture – usually at dawn or dusk. Reflective fore-grounds can also be useful. Use a stretch of water or a wet sidewalk to repeat some sub-ject colors at the bottom of your picture.

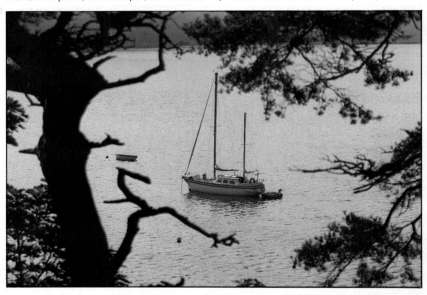

Filling the space
Trees frame a distant subject (above) in what would otherwise be empty surroundings. The branches are suffi-ciently out of focus to give depth and avoid confusion with the mast and rigging. The picture of the horses (right) was shot so that one horse fills and balances the space. It helps lead the eye to distant shapes, silhou-etted on the skyline.

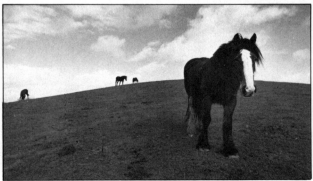

Coping with bad weather

It is a mistake to put your camera away in bad weather. Modern cameras and films now allow you to photograph under very dim conditions and, provided you protect your equipment from the worst of the elements, it is possible to obtain dramatic and unusual results.

The all-weather kit

For shooting in bad weather you will need a waterproof bag, tough tripod, a protective UV or other filter for the lens, and a hand meter for measuring exposure without risking the camera. Be prepared to work quickly and shoot a lot of film, as conditions and subjects may change rapidly. The blending of colors and contrasts in bad weather can produce excellent results, especially in prints made from slides. In mist or fog conditions photograph subjects that are either backlit or sidelit. Include close foreground detail so that differences in tone give a strong sense of depth.

Exploit movement, too. In high winds, rain, or snow, experiment with shutter speeds between 1/8 and 1/250, shielding the camera and tripod. Take close-ups of all kinds to imply the overall conditions –

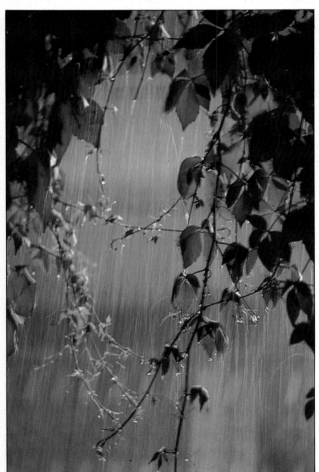

Photographing rain
Rain is uncomfortable to work in but can give rewarding pictures. In the picture on the left, pattern encapsulates a typical downpour. The shot is backlit and exposed at 1/15 on slow film. Try to bracket this type of picture, varying your shutter speed.

Protective bag For protection against blown sand, rain, or snow, place a plastic bag over your camera (below). Cut a hole for the lens, which you should protect with a hood and UV filter. Seal the plastic to the back of the hood. You can then insert one hand through the mouth of the bag from under the camera.

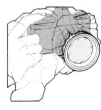

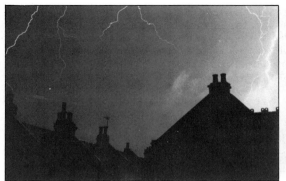

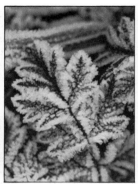

rain-soaked faces, for example, or frost patterns on glass. If you find a rainbow try to photograph it against a darker background. Underexpose rather than overexpose to preserve its range of colors, and try to include landscape features at the bottom of the arch. A wide-angle lens is useful.

Lightning flashes For the shot above left, a small aperture was used and the camera left pointing in the right general direction with its shutter open.

Frost patterns In the picture above, a mixture of sharp and unsharp detail adds variety to the natural pattern.

Photographing snow
Snow in overcast conditions usually appears slightly bluish and sometimes leaden. You can warm up this color by using a pale pink skylight filter or by shooting late in the day when the lighting color is warmer. Low-angled sun is required to show the snow's characteristic texture. Make several local exposure readings – one overall reading can result in the snow appearing gray.

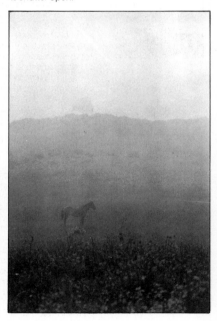

● Overcast weather is often ideal for photographing interiors because of the reduced contrast between inside and outside views.
● Some underwater cameras are designed for land use, too (lenses have separate focusing scales). They make excellent rainproof cameras.
● Spots of rain clinging to the front of a filter give strange focus changes over patches of the image. Look at these through different apertures before deciding to dry the filter – the effect may be worth shooting.
● Black and white film is often more effective than color for capturing stormy weather conditions.
● Bad weather shots often require careful printing if they are not to lose their atmospheric feeling.

HINTS AND TIPS

Mist effects Try to include objects at widely differing distances when shooting in misty conditions. In the picture above, diffused top lighting gives a pearly atmospheric quality. Contrast and detail soften with distance, and depth is exaggerated.

Working in extreme climates

Photographic equipment and materials are designed to work well in typical summer and winter temperatures in temperate climates of the world. But in deserts or arctic regions extreme conditions regularly apply. You do not have to travel to these parts, however, to come across temperature extremes. The temperature in the trunk of a car in sunshine, for example, can exceed 160°F (71°C) and in winter this may fall to −35°F (−37°C).

The worst effects of cold are felt on the mechanical parts of the camera and batteries. In hot conditions there is a risk of lens damage and changes in film response. In both situations, choose comfortable clothing. Whether you wear a light safari jacket to keep cool or a thick three-quarter length insulated coat to retain warmth, make sure it allows you to move easily and has plenty of deep and accessible pockets.

HOT AND COLD CLIMATES

Very cold (down to −10°F/−23°C)

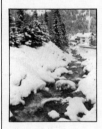

Main problems

As temperatures drop below about 15°F (−9°C) oiled mechanical parts of the camera become increasingly prone to jamming. Metal parts of the body are cold enough at −10°F (−23°C) to "burn" your unprotected hand. The film base also becomes brittle and easily broken. Similarly, canvas or plastic bags turn rigid and are easily torn. Batteries tend to lose their power causing problems with meter readings, shutter timing, flash, and motor drive. If you bring the camera from these conditions into a warm living area, condensation will form on all its exposed surfaces and, sometimes, within the lens itself.

Precautions

Like a car, it is possible for you to have your camera adapted for extreme cold. This means having all oily lubricants removed. It is also a good idea to tape over bare external parts of the camera body, especially the back, which touches your face. If you intend to use a motor drive it will be necessary to power it from a separate cord-linked battery pack. Keep the battery pack warm inside your clothing. On most cameras you can use this pack to power all other circuits. Carry your equipment in a metal case, not a fabric or plastic container. And when you have to move equipment or films from a cold to a warm environment, put it in an air-tight bag first.

Very hot (over 100°F/38°C)

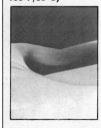

Main problems

Extreme heat causes metal parts of the camera to expand at different rates, leading to mechanical jams. The worst effect of extreme heat occurs with some lenses – the heat can loosen the anchorage of lens elements. Heat is often accompanied by high humidity. This moisture affects the camera's electronics, and gradually the wiring spreads corrosion throughout the camera. Prolonged humidity affects the gelatin coating on the film, so that coils stick together and bacteria may even attack the emulsion. Mould spores may also grow as small white spots within the lens. Film speed and the color balance of your results may also be affected.

Precautions

Insulate your equipment and materials from the environment as much as possible. Keep cameras in foam plastic in reflective silver or white air-tight cases. Wherever possible, place the case in the shade, and allow air to circulate on all sides. Store each day's film in a refrigerated cool box, but allow sufficient time for chilled films to warm up before loading them into the camera (see p. 64). It is a good idea to include bags of silica gel in all cases used to store film and equipment. The silica absorbs airborne moisture and you should dry it out in the oven every evening. After exposure, replace all films in their containers and store them in the refrigerator.

Intensifying colors

Sometimes you may want your pictures to display particularly intense colors. You can achieve this through a variety of techniques – choice of lighting, use of exposure and filtration, and the way you compose and present your images, for example. It is not enough for colors actually to be bright, they must also look bright to the eye, and this often varies according to their surroundings.

Techniques for strengthening color
The color of an object is greatly affected by its surface texture – a glossy book jacket is brighter than a matte one, and a polished car seems more colorful than a dusty one. Similarly, atmospheric conditions and the direction of light alter color. Richest colors occur in clear atmosphere (sunlight after rain, for example) and when the subject is in direct, generally frontal lighting. You will sometimes further improve colors by using

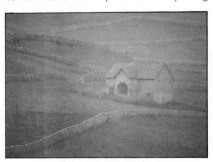

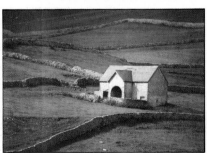

Subject conditions
You can transform subject colors through choice of weather conditions. The top picture was taken in misty rain. A few minutes later direct sunlight gave the colors in the shot above.

COLOR CONTRASTS

Judgement of colors is often affected by adjacent colors or tones. A color always looks lighter against darker surroundings, and darker against lighter surroundings. A pale, pastel color often takes on a slight tint complementary to a strong adjacent color. Both effects are known as "simultaneous contrast". They are used everyday in the choice of bold color combinations for road signs, advertising, and decorative designs, and you can often apply them in photography through choice of background.

Complementary colors The colors of the spectrum are shown (right) as a wheel, divided into red, green, and blue light. Also shown are complementaries, cyan, magenta, and yellow.

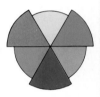

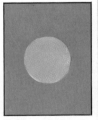

Adjacent colors The two diagrams above show how color is affected by surroundings. Both circles are identical, but in the version right the surround tends to merge with and suppress the center. In the other diagram, contrasting tone intensifies center color.

Color as black and white Colors that appear very different to the eye sometimes merge as similar grays in black and white. The color patches below are also shown as they would reproduce in a print made from normal panchromatic film.

Spectrum

Panchromatic

a polarizing filter. This reduces surface glare and scatter from surfaces angled to the light, allowing true colors to show through. (For the opposite effect, shoot against the light in hazy conditions using a distant viewpoint and telephoto lens.)

Richest colors are seen when the subject is translucent and lit from behind. Stained-glass windows, spring foliage, kites, and hot air balloons all show their colors free from surface reflections in this way. When shooting slides, further improve colors by slight underexposure. With color negatives, have your prints made on glossy paper instead of matte.

Composing in color

Colors can look richer according to the way you present them. A small patch of color against dark neutral or muted hues often looks brighter than one color filling the frame. Similarly, a small area of color stands out boldly from surroundings that have a complementary tint.

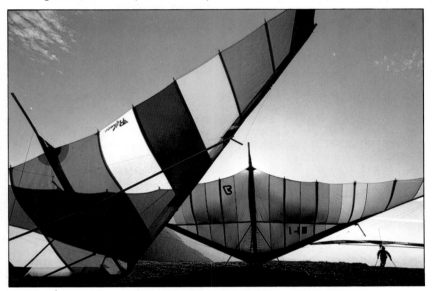

Translucent materials The photograph (above) of hang gliders was taken directly into the sun. The intense light streaming through the thin fabric reveals and strengthens the already bright colors.

Color filters Filtering when shooting or printing strengthens some colors while suppressing others. In the view (right) foliage is black and the building is a deep pink.

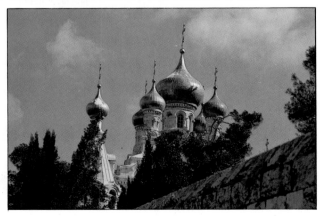

Showing colors as tones

Black and white film records colors as different tones of gray. You therefore have to imagine how the colorful scene in your viewfinder will look translated into a mixture of tones. Sometimes it is helpful to manipulate normal black and white reproduction – either by filtering the lens or lighting, or by shooting on a special film which has a different reaction to the colors of light.

Working with image tones

The best way to learn how colors convert into tones is to find a colorful program on television, and keep changing the control between color and monochrome. Notice how the white clouds in a pale blue sky tend to disappear when color has gone, and some visually contrasting colors become very similar grays. In photography, you can alter the values of one color against another by using a lens filter (see p. 174). The filter must be the same hue as the colors you want to lighten, and as opposite as possible to the colors you want to darken. You can also color the lighting (flash or lamps) in the same way. Orange light (at sunset, for example) darkens green, but yellow and red remain relatively bright. Red lighting makes reds indistinguishable from white, but turns strong greens black. Filtering the light or lens is often necessary when copying colored lettering or drawings. Bold red lines on white paper, for example, will photograph as pale gray against white unless you use a green or blue filter to turn the red black.

Using special films

All regular films have panchromatic sensitivity – they respond to all colors in various gray tones (see p. 78). But a few special-purpose films give more distorted values. Ortho film (such as Agfaortho 25) records reds as black – results resemble pan film exposed through a blue filter. And infrared black and white film gives a particularly strange response. When exposed as intended, all healthy vegetation reproduces as white, and blue skies as black. Grass and leaves take on a dream-like, luminous quality and faces look deathly pale.

THE EFFECTS OF FILTRATION ON COLORS

When you filter the lens or light source for a black and white photograph, ignore the overall color it gives to the image. Instead, look carefully at how some colors go lighter, others darker. Filters have virtually no effect on neutral gray, white, or black parts of the scene (although heavy filtering can alter the general contrast of the film). You will get similar results whether you use filters when photographing the actual subject, or while copying an originally unfiltered color slide on black and white. Compare the three monochrome images below with the original colors of the scene shown on p. 130.

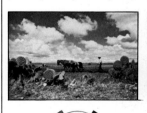
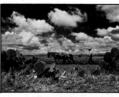
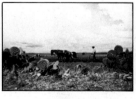

No filter This copy of the color picture on p. 130 was taken unfiltered on panchromatic film.

Red filter Blue sky becomes almost black, dramatizing clouds. Plants also darken.

Blue filter This filter lightens the sky, suppressing cloud shapes.

CHOOSING COLOR FILTERS

Subject	Effect required (using pan film)	Filter color and (Kodak) number
Blue sky in relation to white clouds	Natural	Yellow (8)
	Darkened	Deep yellow (15)
Blue sky as background to pale subject	Dramatically dark	Orange (21)
	Almost black	Deep red (29)
Sunsets	Increased brilliance	Deep yellow (15)
Landscapes	Less palor in far distance	Deep yellow (15)
	Maximum penetration of bluish haze	Deep red (29)
	Pale foliage	Deep green (58)
Scene containing mostly warm colors – red, orange, bronze	Lighter – to show detail	Red (25)
	Darker – for less detail	Blue (47)
Scene containing mostly cold colors – blue, green, purple	Lighter – to show detail	Blue (47)
	Darker – for less detail	Red (25)
Poster with green and magenta lines on gray	To make green black, magenta white	Magenta (33)
	To make magenta black, green white	Deep green (58)

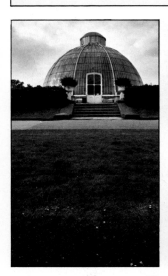

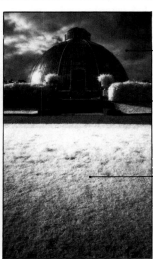

Sky darkens dramatically, and clouds are emphasized. Reflections from glass increase.

Shadows mostly record darker, because the only light that they receive is from the blue sky.

Grass in direct sunlight reflects infrared strongly, giving a "frosted" look.

Infrared film Black and white infrared film must be exposed through a deep red or infrared (black-looking) filter. Unlike normal film, it only responds to red and to the infrared radiation reflected from chlorophyll in plants. As the result above right shows, grass reproduces as though lightly covered in snow (see p. 130). Detail has a "smudgy" look, shadows lack detail, and contrast often increases. The same scene shot on regular film is shown above left for comparative purposes.

Avoiding inaccurate colors

Usually in photography close color accuracy is unimportant. No one is likely to hold the picture up against the original and compare colors and tones. But for some subjects – copying paintings and illustrations of food, for example – colors are critical. You must then aim for special accuracy by using a very careful technique involving choice of film, exposure, and lighting.

Film choice

Color slides give you least margin for error – there is little chance of correction later. Whether you use slide or negative film, try and include something recognizable in the image to help you or the printer assess the results. Shoot any series of pictures (including any test pictures) on the same brand and batch of films, and have them all processed by the same laboratory. When shooting on (daylight) color negative film in tungsten lighting, try to use a blue conversion filter on the lens. If you shoot slides on film not expressly designed for your lighting source, you must use a conversion filter. But even then, make some test exposures. Have all films from the same session processed at about the same time.

Exposure

Take several exposures of each shot if possible, bracketed at half-stop differences.

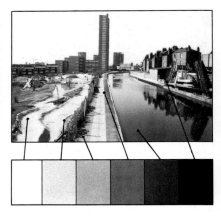

Gray scale You can include a gray scale and then compare it to see if copy prints are underexposed (dark tones with degraded whites), or overexposed (light tones with no tone darker than gray).

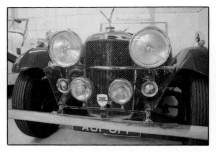

Fluorescent lighting
No color film is correctly balanced for fluorescent lighting. The picture above was shot on daylight film and shows the typical greenish result given by most fluorescent tubes. For the version left, the magenta and yellow correction filters recommended for these tubes (see p. 207) were used over the lens. Results are acceptable, but reds still lack some richness. For best results always try to use the correct color light source for your film.

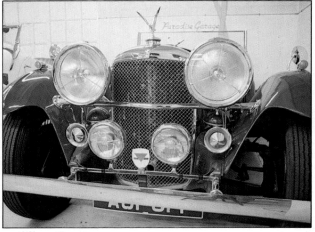

LIGHTING FOR ACCURACY

Photography often exaggerates lighting differences. Mixed light sources and lighting unevenness distorts the colors and detail in the picture below right (shot on daylight film). For the more accurate version (right) several corrections have been made. A blue conversion filter over the lens removed the table lamp's orange cast. The other tungsten light on the left was moved further away and re-angled to eliminate unevenness. A white cardboard reflector was also added to the right of the camera lens to reduce contrast.

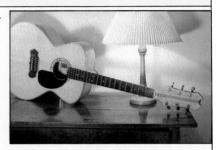

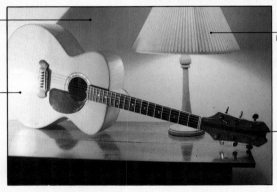

Unevenness from left to right. No one exposure can expose the whole picture correctly

Glare patch destroys color and detail

Household lamp does not match film response, records with strong orange cast

This end of the guitar is shadowed and lacks detail

Read any exposure time recommendations packed with your film. For the greatest color accuracy adjust lighting and aperture so you do not give exposures longer than 1 sec and, ideally, no longer than 1/10.

Lighting

The color of your lighting must be correct for the film and even over the whole subject. Avoid patchy lighting due to cast shadows, or having the light source too close to one side. To improve evenness increase the subject-to-light distance. You can compensate for dimness with extra exposure. Take special care to avoid colored reflections from surroundings. If you are using daylight as your main light source try to work during the middle of the day. Avoid shaded areas if most of the light is coming from the blue sky. Flash is one of the most accurate light sources because of its consistent color and intensity.

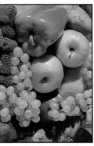

Exposure time The green cast in the photograph above was due to an exposure time of 20 sec on slide film designed for optimum color quality at times not exceeding 1/10. Old or badly stored films sometimes give similar casts.

● All tungsten lamps change their color with voltage fluctuations. If your supply varies use flash.
● Subjects that are either neutral or pastel in color are more likely to suffer from color casts.
● Some lenses of different brands vary in color bias. Do not mix brands.
● If you are shooting a series of a critical subject, test and then standardize your light source, film, and exposure times.

Controlling contrast

Shadows and dark areas in pictures are often important. They help to show shape and form and they can subdue assertive parts of a subject so that other areas are stressed. But when you want detail in both bright and dark parts of a scene, you may have problems of contrast – the ratio of these two extremes. If you can recognize this type of situation in advance, you can either accept it (and therefore some resulting loss of detail in one area or the other), or take steps to reduce contrast. The way you achieve this reduction depends mostly on the size and distance of your subject.

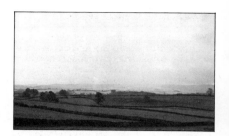

Basic limitations
The basic problem is shown by the landscape on the right. If a whole scene is dark, you can produce detail by increasing exposure. If it is entirely bright you can reduce exposure. But when both are present in the same scene, the best you can do is compromise between the two readings. If shadows require four f numbers or shutter settings more than bright areas, contrast is beyond the range of most films. You must then choose to have shadows dark and featureless (to preserve highlight detail) or accept burnt-out highlights (for the sake of shadow

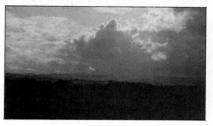

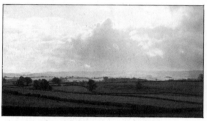

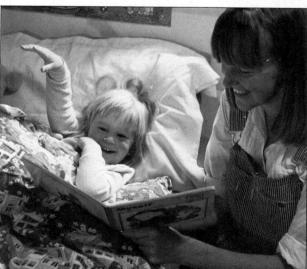

Controlling detail In the backlit landscapes above sky is about 60 times brighter than the ground. The top picture was exposed for the land and the center one for the sky. The version above was shot with a gray lens filter shading the sky alone.

Using local reflectors For this contrasty shot (left) bedclothes and book act as reflectors to lighten the child's face. Always look out for ways of reflecting light back naturally. Often, a slight adjustment of subject or viewpoint can minimize contrast.

CONTRAST RANGE

With close-ups, such as the dolls below, you can control contrast with a reflector near the camera. White cardboard or paper gives the softest fill-in, but is less reflective than crumpled foil. Use a large reflector for an even result. The closer the reflector the more contrast is reduced – vary its distance if you are unsure of the results.

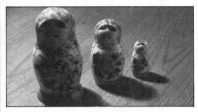

No reflector Here diffused backlighting from a small window was used. Exposure was read overall.

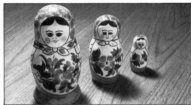

Distant reflector
White cardboard was held 2 ft (0.65 m) from the dolls.

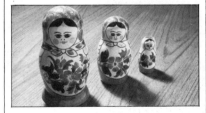

Close reflector Here reflector distance was halved to further reduce contrast.

information). The alternative is to find some way to reduce the subject contrast itself.

Methods of control

The most practical way to reduce contrast, outside of the darkroom, is to add some light to shadow parts. You can do this to the subject itself or manipulate the image as formed by the camera lens.

A reflector, either matte white or crumpled silver, will reflect some light to shadows when a subject is sidelit or backlit. Place the reflector near the camera if you are working close or include it in the picture as a natural feature. Indoors, you might shoot in a smaller room with lighter decorations, diffuse the window or lamp, or move the subject away from the light source and close to a reflective wall. Another approach is to add frontal light – a lamp or flash – preferably diffused so that confusing extra shadows are not created. For a still-life, stop well down or use a neutral density filter, and then use a flashlight to "paint with light" from the camera position during a time exposure.

Lens and film

These methods do not work with distant subjects such as landscapes. If you cannot wait for softer, natural light, use a gradated gray filter (see p. 174) to dim the sky, or a mild diffuser, which will spread light into the shadows. With color slide or black and white films, you can halve the ISO rating, then have processing adjusted to reduce contrast (see p. 62). It also helps to use fast films. These are better able to record a wide contrast range.

> **HINTS AND TIPS**
> ● When shooting in color make sure any reflector is neutral in coloration.
> ● You must be more careful to expose accurately with contrasty subjects. Think carefully where detail is most essential.
> ● If in doubt about contrast it is better to overfill. The photographic process has a contrast-increasing effect.
> ● It is easier to predict final contrast by viewing your subject through a dark gray filter or a stopped-down camera lens.

Dealing with reflections

Reflections are sometimes a nuisance, but they can also form the very core of a strong picture. Use them to double the color or pattern from other parts of the scene, or to bring together two physically unrelated views. Reflections also allow you to relate a person and a place, for example, or to create many different abstract designs.

Controlling results

A reflection alters its appearance with every change of viewpoint and lighting. Light reflects off a smooth surface at an angle equal but opposite to the one at which it arrives (see right). Knowing this, you can forecast that to see more sky reflected in a window you must lower your viewpoint. A higher viewpoint will reflect more ground. How strong a reflection appears depends on the brightness of the object reflected, compared to your reflecting surface and its surroundings. The sunny side of a street, for example, shows brilliantly in reflective surfaces on the shaded side – but on a dull day both sides may have equal values. So pick your time and lighting as carefully as viewpoint. Where you have no choice and you must reduce reflections, use a polarizing filter attachment. In some situations you can spray the reflective surface with a dulling substance, block the

SURFACE AND REFLECTION

There are two main types of reflective surface – glossy, very directional (polished metal or glass, for example) and matte, non-directional (white cardboard, for example). Gloss surfaces give you mirror images, glare spots, and usually harsh contrast. Reflections at right-angles to you will produce reflections of the camera and any on-camera flash. Matte surfaces produce scattered light. There is no reflected image or glare, just general illumination. All light-reflecting objects have surface qualities somewhere between the two.

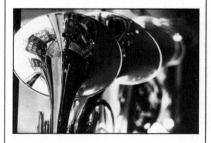

Gloss surface Angles made to the surface between incoming and reflecting light are equal. The surface shows highlights and reflections as in the picture above.

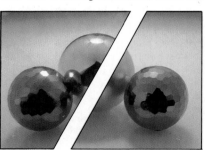

Altering surface qualities Subjects with gloss surfaces (above left) reflect the light source as a bright highlight. After treatment with a dulling spray (above right) the same surfaces mostly scatter light instead. What was highlight becomes sheen, and contrast is generally reduced. You can see similar differences between glazed and dusty surfaces and still and rippled water.

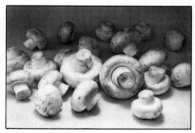

Matte surface When light reflects off a finely textured irregular surface it is scattered. As shown in the picture above, there are no glare spots and very few dark areas.

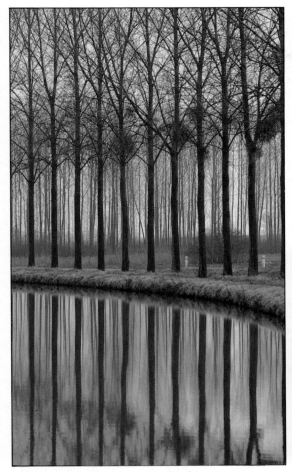

Doubling pattern The strength of the telephoto shot left is the subtle difference between the trees and their simplified reflected detail. The stillness of the water adds greatly to the effect.

Extending color For this picture (below) the photographer chose a position within the shadowed half of the street. He lowered his viewpoint until colors from the sunlit buildings opposite were reflected from the water in the road. By measuring and setting exposure for the brighter areas only, the water appears to gleam from the dark shadow. It forms a strong foreground and helps balance the overall composition.

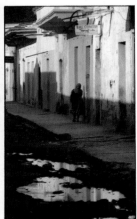

reflection with something dark, or angle strong light (like flash) from the camera.

Focusing the reflections

When shooting pictures that include reflections bear in mind that your subject and its reflection are at different distances from the camera. If both subject and reflection are distant, then depth of field at most apertures will probably be sufficient. If the reflective surface is close, however, you must decide whether to focus on the reflection (showing the surface and its surroundings unsharp) or choose the reverse effect.

Coping with different distances The diagrams on the right show the problem with trying to focus on both the subject and its reflection. The broken lines show the distance between the camera and the reflection, while the solid lines indicate the (sometimes) much shorter distance between the camera and the subject.

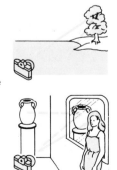

Shooting against the light

Shooting toward a bright light source like the sun gives pictures a dramatic backlit effect. This strengthens shapes, simplifies details and increases depth. However, it also creates technical problems – flare, extreme contrast and exposure reading errors.

Advantages of backlighting

Working with the sun ahead of you, rather than behind or to one side can transform a scene. Some objects turn into clear-cut silhouettes, with details and colors suppressed. And shadows all fall toward the camera, often casting interesting patterns across the foreground. This will be a problem if you want to show detail in the subject or surroundings. But you can turn it to your advantage in situations where detail is not so important.

Backlighting is often the best way to give an impression of brilliance and heat. It shows up the luminosity and sparkle of subjects which reflect and transmit light. A

Backlighting to reveal structure Most plant leaves are translucent, and reveal their structure when backlit. The picture below was shot almost into the light, against a distant, dark background. Rim-lighting picks out the leaf's edge, but some illumination still passes through.

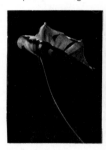

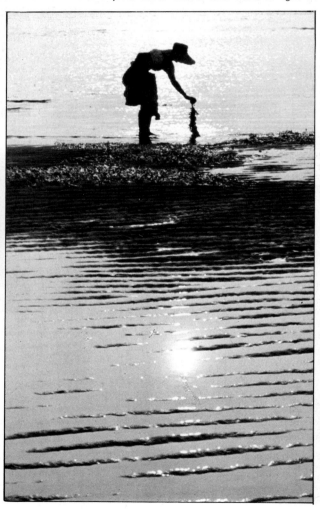

Creating a silhouette The picture right was taken toward the setting sun using a well-shaded lens. The figure was positioned to place its silhouette against the lightest part of the scene for the most dramatic effect. Exposure was read off the part of the sea that reflected only sky.

CONTROLLING FLARE

Flare is light spill, usually into the edge of the lens. In mild cases just the blackest parts of your picture look slightly gray. With more extreme flare, a whole ring of light forms, and often several ghost reflections of the lens diaphragm too (see pp. 57 and 59). When shooting against the light, stop down to your working aperture first and look for flare. Flare is more likely if your lens is old, or the lens or filter is dirty. Fit a hood designed to suit the focal length of your lens. If this is insufficient, extend it by using your hand as a shade or shift your viewpoint slightly (see below).

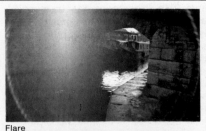

Flare

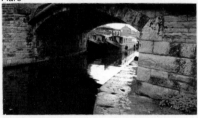

Flare corrected

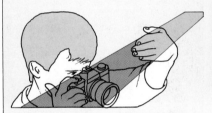

Making use of shadows The oblique shadows in the foreground of the simple still-life shot (right) are caused by light from the rear left. Reflective surroundings nearby return some soft lighting, reducing contrast. A wide-angle lens was used to exaggerate the closer parts.

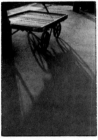

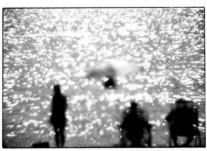

Shooting sunlight on water The glitter of sunlight off disturbed water is sometimes best conveyed out of focus. The shot above was taken with a wide-aperture mirror lens focused further than anything in the scene.

backlit portrait will show rimlit hair and shoulders, strongly separating the figure from the background. And it will avoid the problem of the subject squinting directly into the light.

The problems of contrast and exposure

Lighting contrast greatly increases when you turn toward the light. Watch out for light flaring into your lens (see above), because the exposure meter will give faulty readings if it does (see p. 44). For best results, have light-toned surroundings behind you; these will softly reflect the light back into shadows to reveal detail, while still preserving the backlit effect. With close-up subjects position white paper as a reflector, or fill-in with weak flash from the camera (see p. 156). Another approach is to expose for the deep shadows so that everything else is completely "burnt out". For distant shots it is generally best to accept that solid objects will appear as black shapes, and expose for the lighter parts of the scene only. Many older TTL meters are "blinded" by intense, direct light from the sun and give faulty readings for up to a minute later.

89

Photographing the sun and sky

The usual advice given to a beginner is to keep the sun behind the camera. But often you can dramatize a picture by including the sun – as the focal point of a landscape, for example. Use the sun to symbolize light and heat. And at dusk or dawn you will find the sun a source of rich, changing sky colors. Sky and clouds alone sometimes give magnificent "skyscapes" that are well worth capturing. As with all subjects shot toward the light (see pp. 88–9), the main problems are contrast and exposure. The contrast latitude of films varies greatly, so if you are in any doubt it is a good idea to bracket your exposures.

Coping with contrast and skies
Contrast will be greatest when you take a shot that includes the sun in a clear, noon sky. To get an effective result try greatly underexposing the land, and build a "moonlit" picture from the sun's disk plus the reflected glint from surfaces such as rooftops or water. If you expose for land detail instead, you will obtain a burnt-out, featureless sky. To lower contrast, select a viewpoint that tucks the sun behind some

element that you want to emphasize. A gray graduated filter will dim the sky and allow you to expose for the land. Or you can wait for hazier conditions when natural contrast is much reduced.

The appearance of skies varies most in spring or autumn, during weather changes, and early or late in the day. To emphasize delicate clouds use a polarizing filter (see p. 130), or a yellow filter if you are shooting

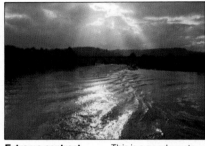

Extreme contrast Although the shot above was taken in the mid-afternoon, it looks like a dusk scene because of the large underexposed areas. This is a good way to treat extreme contrast. Here, the sun itself was just excluded from the frame. Watch out for flare in contrasty lighting.

MAKING A FEATURE OF THE SUN

You can vary the size of the sun in a picture by changing lens. A wide-angle lens makes it a pinpoint, a telephoto produces an enlarged disk. Another way to increase its size is to use a starburst attachment, which spreads "rays" across the image. At dawn and dusk the sun seems bigger and more dramatic. It appears closer to ground detail, and haze makes the disk dimmer in relation to the surrounding sky. For sunset pictures you can often select ground features, then arrive early and shoot several pictures as the sun changes. Underexposure makes a sunset look richer.

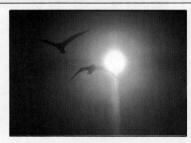

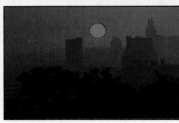

Burnt-out sun Overexposing the sun gives an atmospheric result with strong foreground shapes (left). Flare reduces contrast, turning silhouettes gray.

The effect of haze The setting sun in a telephoto shot (below left) looks larger close to buildings. Haze reduces disk brightness and scatters light throughout the sky.

Shading the sun For this shot (right) the sun is hidden behind foreground foliage. Correct exposure was critical to preserve sunlight and mist.

in black and white. Storm cloud formations look dramatic when rim-lit in front of the sun (see p. 92).

Measuring exposure

Decide which part of the sky you want to appear midway between the darkest and lightest elements, and read exposure from this. For a sunset you might read from sky immediately overhead. If you want a burnt-out sun, measure from the land. Try to use slow film, and fit a neutral density filter if necessary to avoid overexposure. When including the sun, try making your first exposure on an automatic setting then switch to manual (or select exposure override) and take several progressively underexposed versions. Always be especially careful when looking through the viewfinder at the sun – it can damage your eyesight.

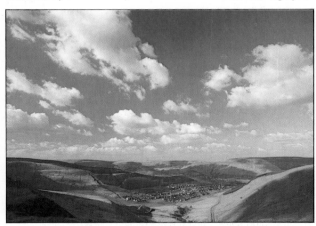

Sky in landscape In the picture left, the exhilarating pattern of white clouds is echoed by their shadows cast across the landscape. It was shot with an extreme wide-angle lens to include a large area of sky and to help dwarf the town in the valley below. The side lighting gives the clouds shape and varied tone values, while the use of a polarizing filter has darkened the blue sky at right-angles to the sun.

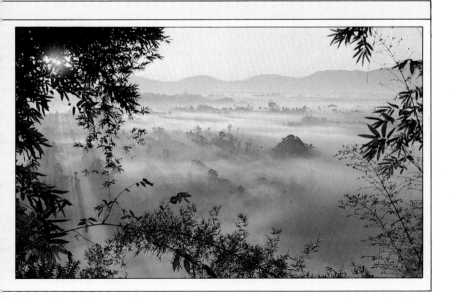

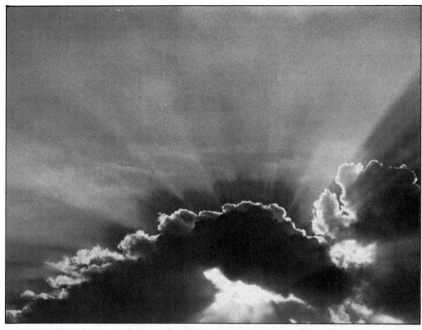

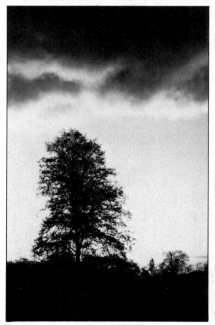

Shooting clouds at sunset The landscape left was photographed a few moments after the sun had sunk below the horizon. The rain clouds are lit dramatically from below.

Exposing for radiant light If storm clouds briefly cover the sun, you may get a radiant light effect (above). Measure exposure from the blue sky, and use a yellow filter to darken its tone.

● Looking directly at brilliant sun can damage sight. The risk is greatest with a telephoto. When composing through an SLR, stop well down and keep the preview button depressed. Alternatively, fit an ND filter.

● Watch out for the effect of overall or patchy flare, particularly when the sun is just out of frame. Test at working aperture.

● Some meters are temporarily "blinded" when exposed to bright sun. It may be best to take a reading first, and then switch off the meter while composing your picture.

● Sun and sky shots need careful printing. If your results are too pale and gray, ask your laboratory for reprints.

Photographing at night

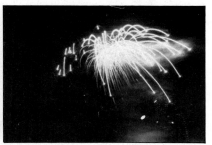

Taking pictures at night is not as difficult as it first sounds. Technically, all you require is a camera with a B shutter setting. Commonplace subjects can seem much changed at night. Towns and cities with their traffic, buildings, and illuminated signs can be particularly rewarding, as can fairgrounds and firework displays. You can even use camp fires or candle light as a light source for unusual portraits. A good TTL meter will measure accurately dim light at night, but excessive contrast is always a problem.

Essential materials and equipment

Work with fast or medium-speed film. Fast types will give more grain but are better able to handle the harsh lighting contrasts at night. With color slides try to use tungsten-balanced film for light sources such as

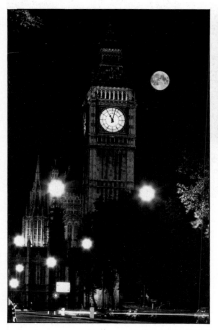

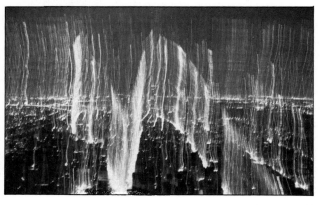

Static camera and subject In this picture (left) a 135 mm lens used from a distant viewpoint makes the clock face and moon similar in size. The moon's brightness also relates closely to the floodlit building. Exposure was measured from the building.

Moving subject For this picture of fireworks, the lens was set at f 16 (ISO 125 film) and the shutter held open for 4 sec. This type of shot always requires a tripod, and for best results in color you should use daylight-balanced film.

Moving camera The shot of Manhattan (right) was made simply by moving the camera during the exposure. The camera was hand held but pressed against a wall on top of a tall building with the shutter open on B. For the first 4 sec the camera was held steady, and then tilted downward slowly before the shutter was closed. The lens aperture was f 8 using ISO 125 film.

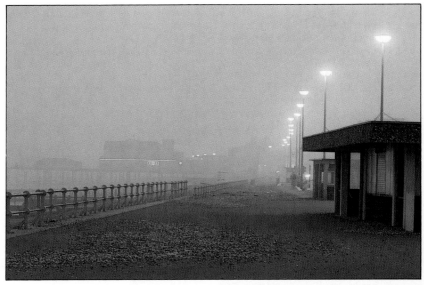

Shooting at dusk By shooting at late dusk night scenes have reduced contrast. In the picture above this is further helped by sea mist. The unreal color is caused partly by the street lights and partly by the bluish quality light takes on at dusk.

Day for night The picture on the right was taken mid-afternoon, and given 4 stops underexposure. A pale blue filter has added to the effect. For similar moonlit results you must underexpose and shoot toward the sun. Bracketing is always a good idea.

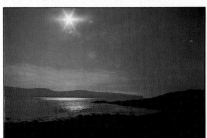

decorative lamps, candles, and fire light. Street lighting, moonlight, and most floodlighting is recorded best on daylight-balanced film. Slides are particularly effective for night photographs – when projected they re-create all the sparkle and vitality of the original scene.

Other essential equipment for night photography includes a tripod and cable release. Use your wide-aperture standard lens for pictures featuring people and a zoom lens for light-blur effects.

Measuring exposure

Programmed or aperture-priority meters, which give time exposures of many seconds, are excellent for measuring exposure for night shots. Time an automatic exposure and then change to manual and produce a bracketed series. Low light is usually less of a problem than contrast. Help yourself by picking scenes where all important elements are about the same brightness, and always take a reading from close up to the main subject. Another way of minimizing the contrast problem is by shooting at late dusk when there is more ambient light. Notice also how wet surfaces, light from buildings, traffic lights, and even haze all help to fill in detail in dark areas. Small but intense areas of light in front of the camera lens, however, may cause an unacceptable amount of flare. Sometimes, this flare can add a point of interest.

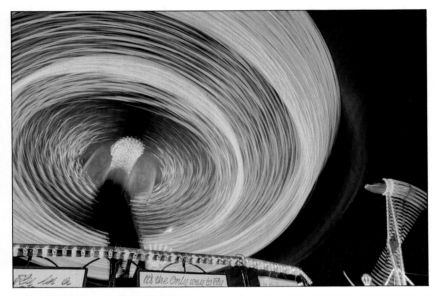

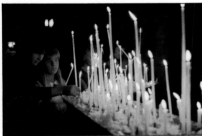

COMPENSATION FOR LONG EXPOSURE				
With prolonged exposure times, film has a reduced ISO speed. This table shows		typical exposure compensations required, by widening the aperture.		
Time indicated (sec)	1	10	20	30	40
Increase in aperture (f stops)	$\frac{1}{2}$	1	$1\frac{1}{2}$	$1\frac{1}{2}$	2

Slow and fast film

Slow film is ideal for long exposures to blur moving lights at night. The fairground shot (top) was given 10 sec exposure at f 11 on ISO 64 film. The foreground ride was moving quickly with flashing lights, the distant dive-bomber barely moving. In the picture above, fast ISO 400 film was required. The camera was hand held at 1/60. Even at this speed an aperture of f 1.8 was necessary.

HINTS AND TIPS

● For moon pictures, use your longest lens and try to include parts of trees and buildings. A general meter reading tends to lead to overexposure. Bracket shots at around 1/15 at f 8 on ISO 100 film.

● The moon passes across the sky quite quickly. Shots exposed longer than about 30 sec will show some blurring.

● Turn moonless starlit skies into many curved star paths by exposing for about one hour.

● With static subjects, add light to chosen parts by firing a flashgun from different parts of the scene. Place the camera on a tripod with the shutter held open on B.

● Try shots of signs using a faceted lens attachment, or by zooming slowly during the exposure.

● For shots of people, pick a viewpoint facing a lit surface and aim mostly for silhouettes.

● Shoot candids at wide apertures to help separate people from any possibly contrasty surroundings and also to reduce camera shake. An infrared autofocus camera is useful for night photography when visual focusing is impossible.

95

Making the most of subject detail

The subject and your personal approach will dictate whether you aim for the highest photographic quality and resolution, or go for an atmospheric result. Make yourself familiar with the techniques involved in both these treatments. You can then start off with the most suitable materials and methods to produce the picture you want.

Suppressing detail

To make a picture look less clinical, break up detail with grain. Shoot a flatly lit image on fast film, give it push processing, and then enlarge it. Use a diffuser attachment or keep the image moving during exposure. Keep the area in focus to a minimum – restrict depth of field and light, and expose only for those parts of the subject you want to identify in the final image.

Emphasizing detail

For a crisp, sharp image use a slow, high-resolution film (see pp. 54–6). Lenses and filters must be very clean and you should use a lens hood. Use a tripod and release, or shoot with flash. Make sure that depth of field is ample. Lighting must emphasize your subject's fine textures. Avoid dense shadows and burnt-out highlights. If necessary, use reflectors or fill-in flash. Take care to expose film accurately – bracket your shots if possible.

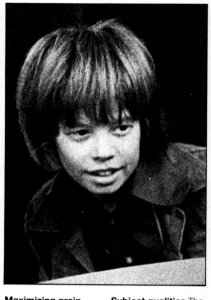

Maximizing grain This image was enlarged from part of an ISO 1250 push-processed negative. Soft lighting allows the use of harsh-contrast paper to exaggerate the grainy pattern, always strongest in gray tone areas.

Subject qualities The picture facing page uses fine photographic detail to stress the subject's own qualities. Lighting is directional but not harsh. Accurate exposure retains highlight and shadow detail. Slow ISO 100 film minimizes grain.

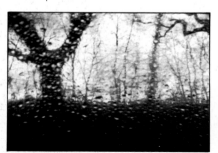

Improvised diffuser Often you can soften image detail using an improvised diffuser. The picture above was shot through a rain-spattered window. Try photographing a distant subject through open-weave fabric, or reflected from a wet surface. Depth of field will greatly affect results – use the preview button or shoot at different apertures.

- To soften optical detail try holding transparent plastic wrapping over the lens. Or use a UV filter and breathe on it just before pressing the shutter.
- To reduce detail, copy a slide giving half the exposure with the image out of focus. Alternatively, place a diffuser between slide and camera, or back the slide with tracing paper or translucent textured material.
- For maximum subject detail and color try using a polarizing filter. It will also reduce flare from sparkling reflections. You will, however, have to increase exposure.
- If possible, avoid overexposing negatives when aiming for maximum subject detail. In dense images light "spreads", softening and flattening any bright highlights.

HINTS AND TIPS

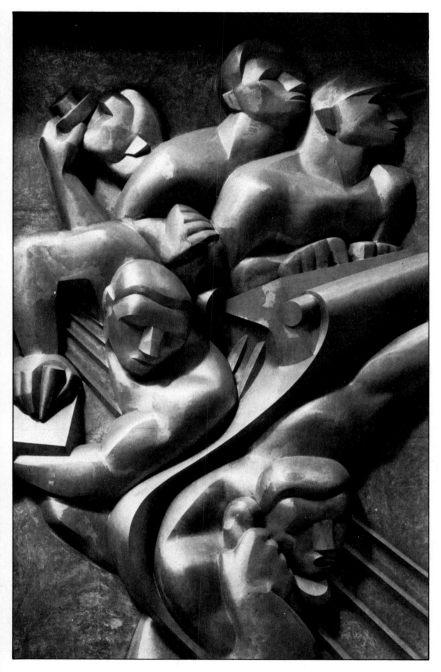

Creating a sense of movement

Even though you are taking still pictures, movement can be suggested in several ways – some technical but others mostly implied through viewpoint and framing. Blurs and streaks, dynamic lines and shapes, overlapping images and sequences all give a sense of action. They are especially useful for subjects such as athletics or dance.

Simulating movement

Blurred detail in a picture matches the eye's impression of movement. On film you must use techniques such as subject or camera movement during a slow exposure, or use a special effects attachment. If the background is plain and dark a moving subject spreads highlights across it. Against a light background the subject appears "eaten into" and may almost disappear. Zooming the camera lens during a slow exposure is another method of creating dynamism.

Multi-images in one picture are easily created using a parallel-faceted lens attachment. Or you can fire your flashgun at intervals in complete darkness while you hold the camera shutter open on the B setting. Another approach you can try is to shoot a series of pictures and present them in strip form like a cartoon.

COMPOSING MOVING SUBJECTS

The way you position your subject in a picture has important effects on the feeling of action. By leaving most space in front of a moving figure, you suggest it is entering the frame, and action is beginning. Sometimes giving more space to trailing dust or snow creates a stronger sense of movement. Similarly, if you pick a camera position that gives an impression of diagonal or converging lines (rather than parallel lines) you will create an active effect. A wide-angle lens and close viewpoint may be helpful, too.

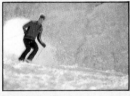

Space in front This framing suggests movement by showing the distance the skier still has to travel.

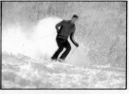

Central placement This most common form of framing contributes least to the sense of movement.

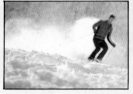

Space behind Framing now suggests how far the skier has traveled. Makes good use of the trailing snow.

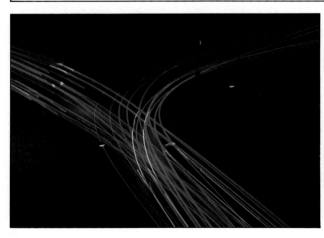

Time exposure The semi-abstract traffic patterns (left) were created using a 45 sec exposure. Red predominates because the vehicles were moving away from the camera.

Lens attachments In the picture on the facing page two static figures give the impression of animation. The photographer used a lens attachment with vertical facets to fragment the image, creating a diagonal thrust.

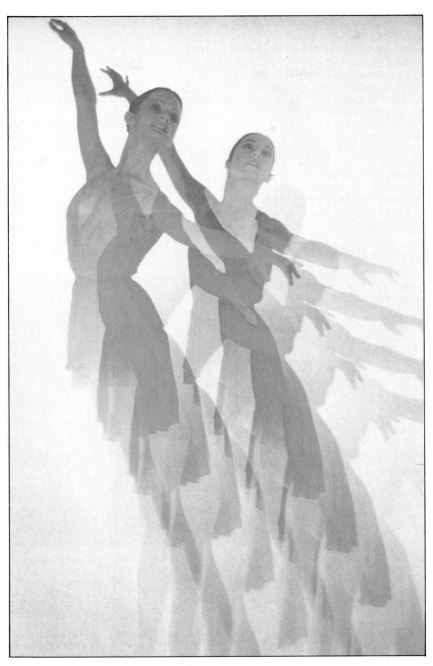

Using window light

Even when shooting indoors, daylight is still a valuable light source, provided that it is not too harsh or uneven. Painters have traditionally used the diffused even lighting offered by a large window opening away from the sun. Similar "window light" can be improvised and is often ideal for shooting portraits and still-life subjects of all kinds.

Creating soft shadows
The main feature of window light is the absence of hard-edged shadows. Its even, gentle quality is excellent for revealing the shape and form of subjects, especially if the light comes from one side. You can see the effect near any large window on an overcast day. In other situations you can adapt

lighting to produce the same type of result. For example, muslin or tracing paper over a window facing direct sunlight diffuses its harsh light. Lamps or flash pointed toward a large matte-white surface such as a wall, or shining through a large sheet of tracing paper, give a similar effect.

Applying the technique
Window lighting gives a pleasing natural effect – the illumination is all from one general direction, and there are no "stagey" highlights or conflicting shadow edges to confuse subject detail. This is especially important when photographing groups of objects, where shadows from one element easily become cast across others. The softness of the light is excellent for shiny

SIMULATING WINDOW LIGHT

A window that is not receiving direct sunlight gives diffused, scattered illumination. The larger the window and the closer it is to the subject, the softer and less distinct the shadows become. With close-ups you can scale everything down using a sheet of tracing paper just outside the picture area and shining a lamp through it. Results are also greatly affected by the direction of the light – from the two extremes of frontal lighting for maximum detail to backlighting.

The basic principle
The smaller and farther away your light source the more distinct shadows and contrasts in your subjects will appear. A small, high window gives quite hard lighting indoors even on an overcast day (see right). A larger, closer window gives light from a wide range of directions, and so illuminates more of the shadow areas. When the window is very large and near (bottom right) it almost envelops the entire subject.

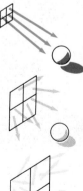
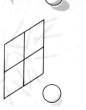

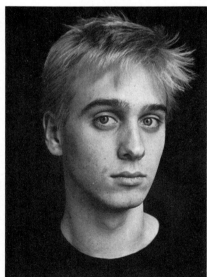

Frontal This shot was taken near a large window to the camera's right. A screen on the left helped to lighten the shadow side. Detail is excellent. Compare with the subject on p. 104.

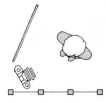

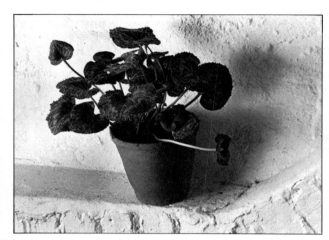

Still-life Window light quality is helpful when the subject itself is contrasty, like these dark plant leaves against a white wall. A conservatory window out of frame on the left gives soft directional lighting. The wall itself acts like a reflector, providing fill-in. The result is detail throughout, without excessive flatness.

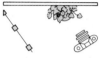

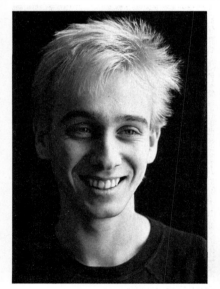

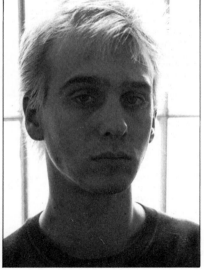

Side The subject for this shot was turned and moved further from the window, and the reflector was removed. Each of these changes increases subject contrast.

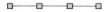

Rear In this version the subject had his back to the window. A large white screen behind the camera returned some of the light to the face. The result, though, is still quite natural, but flat.

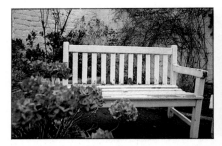 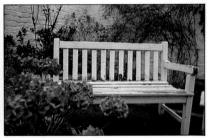

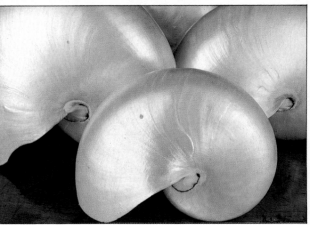

Color correction The pictures above were taken in a conservatory using daylight from a pale blue sky. To correct the dominant blue effect this produces on daylight film, a pale yellow CC10Y filter was used (above).

Accentuating color The still-life shot (right) shows how frontal use of soft diffused window light emphasizes subject sheen and delicate coloring.

reflective objects such as polished metal or glazed ceramics. The glaring highlights these surfaces produce in harsh light are spread out into a sheen. Window light directed from the side or rear can give a moody interpretative effect.

Avoiding problems

Although shadows are soft, you may still have to add some light to darker areas, especially if the window is very much to one side. Use a white board or sheet on the shadow side to reflect back enough light to reveal some detail. You must also be careful about the color of window lighting. If the light outside is all from blue sky, for example, it will create a blue cast on the film. This is particularly important on slide film, where you might have to use a pale color correcting filter. Bounced flash is more consistent in this respect as its color is always balanced to daylight.

HINTS AND TIPS

- To create window light quality with flash use a powerful unit. Either direct it through a translucent umbrella or bounce it off a large surface.
- Take care over light evenness – brightness tends to fall off across the picture. This happens when the window light is too close, so sometimes you must compromise between softness and evenness.
- You can create soft illumination similar to window light with a small lamp, using a "painting with light" technique. Work in a darkened room, give an exposure of several seconds, and move the lamp continuously within an area the same size as a window.
- The color of decorations such as walls and ceilings or furniture can easily give color casts.
- Window light is dimmer as well as softer than direct light, so be prepared to use wider apertures or more sensitive film.

Mixing different light sources

Some scenes contain a mixture of light sources, especially at dusk. Color films are balanced for particular forms of lighting, therefore only one source will record correctly. You can decide which one through choice of film or filters.

Controlling results

A typical mixture is tungsten lighting (domestic lamps, for example) and daylight. If you shoot on daylight film, colors will be correct in parts lit by natural light or flash, but lamps will appear orange (see p. 52). The same shot on tungsten light film (or blue-filtered daylight film) shows the lamp-lit parts correctly, but daylit or flash-lit areas are blue. Usually it is best to use a film or filter that gives the correct color for your main subject. This is most important with slide film – it is possible to adjust color negatives during printing by dialing in different strengths of filters on the enlarger.

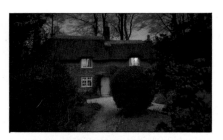

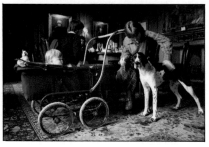

CHOOSING COLOR FILTERS

Light source	Daylight film	Tungsten film	Daylight+ 80A filter	Tungsten+ 82B filter
Noon daylight/Flash	Correct	Blue	Blue	Very blue
Studio lamps	Orange	Correct	Correct	Bluish
Household lamps	Very orange	Yellowish	Yellowish	Correct
Skylight after sunset	Bluish	Very blue	Very blue	Very blue
"Cool white" tubes	Greenish	Green	Green	Cyan

Choosing film Both images above were taken on daylight film. The exterior was lit by the blue light that follows sunset. The foreground of the interior shot was lit by daylight, the background by domestic lamps. On tungsten film daylit parts would be blue.

Unusual mixed sources Most street lamps and floodlights produce tinted illumination, with some colors missing altogether. The daylight film shot of Notre Dame (right) shows green-deficient sodium lighting on the building, while streets are lit with red-deficient vapor tube lamps. Results are similar to the visual appearance of the scene. No filter could correct both sources. Avoid using unusual lighting for portraits and close-ups.

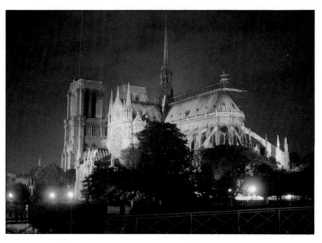

Lighting for dramatic effect

Dramatic lighting can create an eye-catching and spectacular scene from something quite ordinary and mundane. A splash of light, a silhouetted shape or pattern of shadows attracts the eye through their contrasts of highlights and shadows. The type of light source for this is usually harsh – direct sunlight, flash, or spotlighting, for example.

Using localized lighting

Often the most dramatic effects come from localized lighting. A pool of light under a street lamp or shafts of sunlight from a window or gap between the clouds acts like stage lighting. A similar thing happens when the picture contains the light source – someone in dim surroundings lighting a cigarette, for example. Lightest and darkest parts close together seem immediately to create a center of interest. Another way of dramatically picking something out is by backlighting. This allows you to rimlight a

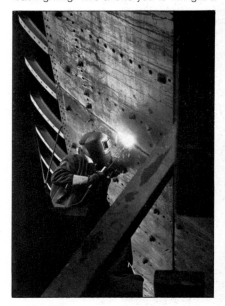

Including the light source For this shot exposure was read from the ship's plates, but excluded the weld-ing torch. Overcast daylight is just strong enough to give background detail and shadow fill-in.

Frontal Lit by one small lamp just above the lens, this result is the most natural of the series. But it has a dull flattening effect, similar to flash used on the camera. There is little sense of subject texture or form.

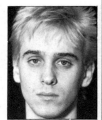

Light from below Here the lamp was pointed upward from subject chest level. The nose casts a shadow upward, giving a stage footlights effect. The face now has a dramatic, slightly menacing appearance.

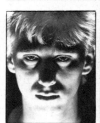

Double side light For this version two matching lamps were used, 90° to each side of the head. Skin texture is good and the face has roundness, but the large central shadows give a dead look. The result is highly unnatural.

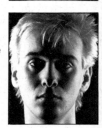

Backlight Here the lamp was directly behind the subject's head. Some light is reflected back from a wall behind the camera, giving soft, flat light over the face. Contrast is limited to the hair so that it dominates.

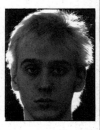

person's shoulders and hair against a dark ground. Or you can silhouette their shape by having a lit patch of background such as a window or open door behind them.

Technical problems

You must take particular care over contrast and exposure. Decide where you want detail, and where it will be best to leave areas mostly featureless dark or light. With a silhouette, for example, you have to measure exposure mostly from the background. This will result in a predominantly dark and underexposed shape. For a portrait, such as someone sitting close to a reading lamp, measure exposure from the face and let the illumination source overexpose so that it seems to spread and glow. Learn to recognize when contrast will be excessive. With close shots you can use a reflective surface near the camera, or bounce flash, to give detail in the shadows.

Light patterns Shafts of sunlight sliced by the overhead grid, show up in the dusty atmosphere (left). They silhouette the figures, creating a picture with a dramatic sense of pattern and depth with shadowy surroundings. Exposure was measured from the sunlit background parts of the scene only.

HINTS AND TIPS

● To see how contrasty your picture will be, squint slightly or look through the camera with the lens stopped down. This also helps identify the part from which you should read exposure.
● Always aim for lighting that is a little less harsh and contrasty than you want in your picture.
● Shadow areas reading one-eighth (three f numbers) darker than the part from which you read exposure, will record dark and featureless. This is because lighting differences of this magnitude are beyond the recording capability of the film.

Recording surface texture

Emphasizing texture is the best way to give an impression of how a subject would feel if you could touch it. Texture – smoothness or roughness, cracks and bumps – is always visually dependent on lighting to reveal it. (Unlike pattern, which can be formed on a flat, texture-less surface.) Sometimes texture can make a satisfying photograph on its own, but mostly it is an important component in successful pictures of landscapes, people, or natural history, adding an extra dimension to the composition.

Finding the right lighting
The direction and quality of lighting affects the appearance of texture. Hard, glancing light skimming across the surface of a subject dramatizes and exaggerates rough texture. At the opposite extreme, soft light from a less acute angle will reveal sheen and enhance undulating surfaces. You may have to wait for the right time of day and weather conditions in order to use natural lighting. For close-up work you can

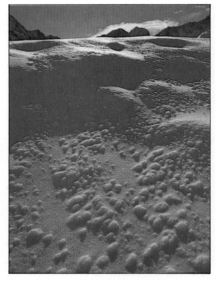

Snow texture Harsh sunlight from the rear exaggerates texture and sparkle. The surrounding deep blue sky tints the shadows.

USING CONTROLLED LIGHTING

Working indoors you can control completely lighting direction to alter the appearance of texture, especially with still-life subjects. Using a lamp allows you to see the precise effect of every change. According to the angle of the light some textures are exaggerated. Others are suppressed by being flatly lit or cast into

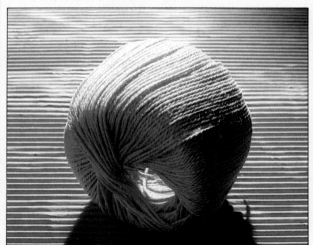

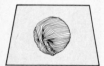

Rear lighting In this still-life shot the light was placed behind the ball of string. This lighting scheme emphasized background texture and the top of the string.

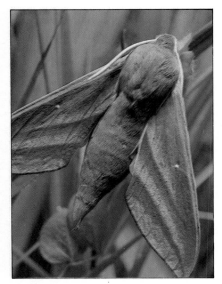

Hawk moth Fur-like texture in this shot is gently picked out by soft directional light. It was top lit through a diffuser.

use electronic flash. This enables you to position lighting for the best effect and also helps freeze subject movement.

Choosing the best lighting for texture is easiest when most of your subject is all on one plane, like the snowfield (left). When you have many surfaces at different angles – some vertical, others horizontal – lighting which enhances one texture may shadow and suppress another. You must then decide whether to emphasize only the most important part, or to compromise by choosing softer, more generalized lighting.

Coping with contrast

Harsh, directional lighting dramatizes texture, but it also creates the problem of extreme contrast between lit and unlit parts. In natural sunlight there may be enough light from the sky to stop shadows becoming a featureless black. And when shadowed areas are quite small, you can ignore them. If you are shooting close-up, reduce contrast by using a white reflector such as cardboard on the shadow side.

shadow. These changes are greatest when you use a hard light source, such as a spotlight or a small floodlight some distance away.

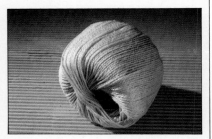

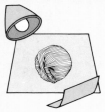

Side lighting In this version of the picture the lamp was moved to the left of the subject. Here, the light suppressed corrugations and revealed more texture of the string itself. A reflector was added.

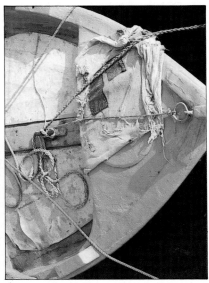

Weathering Texture helps show the character of worn and weathered materials. The boat was lit by the last weak rays of the setting sun and general skylight.

Lighting small objects

You can use various everyday light sources to light and photograph small still-life objects. You will already have many of the items you need for this type of "studio" work at home. They include background materials, shaders, reflectors, tape, and string. It is helpful to know some simple professional lighting techniques, especially for difficult subjects. You can work at home or photograph in museums and exhibitions.

Selecting equipment
You will not need a bright light source if you have a static subject and you place your camera on a tripod. A desk lamp or carefully directed room light, or even a hand lamp, can give enough illumination. For color photography the lighting color is important. A slide projector or a small photographic lamp are good lights for tungsten film. When the source is mostly daylight, augment it by using a blue-tinted display lamp, blue acetate in front of a tungsten lamp, or flash. Whatever your source, you will often have to soften its quality or reduce its contrast with diffusers and reflectors.

Choosing lighting techniques
When photographing small items in a darkened room at home, you can build up the necessary lights and reflectors one at a

time (right). You can usually use a standard lens, but sometimes you will need an 80 mm or 100 mm lens (perhaps with extension tubes) to distance your camera from the subject and allow room for lighting.

Strong, textured objects respond well to hard, oblique lighting from a projector or distanced tungsten lamp or flash. You may have to enclose polished silver and mirror-finished subjects in a light-diffusing "tent" of muslin or plastic, with the camera lens looking in through a hole. Glass is often best lit as a silhouette (see p. 88). Subjects with deep enclosed spaces, like the inside of an electronic chassis, require very frontal lighting. Use ring flash, or light directed by 45° glass. It is best to use flash for any close-up subject which may shift its position during exposure, such as flowers or delicate paper structures.

- Try to read exposure from a close position, filling the frame with the main part of your subject. Do not refocus – your result will be more accurate if you measure the area unsharp.
- To make lighting softer and more even with a static subject

move the lamp during exposure.
- The most useful aids for lighting small objects *in situ* are white paper (to lighten shadows) and black paper (to restrict light and prevent reflections appearing).

HINTS AND TIPS

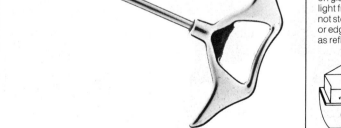

Reflective surface
With reflective subjects (left), make a white cardboard enclosure (below). For a shadowless background, place subject on glass and bounce light from below. Do not stop down too far, or edges will appear as reflected detail.

IMPROVISING A MINI-STUDIO

Try to exclude most existing light from your working area and then arrange your own lighting with everything under complete control. Set your subjects some distance in front of the background surface. This will give you enough room to light the background independently – to control its tone and also eliminate any unwanted shadows. Start building up lighting by positioning one main light source. Then add white reflectors to reduce contrast. A second light may be required for rimlighting.

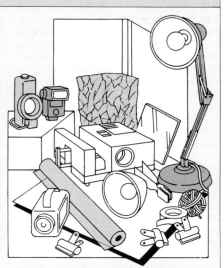

Useful items Some equipment for setting up and lighting small still-life objects is shown right. Use white, gray, or black cardboard for bases and backgrounds, and kitchen foil as reflectors. The desk lamp and chair clip-on lamp act as floods, further diffused by tracing paper. Use the slide projector as a spotlight. The flashlight will illuminate small areas or soften shadows.

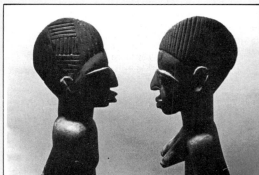

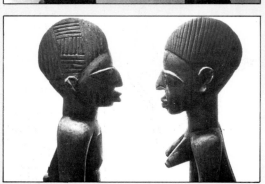

Simple set-up First, decide the placing of your main light. For the subject left, an undiffused desk lamp was placed almost overhead. Shadows are heavy, but this is satisfactory as an interpretative photograph.

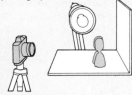

Building a scheme To show more structural detail in the figures add illumination from the front. Curved white cardboard either side of the camera reflected some soft top light. A projector lit the background.

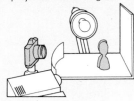

Photographing through glass

Photographing through glass can produce interesting semi-abstract images if the glass is patterned or faceted. Often, though, you are forced to photograph through plain glass in order to record paintings, fish in glass-fronted tanks, scenes through car or shop windows, and various museum-type objects in glass cases. Here you must minimize the problems caused by the glass itself.

Overcoming the problems

Pick a viewpoint to minimize reflections from your side of the glass. Sometimes, given the correct angle, a polarizer will be sufficient. Or you can use a powerful flash from the camera, provided that you are not square-on to the surface. You can minimize camera reflection using a telephoto and moving back, or by shooting through a hole in black cardboard. To shoot distant scenes through a window, have the camera square-on with the lens hood almost touching the cleaned glass surface.

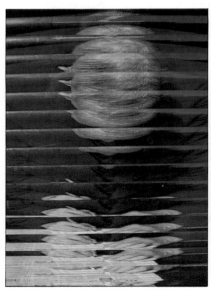

Abstract view This figure behind molded glass was photographed from some distance. The pattern consists of slightly different "squeezed" views. Faceted lens attachments work in a similar way.

DISTANCE AND ANGLE

Time may not always permit control over reflections other than by choice of camera distance and angle. With flat glass, altering your angle to the surface can shift a bright reflection out of the picture. Or have someone in dark clothing stand next to you to block it out. Curved glass is more difficult. Some reflections may have to remain – so make them add to rather than detract from your picture. Review results at your working aperture.

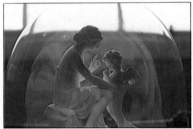

Close viewpoint The picture above was taken close up with a 50 mm lens. To reduce reflection, it had to be shot from a low angle. Widest aperture was used to make remaining reflections unsharp.

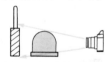

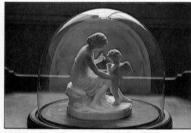

Moving back For the version above the lens was changed to 135 mm and the camera distance increased. Its reflection is now too small and dark to show. This allows a higher viewpoint and simpler background.

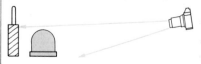

Copying techniques

Copying – photographing slides, prints, drawings, and paintings – is an often underrated technique. Yet copying allows you to duplicate, manipulate, and even improve originals in various ways. Methods of shooting opaque-based objects like prints differ from copying film originals (see p. 112).

Applications

Copying paper-based originals allows you to record large paintings, small stamps, engravings or pictures from books. Lettering can be turned into slides to title shows. Montages and retouched or colored photographs become pictures without joins or surface defects. Old photographs can be preserved as new prints – and any stains removed if copied (in black and white) through a filter matching the color of the stain. By copying slides you can duplicate originals, or turn them into negatives.

There are many ways to manipulate your original image. You can copy through a diffuser or shift focus during a time exposure to soften detail. Double exposing one

---

COPYING OPAQUE-BASE ORIGINALS

It is vital to have your camera centered and square-on, and the original evenly lit. This is made easier using a converted enlarger or copying stand. Other aids include a tripod cross-bar or a simple camera stand. Large originals for copying will have to be hung vertically on a wall.

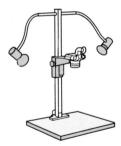

Copying stand

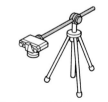

Tripod and cross-bar

Squaring up It is easy for the original to reproduce with converging instead of parallel lines if the camera is slightly off-center. One way to avoid this is to place a small mirror flat against the original. Then move the camera (keeping its back horizontal) until you see the lens reflected in the center of the viewfinder. Another aid is a small weighted plumb line attached to a lens cap. Adjust the camera until the plumb line hangs over the center of the original.

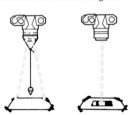

Projected light You can align an SLR camera by first setting it parallel to the original and then projecting light through the viewfinder. Do this in a darkened room, holding a small flashlight close against the eyepiece. An image of the focusing screen is projected from the lens. It is easy to center the original in the light patch,

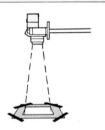

adjust camera height to fill the frame, and focus the lens until marks on the screen appear sharp on the original.

Even illumination Illuminate the original with two light sources angled at about 45° and directed so that the center of each beam points at the opposite edge. You can help test evenness by holding a pencil or rod at right-angles to the center of the original. The two shadows should be of equal tone and length.

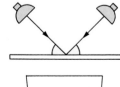

COPYING SLIDE ORIGINALS

Slide copying is made easier by the standard size of the originals and by various close-up attachments designed for copy work. You must still take care over focus, exposure, and light evenness coming from behind your original slide.

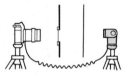

Improvised set-up For a slide copying set-up (above) you require a close-up lens or extension tube that permits 1:1 reproduction. Have the camera square-on to the slide taped over a hole in black cardboard. Flash offers the most consistent light source. Align the lens and flashgun unit, which should be diffused with colorless tracing paper, and positioned well back from the slide. To maximize grain, remove the tracing paper and substitute a small aperture in cardboard in front of the flash.

Tube copier A tube copier is the simplest equipment designed for slide copying. You clamp the slide over one end of

the tube behind a light diffuser. You then attach the other end of the tube to the camera body and a lens halfway between the slide and film forms a 1:1 image. You can point the unit at any suitable light source. With this set-up camera shake is almost impossible because the subject is secured to the camera.

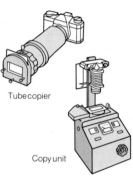

Tube copier

Copy unit

Copying unit Several self-contained slide copying units are available that incorporate their own light source. The one illustrated above contains an electronic flash and a modeling lamp positioned under the slide. You read exposure from the modeling light using the camera's meter or a swing-over measuring cell. Some

units have built-in correcting filters of various tints, which you can dial in. You can move the camera up or down on guides and the unit has bellows that allow you to copy any small parts of the original slide at will.

Image conversion Copying allows you to convert your slides into different forms of images. Color slides can be changed into color negative or black and white negative film images. You can make dozens of instant picture slides from one original image, or you can convert a color slide to a high-contrast black and white result. Both versions below were produced from the color slide found on p. 98.

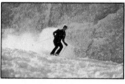

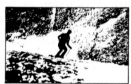

image on another is more controllable than when shooting the original subjects. Colors can also be adjusted using correcting filters. To create a grainy image, back a color slide with specially etched slide mount glass. Then copy it, illuminated by a small lamp or flashgun placed behind.

For most work it is best to copy on low-contrast film – if necessary overexpose and then have the laboratory hold back (see pp. 62–3) processing to avoid excessive contrast. Measure exposure with a TTL meter in the usual way, but bear in mind that some originals will fool the meter as they contain large light or dark areas.

HINTS AND TIPS

- Surround opaque-base originals with wide strips of matte black cardboard.
- When copying an old photograph with a faded sepia or yellowish image in black and white, you can improve results using a green or blue filter.
- If your original has a color stain use a similar colored filter to remove it on black and white film.
- Montages, mosaics, and retouched photographs should always be made large. After copying make reduced-size prints.
- Slide duplicating film is a special low-contrast material designed for copying slide originals.

TACKLING
SPECIAL PROJECTS

The previous section dealt with solving problems mostly concerned with composition and shooting conditions, and applicable to a wide range of subjects. This next section concentrates on points that are special to specific subjects. It starts with the most popular camera subject of all – people. The challenge here is usually obtaining the co-operation of the person you are photographing, finding the right setting, and then solving the problems of lighting and camera technique. Children and animals are the next topics, and here the additional qualities of great patience and organization are essential to successful results. You may, however, be more interested in totally unposed pictures of strangers or the more specialized area of sport.

Landscapes and general views call for patience of a different kind – ability to plan and wait for exactly the right weather conditions and time of day for the effect you want. Much the same applies to travel photography, except that time is often even shorter. Other challenging subjects such as nudes, architecture, and varied forms of natural history are also discussed in turn. Another area entirely is concerned with still-life images, arranged and lit indoors where everything is under the control of the photographer.

Portraits

A good portrait should be something more than just a likeness – it should capture some aspect of the individual's personality. Apart from candids, most portraits are taken with the knowledge and co-operation of the subject. You must, therefore, expect to direct the picture to some extent – deciding the setting and picking the vital moment for both pose and expression.

Organizing the picture

Portraits can range from close-ups, with the face cropped tight by the picture edges (see p. 117), to a figure in an environment where the surroundings take up much of the space. A plain background such as the sky or a wall is safe, but can be boring. By including surrounding details, especially indoors, you can add information to a portrait, suggesting life style, occupation, or interests. Decide whether to choose a formal or informal approach. Watch how your subject tends to stand or sit and the natural positioning of hand and legs when relaxed. Look for mannerisms in expression. Often this means spending time talking to the person and, if possible, giving him or her something to do. It helps if you can create an atmosphere of confidence, but do not

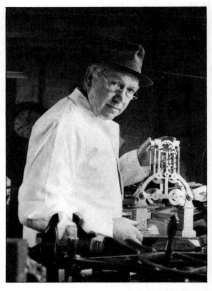

Working surroundings For the portrait above the clockmaker was told to look up briefly. Soft directional light separates the subject's head from the darker surroundings.

Outdoor setting For the portrait of a friend dozing in the sun (facing page) the photographer made strong use of the leaf pattern setting. The result suggests great privacy.

LENSES FOR PORTRAITS

Avoid lenses shorter than about 50 mm for nearly all portraits. If you use a wide-angle lens, you will have to be close to your subject to fill the frame. Then features such as the nose will appear too large. A 100 or 135 mm lens allows you to work further back, producing a more natural perspective. If you use a compact camera, choose its longest focal length, or keep back and have a selective enlargement made.

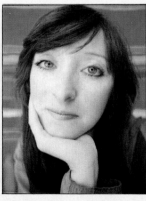

28 mm Head shots taken with a wide-angle lens distort facial features.

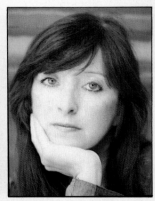

100 mm The same framing from four times further back gives more natural perspective.

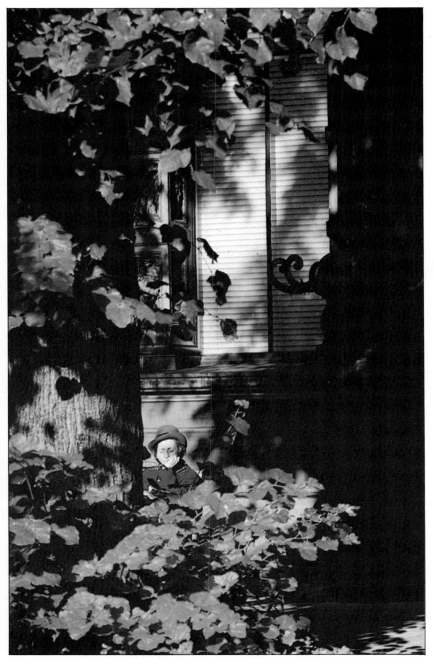

ORGANIZING GROUP PORTRAITS

People often prefer being photographed in groups – within a crowd they feel less under inspection. But you must organize things so that every individual can be seen, and that the group as a whole has shape and structure. Groups such as bandsmen or football teams can be arranged formally around their leaders. Center family groups on the parents or the youngest member. You almost always have to move people closer to each other to avoid gaps in the picture. And be prepared to capture people's attention by devices such as blowing a whistle or waving at the vital moment. To be safe, take two or three shots.

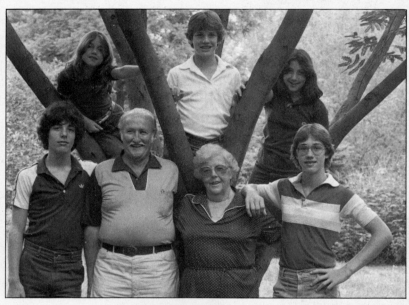

Variations of approach Two successful approaches to a family group can be seen here. For the informal version (right) parents were positioned at opposite ends, and then everyone else squashed themselves in. In the other version (above) the photographer exploited the shape of the apple tree, and located the parents centrally. The smallest children, raised up behind, helped to create a compact grouping.

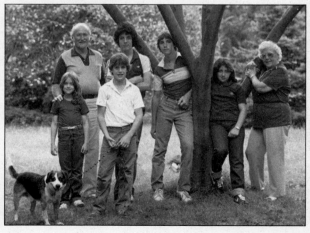

116

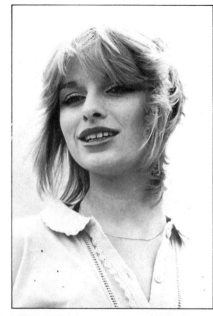

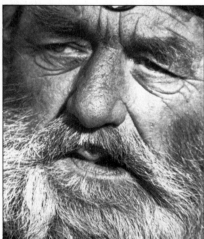

dominate or over-stage situations. To avoid self-conscious pictures, try and catch your subject fully absorbed in something or relating to you at the moment of shooting.

Choosing the best technique

Choose between a face shot, head and shoulders, half length or full length. You can encourage certain kinds of poses by the way you stand or seat people. Using the camera on a tripod helps eliminate the barrier created when equipment covers the photographer's face. After setting up and focusing you can converse directly from one side of the lens. Shifting your own position (up, down, left, or right) gets the sitter to change position of head or eyes naturally.

Try to work in existing lighting using, if necessary, reflective surfaces or flash to reduce contrast. Use soft diffused light directed from slightly above your subject unless you want an unnatural effect. Generally, the fewer light sources the more natural the result. Avoid lighting schemes so inflexible that your subject is unable to move easily, and so appears wooden. Have the lens above subject eye level, and to minimize a double chin shoot from a slightly higher position. Similarly, a lower viewpoint helps to hide baldness. Lens diffuser attachments are useful if you must avoid recording any facial blemishes.

High key, low key
Portraits that are generally light in tone with pale backgrounds and soft lighting, give a delicate high-key type of result (top). The opposite, low-key

effect, with harsher lighting and darker detail often suits a masculine portrait (above). This does not mean, however, that you should not experiment with lighting.

HINTS AND TIPS

● In portraits always focus on the sitter's eyes.
● Use the slowest film that the lighting conditions, subject, or camera movement will permit. Reserve grainier films for special effects.
● With most portraits take as many shots as possible, especially of groups where it is difficult to capture good expressions on everyone at once.
● Try self-portraits. Shoot into a mirror or use a long shutter release, or your camera's delayed action release.
● A wide-angle lens (or compact camera with short standard lens) is useful for showing the environment and setting.
● Most frequent faults in portraits are self-conscious expressions due to poor timing and direction, squinting or shadowed eyes due to harsh sunlight, and pictures shot from the wrong angle.

Children

Children are marvellous subjects – they can react to situations with obvious joy, rage, or curiosity. On the other hand they can be introspective. However, children are less controllable than adults, so you must have patience. You also need the skill to react quickly to brief situations, as well as most of the requirements for photographing adult subjects (see pp. 114-17). Props, such as books or toys, can also be usefully employed to stop your subjects becoming bored. These props can form part of the picture.

Working with children of different ages

Young babies may not be able to sit up, and you will have to provide unobtrusive support. Active two-to-five year olds are so mobile that you must move quickly to follow their play. As they grow older, they become absorbed in reading and make-believe, and eventually grow more self-conscious. Try to photograph each of these stages. Show babies at key moments in their daily routine such as feeding, bathtime or a play session. And select actions and expressions which suggest character, including tantrums. Record achievements such as a baby's first faltering steps. Ask a helper to encourage the child to become involved in an activity. Children of about four to eight years old are ideal subjects – you can catch spontaneous moments while they are still relatively free of self-awareness. With older children, look for pensive moments and social relationships toward other children

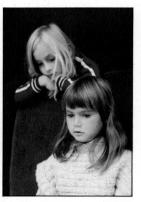

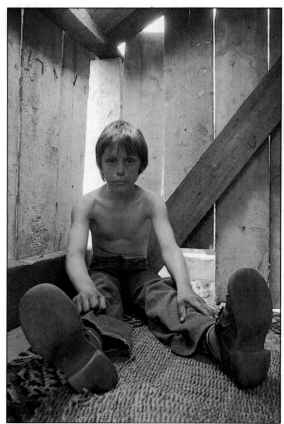

Character and expression In both these pictures expression and setting help to show the character of the children. The boy (left) is king of his tree house. The photographer used a wide-angle lens in the confined space to make legs, arms and the background timber boldly lead in to the child's face. The two girls (above) were absorbed in reading a picture book. Pensive expressions, soft frontal lighting, an uncomplicated background, and the flatter perspective that a longer focal length lens gives, all combine to produce a quieter, more studied mood.

BABIES AND TODDLERS

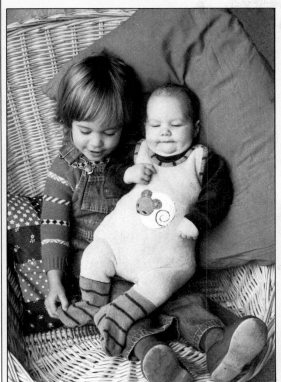

A young baby needs physical support, but you can make use of this fact to show its relationship with other family members. To photograph a toddler, set up a simple, natural situation (like a new toy) and wait to see what develops naturally. Vital expressions are extremely brief, and you must be ready to shoot at once. Never try to force a child to take part in a photo session – stop and take more pictures on another day.

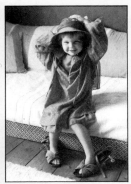

Setting up situations
Leave a baby and child together in a safe chair (above left) for interesting combinations of expression and action. A simple mirror (left) will encourage a baby to examine his own reflection, and also show the mother and baby relationship well. Toddlers nearly always love dressing-up (above). Sometimes the right moment is a result of a child's reaction to you and the camera.

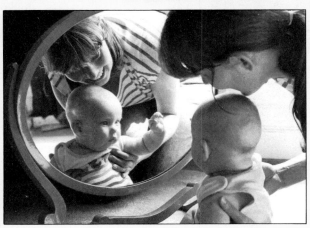

to photograph. Some children are natural performers and over-react to the camera. This is usually short-lived, so be patient and only pretend to take pictures initially.

Choosing techniques

Use a normal, wide-aperture lens and ISO 400 film for most pictures. Indoors, work near a large window for diffused light, or use bounced flash. With active children at play, try some shots at 1/15 to convey the impression of movement. Or use a fast shutter speed and try to freeze the peak of the action. Often it is best to shoot from a child's-height viewpoint, rather than full adult height. Take plenty of pictures, or try to be around with your camera long enough for the children to lose interest in it.

Avoid changing camera settings too frequently – take an exposure reading from the face and try to keep to a shutter speed of 1/125. Always focus on the eyes, and with close-ups do not keep resetting focus. If the child moves about, shift your position backward or forward until the viewfinder image looks sharp again.

Series approach One possible approach to child photography is to contrast activities, or to build up a series of shots taken throughout a child's day. The picture below captures the peak of the action. Backlighting emphasizes the water spray. The shot of the sleeping boy was taken on a summer evening, using fast film and daylight. Pictures like these will help you to create strong album sequences.

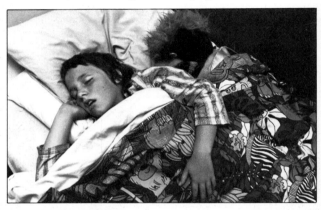

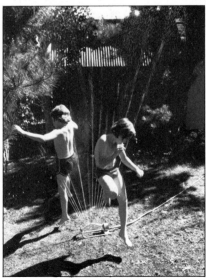

● It is safe to use flash to photograph newly born babies. But bounce light if possible for gentler modeling.

● Look out for close-up pictures which compare adult and baby-size hands, feet, or profiles. And be ready for the way a hand grasps a parent's finger.

● There are often good opportunities to photograph children's expressions at swings and slides, watching TV, or playing with a pet.

● If you choose a formal approach for a portrait of an older child, take care over clothes, hair, choice of lighting and setting. Consider the use of a lens diffuser. Allow some time for the child to relax with you and the camera before shooting.

● For informal pictures of shy older children select moments when they are absorbed in sports or hobby activities. With a younger shy child try turning a photographic session into a game of hide-and-seek or some other activity.

HINTS AND TIPS

Animals

A good animal photograph should suggest the character of the individual or species. With tame or domestic creatures try to show the strong bonds which often exist between animals and their owners. You must have patience and good organizational skills. And you should be able to anticipate good picture-taking moments. Keep your photographic technique as simple as possible. This will allow you to exploit every possible opportunity.

Picture possibilities

Start with tame animals and birds – children with pets and creatures with their young make rewarding subjects. Avoid dressing up animals or overstaging situations. If you want to photograph less accessible animals in their natural surroundings you will have to use a hide or a remotely controlled camera (see p. 142). Take care over backgrounds, especially at zoos. Choose surroundings that suggest environment, or keep them plain. And select a viewpoint that suits the subject's size. You will find that a large animal looks even bigger from a low angle. And a tiny one appears smaller from above, particularly if you show it within something of a known size, such as a hand or shoe. If you need extra light, flash is least disruptive. Bounce it if you are shooting indoors. It is best to have a helper – preferably the owner – to control the animal and attract its attention at the right moment. Because situations can change so rapidly you should shoot plenty of film.

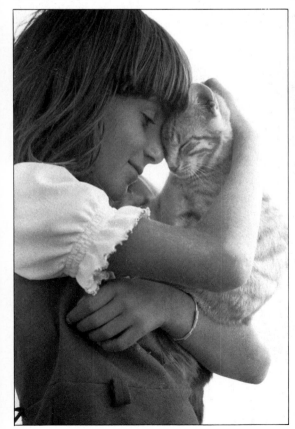

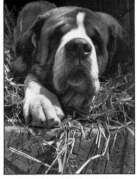

Taking an animal portrait This shot of a St Bernard dog was taken from the bottom of some steps. A low angle and tight cropping helps to stress the animal's size. The straw suggests a farmyard setting. Large dogs are often more placid and easier to photograph than small ones.

Showing relationships The simple picture (left) captures the loving relationship between child and pet. This shot was set up, but then allowed to develop naturally. The photographer waited until the girl's arm formed an intimate, enclosing shape. Soft lighting adds to the mood of companionship between the two.

121

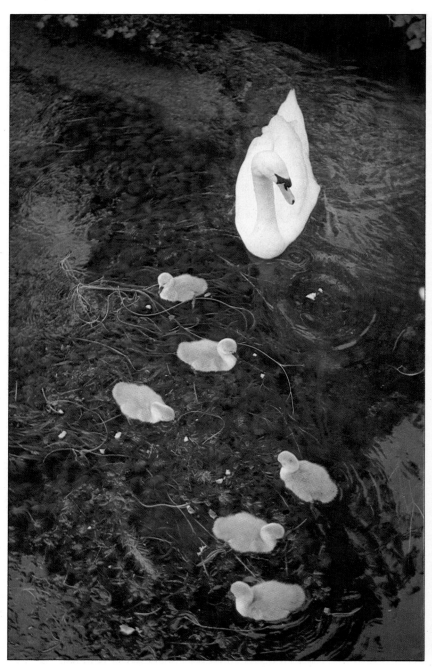

Shooting a sequence
If an animal is extremely active, you can show this characteristic through a series of pictures. The cartoon-style sequence (right) suits the comic nature of this particular dog. Try to keep static objects identically framed in each shot.

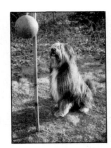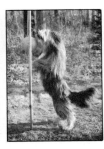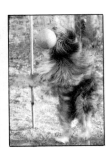

PHOTOGRAPHING ZOO ANIMALS

Overcome problems of bars or glass in the foreground and ugly backgrounds to cages by careful use of viewpoint and shallow depth of field. Find out about the animal's daily routine, and visit when interesting activities combine with good lighting conditions. If possible, show relationships between zoo animals and their visitors or keepers. And try taking animal portraits using a medium telephoto or zoom lens.

Choosing the right moment A high viewpoint limits surroundings to ground detail (right). The polar bears were photographed at siesta time. Their sprawling shapes relate well to the patch of water.

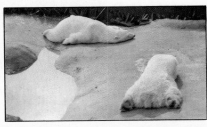

Coping with fences
Netting often forms an obstruction (below left). To suppress it use a telephoto lens and focus only on the subject. Or move in closer and align your standard lens with an open part of the netting (below).

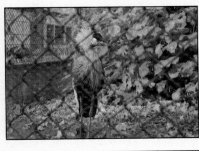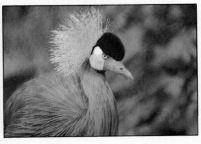

Swan family A swan and cygnets form a simple pattern against dark water (facing page). Encourage young birds to approach your camera position with scraps of bread. To expose light-toned birds correctly, read exposure from the back of your hand.

● In general, use medium or fast film and shutter speeds of 1/125 or shorter. A neutral density or polarizing filter is helpful if you have to shoot at a wide aperture to minimize depth of field.
● A 135 mm or 85-200 mm zoom is the most useful for animal pictures.
● To photograph through a plate-glass-fronted zoo cage, use a lens hood against a clean section of glass.
● Before photographing fish in a tank, slip in a sheet of glass to reduce the front-to-back distance. This will enable you to keep the fish in focus by restricting their movement within the tank.

HINTS AND TIPS

Special events

Photography is an ideal way of recording a wide range of events from weddings to a drama or dance performance. In order to cover this type of subject well you should aim for variety in content and treatment by planning in advance.

Planning your approach
In general, every event has its public and private aspects, and you should try to show both. Staging a party, for example, involves preparing food and washing up afterward. For a full record of the occasion cover these activities as well as taking shots of the guests. Catch people off their guard, in contrast with their formal roles. And give your shots variety by changing subject distance and angle, and using several lenses. Work alongside the official photographer to capture humorous and human interest pictures, ending up with shots of the official group or final performance. Learn from the way that magazines build up their picture stories, often concentrating on events that are open to all photographers.

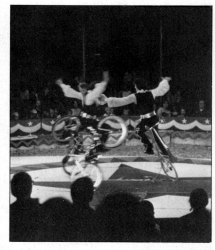

Photographing at a circus Choose a viewpoint several rows back to show the audience in the foreground and gain height.

Dance shots Select a plain background that contrasts with the subject (facing page). Take care with contrasty lighting.

COVERING AN EVENT

Make a list of the aspects you should cover beforehand. If possible, find out what will happen and when. Make sure you arrive early. The pictures below are part of a series taken at an English village summer festival. A general view establishes the setting. Consider shooting comparative general versions at early morning and late evening. Take plenty of close-up, behind-the-scenes shots while people are busy. Try to catch the personality of impromptu performers (bottom). Each picture in this series has a different subject viewpoint and distance to show a different aspect of the whole event.

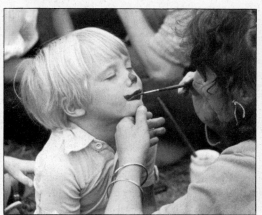

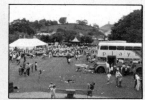

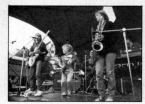

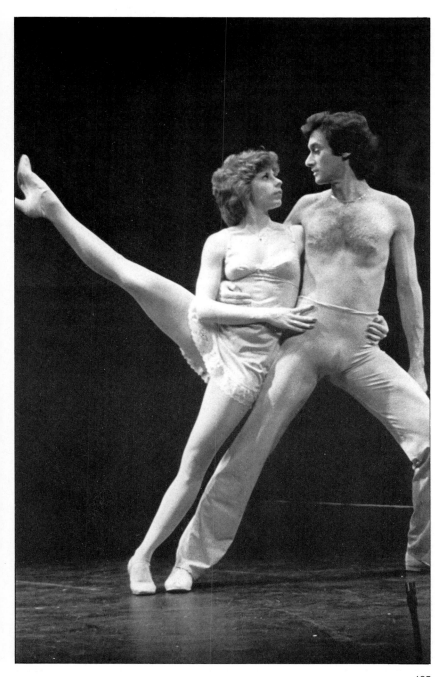

Sports

The most important quality required by a sports photographer is a thorough understanding of the sport itself – its rules, aims, and high points. This knowledge will help you anticipate the action. Also necessary is the right equipment to allow you to show what it feels like to be in with the participants.

Choice of equipment
The most important equipment (apart from the camera body and normal lens) is a medium long-focus zoom and a film winder. Most of the time you will want to fill the frame from a distance, and for sports such as football or sailing this may mean using an extreme telephoto, or perhaps a tele-convertor to produce an optic of 300 mm or longer. A motor drive is sometimes useful, but because of the importance of choosing exactly the right moment to shoot you are most likely to use it on its single-shot setting only. It is also helpful to have a camera offering shutter-priority metering – this allows you to control the blurring or freezing of the subject or to minimize camera movement when using a long lens. Depth of field is usually less important. To photo-

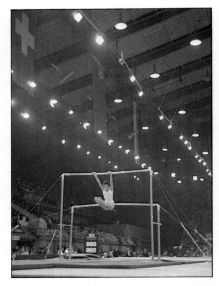

Space and setting The picture above, taken with a normal lens on high-speed film, shows the gymnast's isolation in a huge stadium.

Crowded action The panned telephoto shot below mixes wheels, horses, and jockeys to produce a sense of action and speed.

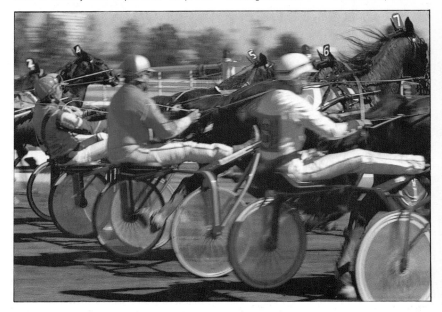

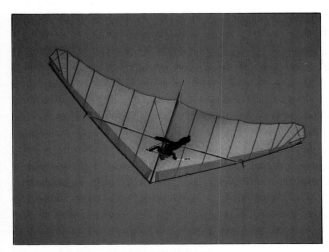

Hang gliding For this shot (left) viewpoint positions hang gliders passing overhead almost against the sun. Exposure was measured for the wing alone.

Baseball and rugby
The baseball shot (below left) shows tension through the frozen stance of the figures awaiting an unseen ball. In contrast, the boys playing rugby (below) are an excited swirling mass of forms.

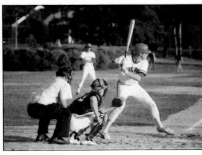

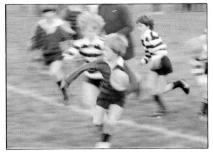

graph events such as boxing, athletics, and swimming, which often take place indoors, use the fastest film and your widest-aperture lens. Flash is rarely permitted. For events such as weightlifting and high jump, where you know the exact positioning of the contestants, a tripod can be useful.

Viewpoint and timing
Successful photographs depend on good choice of viewpoint and timing. Pick a position where you can capture the sense of "taking part". Panning and zooming (see pp. 41 and 168) during the exposure will help this, too. Choose a head-on viewpoint for swimmers and a bend to show horses bunched up or motor cyclists at dramatic angles. Follow team games by looking through the viewfinder. Keep the other eye open to see what is about to enter the frame.

● Some "focus-priority" lenses delay the shutter release while autofocusing occurs, and so may miss the peak of subject action. To avoid this, focus manually or focus-lock the lens on a pre-chosen point where the subject will pass.
● Try to include movement in some sports shots (slower shutter, panning, or zooming).
● Some sports lend themselves to sequences. For example, weightlifting, diving, and horse jumping. Often these are repetitive, so you have several opportunities.
● Use a wide-angle lens for crowds and general settings. It allows dramatic perspective if you can get close to the action – in pole vaulting events, for example.
● Avoid distracting or obstructing the participants in an event. Do not use flash, for example.

HINTS AND TIPS

Landscapes and seascapes

Landscapes and seascapes are subjects available to everyone, but difficult to photograph well. Sense of space, sounds, and the general environment and atmosphere are often as important as any one physical feature. It is a challenge to capture all these aspects of a place.

Exploiting natural conditions

As a general rule, it is best to avoid shooting in the middle of the day when the sun is high and lighting harsh and flat. Dawn and early morning, evening and dusk produce more dramatic changes in lighting direction and color. Shooting just before or after rain, and during seasonal changes can also produce rewarding images. Try to pick conditions that suit the mood you want to convey – early morning mist, for example, to imply depth and distance.

How to structure the picture

Even in a general scene, try to pick out or create some center of interest. It may be a house, boat, a dip in the mountains, or just sunlight glinting off a distant window. Try locating this feature in different parts of the frame and see how the picture balances about it. The position of the horizon is

Where to place the horizon In most cases you produce a more interesting, less symmetrical picture by not having the horizon centered in the frame. Where the horizon forms the base to an isolated feature (top), the feature is emphasized if it breaks up otherwise identical spaces. Drawings center and bottom show how interpretations change when compositions vary between three-quarters land and three-quarters sky. The sky-dominated picture is more open and remote, while the center one has more depth, with the foreground replacing cloud as a main element.

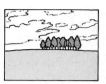

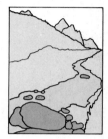

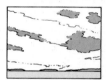

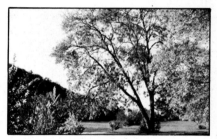

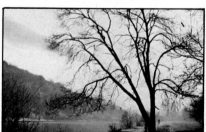

TIPS FOR DIFFERENT LANDSCAPES

Snow
Direct sunlight conditions, preferably from the side or rear, reveal characteristic texture and "glisten". Try shooting in color at dawn or dusk.

Sea
Mood alters with changes of surface pattern and color, according to weather conditions. Avoid large, empty expanses of sea, unless these form a setting to some main element. Fill the frame with a foreground shape, or shoot the coastline obliquely to make a connection between foreground and horizon.

Town
Look for strong angles and use a variety of lenses. Contrast buildings with vegetation. Use foreground objects to screen parked cars or litter. At dusk, lit windows enliven buildings, yet outlines still show up clearly against the sky.

Mountain
Shoot either early or late. Telephoto lenses help give a sense of height to distant mountain ranges and emphasize aerial perspective. Use a UV filter (or yellow/orange types) for blue skies on black and white film. Sunsets are excellent subjects.

Seasonal change The two pictures above highlight the changes in mood the same scene offers at opposite times of the year.

Balancing elements Although relatively small, the boats (facing page) form a focal point, and balance the cloud pattern.

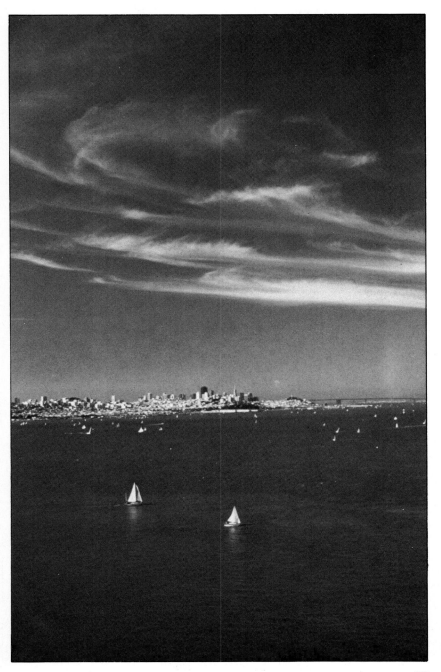

important, too – you can create different impressions by the way land and sea divisions with the sky are cut by the frame.

Not all landscapes have to be distant views. You can show a place purely through close-up elements, and suggest surroundings by concentrating on detail – a close shot of ice-covered rock, sand-blasted wood, or lush tropical growth, for example. Sometimes you can combine a general view and close-up by shooting with a wide-angle lens and placing important detail in the foreground.

Technical approach

For landscape and seascape work, it is a good idea to have a number of filters and lenses of different focal length available. An ultraviolet or haze filter is always useful for color and helps to protect the lens, too.

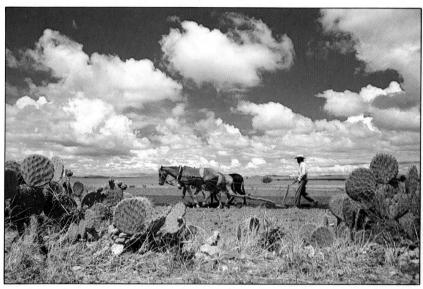

Sky and space The landscape above, with its sense of open space, has a strong center of interest. Cloud formations are accentuated through the use of a polarizing filter to darken the sky without affecting other colors.

Seasonal color The two versions of the scene (right) show how seasonal changes affect colors. A clear, frosty winter's day produces a steely blue tint, whereas evening light in fall emphasises the warm colors of the remaining foliage.

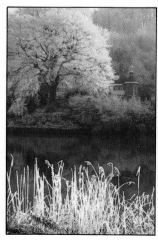

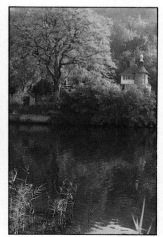

A polarizing filter, plus deep yellow and orange filters for black and white shots will enable you to darken skies. Use a telephoto lens to enlarge distant detail in relation to nearer elements, and a wide-angle lens for the reverse effect.

Interpreting the subject

Try to decide the type of mood you want to convey, not only its formation and detail.

Do not overlook black and white film – simplification of colors into tones can often help mood and atmosphere. You can control impressions such as space, enclosure, calm, and even menace by careful selection of viewpoint, lighting, exposure level, and choice of tone or color scheme. Sometimes, too, a very ordinary scene can be transformed by the right weather conditions or your choice of infrared film or effects filters.

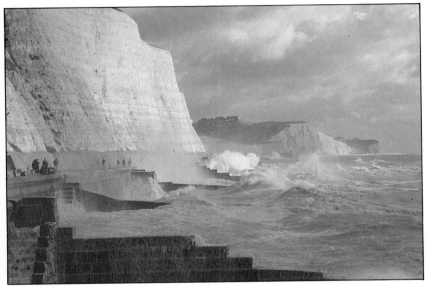

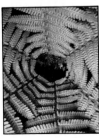

Muted contrast Hazy winter light and spray give soft contrasts and desaturated colors to this coastal scene (above). An ultraviolet filter was used here to protect the lens and prevent an excessive overall blue cast.

Picking out detail
Sometimes, details are as evocative as a broad view. Shots such as a found natural pattern (above right) and a weathered relic (right) give variety to landscape photography.

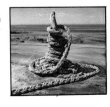

● If possible, carry a small tripod. It allows you to suggest the movement of water or vegetation through the use of blur.

● In general, pick slow or medium speed film for fine detail. Occasionally use fast film for more grainy, interpretative effects.

● When shooting in color, it is usually best to choose soft lighting, rather than harsh sunlight.

● Take special note

if possible of nearby landscapes. These you can photograph at short notice when conditions are just right.

● Experiment with moonlit scenes. Some advanced cameras accurately compute exposure up to 2 minutes.

● Do not shoot just from the obvious spots. Be prepared to explore for better viewpoints.

HINTS AND TIPS

Candids

The essence of candid photography is to show strangers and existing situations as they are, uninfluenced by and unaware of the camera. You must find a fruitful locality and either wait patiently for situations to develop, or grab shots when things occur unexpectedly right in front of you. For this type of photography the right equipment is particularly important.

Subjects and settings

Seemingly unimportant moments often give the most rewarding pictures, especially when they concern human relationships and feelings. Look for unconscious expressions, comparative shapes, or broken patterns. Try juxtaposing foreground and background elements. And make sure that you capture humorous or sad occurrences.

Careful planning will help you to shoot good candids. Begin by working within crowds at markets and public events. This will allow you to come close to individuals without being too noticeable. Another approach is to find a setting – perhaps a notice, store window display, or set of phone booths – which offers a good framework, then wait for people to walk into your picture. Try to work to a theme – for example, people reading or eating, people in

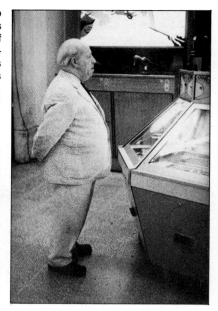

Comparing subject and setting The picture above relies on a strong inter-relationship of shapes for its impact. To show people unwittingly relating to things around them pick your viewpoint carefully and be prepared to respond quickly.

SEQUENCES

A strong setting can lend itself to a picture sequence. You can change the apparent action by the order in which you mount and present results. Keep your framing constant, preferably by placing the camera on a support such as a tripod.

Shooting a sequence For this type of result first frame a strong graphic setting, fixing your camera on a tripod, and then shoot each change of situation. Here, a 300 mm lens created strong perspective and enabled the photographer to take up a distant viewpoint, out of the subjects' notice.

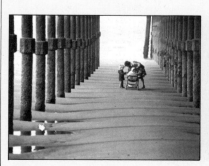
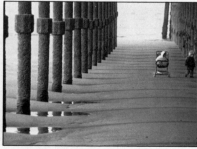

uniform, or stores and customers. If your intended subjects are preoccupied with their own affairs, they are less likely to notice the presence of the camera.

Techniques for candids

Your equipment must allow you to be unobtrusive – avoid carrying a bulging, conspicuous gadget bag. Use a camera with a wide-aperture lens and medium or fast film. Most of the time you will want to use your fast standard lens, but you will find a wide-angle useful for close-involvement crowd work and a telephoto zoom good for isolating more distant figures or head shots. If your SLR has a removable pentaprism try hidden shots from waistlevel. An automatic autofocus compact is excellent for unexpected candids – pull it from your pocket ready to use. Prefocus other cameras for estimated subject distance. Avoid using visible flash or a noisy film winder. Use existing light whenever possible, and improvise a camera support if necessary.

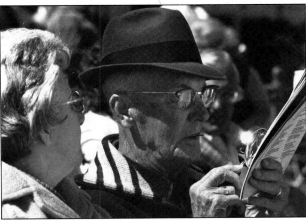

Photographing a crowd To capture this moment of concentration in an open-air concert audience the photographer prefocused the camera on an object a similar distance away in the opposite direction, then quickly swung round. Sunlight reflected from a booklet softly illuminates the man's face. The shot was taken at the fastest shutter speed to program a wide aperture and so isolate individual figures.

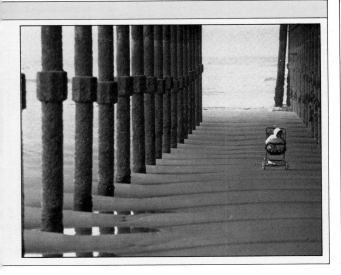

● An outdoor stand or stall is a good working area. Shoot from one end. Avoid including backs of heads.

● When something occurs suddenly, photograph it at once, whatever the camera settings. Then, if possible, correct settings and reshoot.

● Learn to turn on your meter and set focus approximately with the camera still in your pocket or bag.

Travel

If you travel extensively, perhaps on business or vacation, photographs can act as permanent reminders of time and place. The challenge is to sum up the locality, the people, and climate in ways that reflect your personal experiences. As a visitor it is much easier to respond to the unique features of a place than a resident or someone who has been there before. You must, however, always take care to respect local customs.

Capturing different facets

Try to vary your photographic coverage. Think ahead to the way you might lay out a variety of photographs on an album page. General views are often overdone – you can buy postcards of most famous sites, so make sure your shots have extra features you want to remember. Perhaps these will just be concerned with the light, or the view from a particular window, or because they include your companions. Local inhabitants and their ways of life should be featured, and do not forget local architecture, flora, notices, food, transport, or whatever seems strange and new. Be prepared to rise early or shoot late in the evening to catch the best lighting effects. Vary your angles and distances, shoot close-up detail indoors or outdoors where sometimes small objects can express a great deal.

City memories Everyone has different memories of a city. It may be the warm muted colors of Paris at a particular time of day, like this view from Notre Dame (right). Or you can recall a place through selected details. In sharp contrast, the shot below was taken behind a giant stone figure on the roof of St Peters, Rome. The statue hides lightning conductors, and supports holding the sections of the figure together.

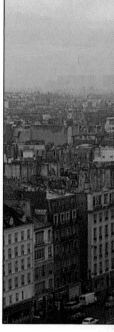

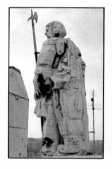

LOCAL CHARACTERS

It is not always a good idea to travel in a group. Alone, or with just one companion, it is easier to get acquainted with the local people. Approached in the right way they will enjoy being photographed, and you can take care to include any relevant surroundings. But do be discreet and avoid intruding into religious or private places without permission. If possible do not use direct flash because of its flattening effect. A zoom lens is an asset because it allows you to fill the frame without drawing attention to yourself by changing position.

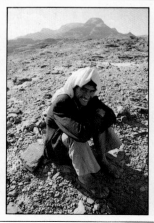

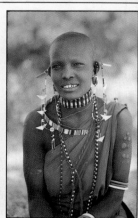

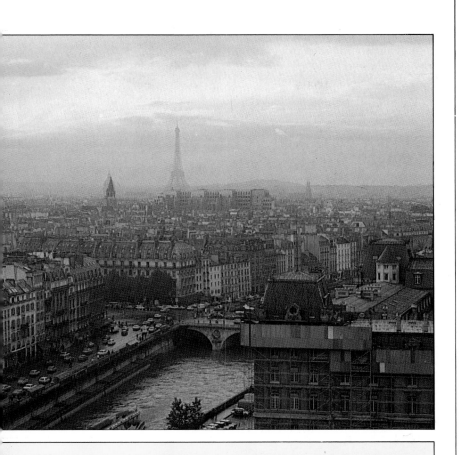

The human approach
By using a wide-angle lens to photograph the Arab guide (far left) a wide expanse of characteristic desert was shown behind him. In the shot of the woman (left), light softly diffused by vegetation reveals the all-important detail. The tough weatherbeaten bagpipe player (right) was carefully framed with an 85–200 mm zoom lens to include the castle and loch in the background.

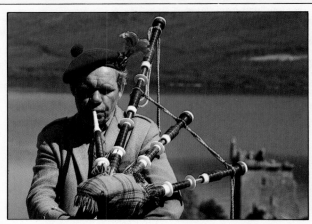

135

Still-life

Still-life subjects are, as the name implies, stationary and often shot close up. Lighting and composition are very considered and controlled. Subjects include "found objects" outdoors, largely natural indoor settings, and totally constructed photographic sets.

Picture possibilities
One of the benefits of still-life photography is that it teaches you a great deal about lighting, design, and composition. A still-life picture may express a feeling of nostalgia, represent a personality, or just present interesting visual qualities others might overlook. These technical skills can also be applied to other forms of photography. Work by selection and elimination with found subjects or, in the studio, collect and put together items related perhaps by shape, color, period, or use.

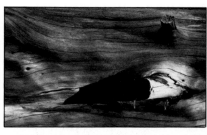

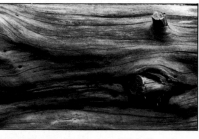

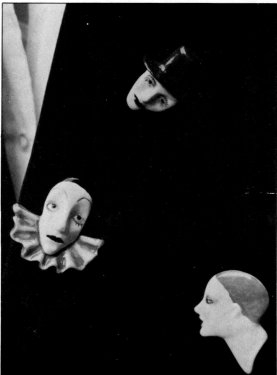

Using natural light Found still-life subjects may change their appearance from moment to moment according to the light. Both pictures above were taken within five minutes of each other as the sun set. Hard glancing sun produced strong shadow and light, but soft diffused skylight (lower version) brought out the "flow" of the wood grain.

Using possessions Sometimes, possessions alone can describe personality. These badges (left), attached to a velvet jacket, suggest that the owner has an eye for stylish color and design. Soft daylight combined with careful framing give a simple but effective composition.

IMPROVING A FOUND STILL-LIFE

The basis of a still-life shot can be found in such things as oddments displayed on a bureau or tools in a workshop cupboard. But you will usually have to do some reorganization. Framed by the camera, the scene typically looks too cluttered or shows unattractive gaps. Simplify the contents by regrouping – removing some objects and perhaps adjusting the lighting. Place the camera on a tripod so you can monitor improvements at every stage.

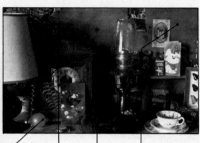

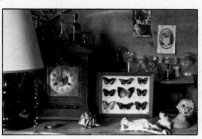

Overly cluttered area

Empty, unattractive area

Modern articles conflict with the period theme

Tops of main objects appear jumbled

An eye for detail
The picture above left records an alcove of bric-a-brac as it was first seen. The many elements lack any overall structure. Removing some objects, repositioning others, and adding some frontal lighting gives the result above. Main shapes now form a roughly triangular composition. For the less accurate interpretation below the lamp was switched on and exposure reduced to further simplify the objects.

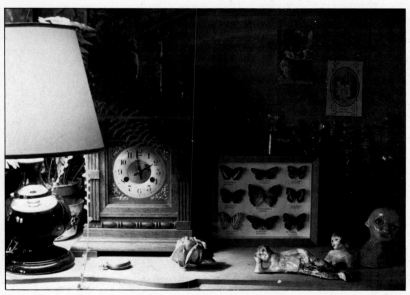

Architecture

The aim of architectural photography is not just to produce good records, but pictures that work well in their own right. Like landscapes, much depends on lighting and weather conditions, viewpoint and timing. To this can be added problems of parked cars, telephone wires, and similar unwanted urban features.

Equipment and approach

The most useful extra items for architectural photography are wide-angle and telephoto lenses, a tripod, filters, and flashgun. Having several lenses will allow you to fill the frame from different distances. A wide-angle lens, tripod, and flashgun are especially useful indoors. Try to avoid too many conventional shots. Often, part of a building – or just a detail – can suggest the whole. Sometimes you can combine detail and a general view in the same shot, perhaps by framing one building within part of another. It is worth being adventurous with lighting, too. Shooting at dusk or night, or in stormy weather can present a familiar structure in a new and dramatic way. Finally, bear in mind that architecture is also lived in. Sight or signs of people will often give life and relevance to your shots.

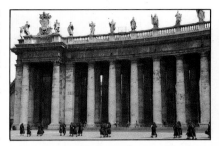

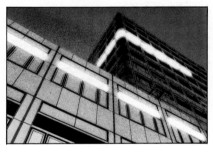

Including people Showing figures adds interest and gives scale. The shot above (top) is of St Peter's Square, Rome.

Infrared film Infrared black and white film was used to photograph this modern office block at night (above).

CHOOSING THE RIGHT LENS

A wide-angle lens is almost essential for architectural interiors, but avoid extreme focal lengths because of their tendency to produce distortions. A perspective control lens is ideal for tall features, but is expensive (see p. 165). Use a zoom or telephoto lens to pick out details or give a "squashed" mixture of buildings by shooting from a distance. Another advantage of a telephoto is that, provided you can get well back from a building, you can often show its entirety without tilting the camera upward. This avoids the problem of converging vertical lines, and the image should not require massive cropping later.

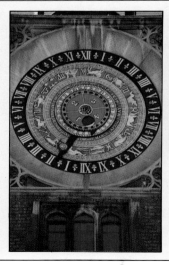

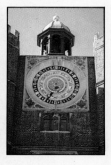

Filling the frame The picture above, taken with a zoom at 85 mm, loses clock detail – the dome dominates. Changing to 150 mm (left) alters the whole emphasis of the picture.

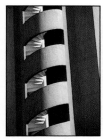

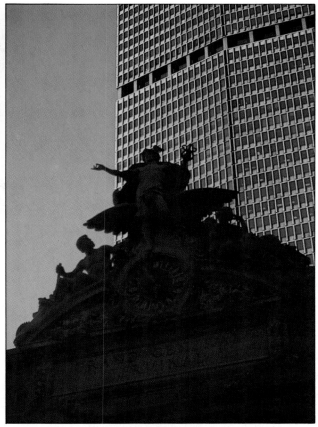

Light and pattern By picking the right time of day you can often emphasize particular parts of buildings. These details from Paris (above) and New York (right) make good use of pattern and shapes typical of each architectural style.

Interiors One of the problems with interiors is unevenness of lighting. You must be accurate in metering, averaging readings from light and dark areas. Although fill-in flash would have given more detail in the shot below, it would also have destroyed the quality of window light across the wall.

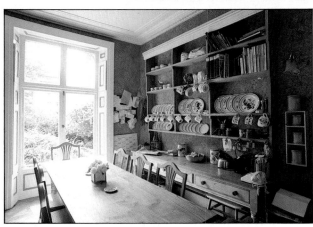

HINTS AND TIPS

● A flashgun is useful for interiors if you can fire it repeatedly.
● Always be on the look-out for interesting architectural detail – either interior or exterior.
● Stained glass should be shot from the inside by day against overcast sky or from the outside at night with the building lit internally.

Nudes

Photography of the nude figure is the classical way of learning the effects of light on form. One of the potential difficulties is the degree of embarrassment between model and photographer. This can be overcome given privacy and clear ideas on the qualities of image you are both aiming to produce. The tone gradations of the nude form are well suited to black and white photography – color easily becomes too objective and clinical.

General approach
Make sure your model is warm enough as cold skin photographs badly. Leave enough time for any marks left by tight clothing to disappear. Soft directional light is usually best to illuminate the body's undulating forms, but harder light can emphasize shape or create silhouette. Underlighting is often better than overlighting, especially if your model has a less-than-perfect figure. Start with parts of the body – the line of the neck and shoulder, back, breast or chest, wrist and hand. Shoot with a short telephoto and use a wide-angle for distortion effects only. Slow, fine-grain film preserves delicate skin texture, but faster grainier film may be more suitable for a male figure.

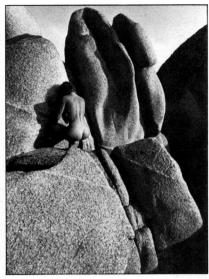

Varying your approach The picture above exploits the rounded forms of both nude and weathered rocks. In contrast, the study below is soft and intimate. It is gently illuminated by a diffused candle in the model's hand and by soft daylight. The picture on the facing page is impersonal and concerned with texture and pattern. Coarse sand emphasizes the skin's natural sheen.

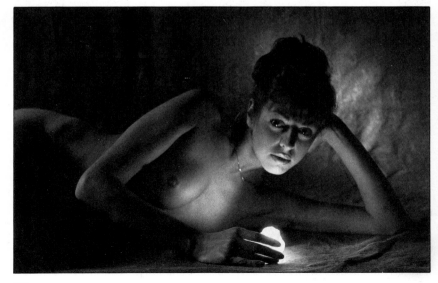

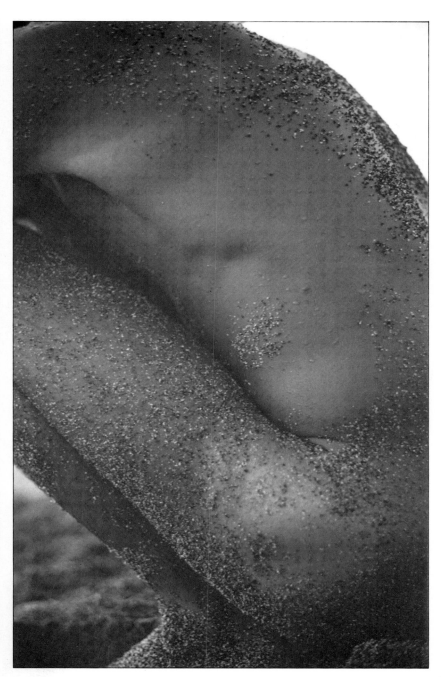

Natural history

Natural history offers you a wide, absorbing range of subjects. Some photographers work in this area because of a scientific interest, others are attracted to it as a rich source of color, pattern, and texture. In fact, the best natural history pictures combine accurate recording and eye-catching lighting and composition. Subjects themselves can be quite simple – many are available in your own yard.

Equipment and organization
A lightweight kit is best if you intend to stay out for a whole day. As well as your basic camera, take a close-up lens or extension tubes, low-level tripod, right-angle viewfinder attachment, and a cable release. A telephoto zoom of about 150–250 mm with a macro mode is also useful. Take a rolled silver or white reflector to improve natural lighting with small objects, and a flashgun with extension lead. Compact binoculars, wire plant clamps, and a sheet of plastic to kneel on are also useful.

Good locations include the seashore, forest, marshland, and lakes. And a great deal of interesting material exists in an ordinary garden. A water bath and a regular supply of food will attract birds. Use a telephoto lens and shoot from an open window partly draped with a curtain. Look for butterflies and insects feeding on vegetation, and a pond soon encourages a range of aquatic creatures.

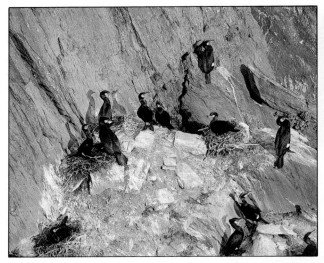

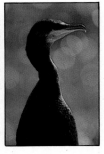

Photographing birds
A normal lens shot from a sheltered position gives a general view of the colony. The 300 mm shot above isolates one bird against the distant seascape.

Shooting through glass An aquarium allows you to shoot under controlled conditions. For the result shown right, the camera was positioned close to the glass, with its reflective surfaces shielded by black cardboard. Flash lit the subject from above, diffused by the water.

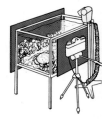

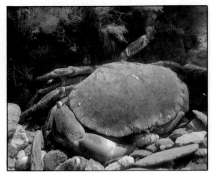

WORKING CLOSE-UP

Working close up can reveal unexpected structures and colors. The main problems are restricted depth of field, exaggerated movement, and lighting difficulties. Flash is the most useful light source with small subjects.

For subjects that will photograph larger than life-size, try using a 100 mm instead of a normal lens, on long bellows. This gives an enlarged image from further back, allowing more room for lighting.

Viewpoint and framing
A flat-on viewpoint (right) minimizes depth of field difficulties. Tight framing accentuates the pattern and shape of the dragonfly. The wing is sidelit by diffused flash, and looks like mosaic glass. In the low-angled close-up below, foreground detail is sharp while the out-of-focus background suggests general habitat.

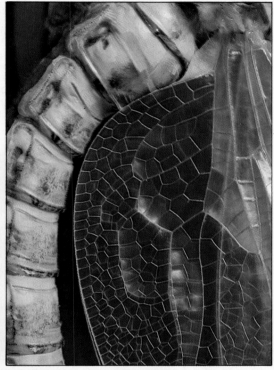

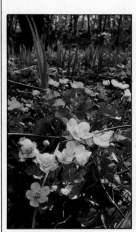

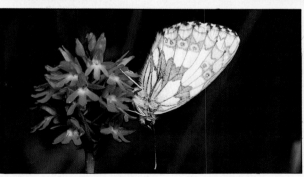

Lighting natural history subjects
Color is a vital element in most nature photography. Here top-lighting with diffused flash, and a shaded, distant background enhance color brilliance. Oblique light across the butterfly helps to show fine texture. The camera was supported on a monopod.

Recording electronic images

Sometimes you may require a still picture record of an image on a television screen, or visual display unit (VDU). This might be part of a home video, a television-displayed slide, or computer read-out.

Television records

For copying a television image, you need a high-resolution flat screen, a tripod-mounted camera, and daylight type film. Darken the room and reduce the television contrast control. Square up the camera, focus, and read exposure normally. Select a shutter speed of 1/8. A typical aperture will be f 5.6 on ISO 100 film.

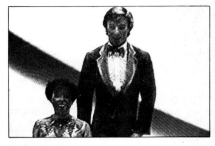

Shutter speed Each television picture takes 1/30 or 1/25 of a second to form completely.

A shutter speed too fast (here 1/125) gives an uneven screen image.

Faults and manipulations The longer your exposure time the more even your picture will be, but action on the screen will then blur (1). Unless you want blurred action, pick a static moment to shoot (2). If your camera is not square to the screen, or the set is badly adjusted, shapes will be distorted (3). Some video recorders on "freeze frame" display a juddering image, giving overall blur (4). It is better to run recordings normally when photographing from the screen.

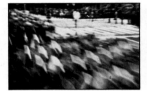

1

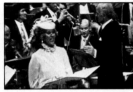

2

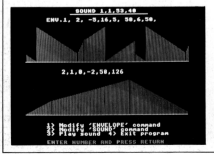

3

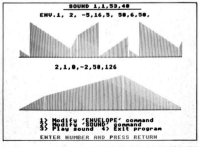

4

RECORDS OF VISUAL DISPLAY UNITS

Visual display units show high-contrast images. Many computers allow you to switch between white or colored lettering on a black background, or the reverse. A black ground display (below) gives higher resolution and contrast. To make a slide with a white ground, shoot on slow black and white negative film and push development. For a print with a white ground (below) shoot on reversal film and have prints made on negative/positive paper. It is best to test for exposure – start with a reading from an area of lettering.

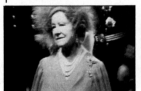

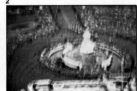

FLASH

Flash equipment and its uses are often underrated by photographers. It is, however, a versatile and convenient method of illumination and well deserves a section of its own.

This section begins by picking out the main features of modern flashguns and their back-up accessories. Exposure and exposure measurement problems are shown to be increasingly solved by the use of a flash sensor or the camera's own metering system. At the same time, errors of one sort or another will crop up from time to time, and a set of the most common mistakes is reproduced.

Once you have a flashgun there are several ways you can use it. Mounted on the camera, most flash units allow you different methods of varying the effect by either bouncing or diffusing the light. Using flash off-camera, but connected by a long flash synchronization lead to the camera, you have a much wider range of lighting options. As you gain experience you may want to combine flash with other light sources – daylight or different kinds of artificial light, for example. This can be a good way of reducing harsh contrasts or improving lighting that is too flat or coming from the wrong direction. The techniques to produce these effects are shown and explained in detail.

Flash equipment

Flash is a portable, convenient light source that is often mis-used by beginners, who either expect it to do too much, or fail to exploit it fully. In fact, you can use flash to give varying degrees of hard or soft lighting from any direction, using one or several units. Guns range from simple built-in or clip-on units to large, powerful, professional systems. Each electronic flashgun differs in detail, but they all have certain features in common.

Synchronization

To enable a flashgun to fire its brief flash of light at exactly the right moment the gun is connected to a circuit inside the camera body through a "hot shoe" socket or electrical cord. Sometimes the flash is built-in to the camera. The circuit leads from the flash connection to a switch in the shutter which

Hot shoe The accessory bracket on top of the camera contains electrical contacts that connect the gun to the shutter. "Dedicated" units have additional contacts that pick up ISO speed and other data from the camera.

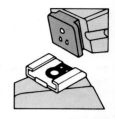

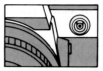

Co-axial socket Some cameras have a simple cord and plug firing connection between flash and camera in addition to a hot shoe.

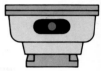

Flash test button A button, usually sited near the base of the flashgun back, short-circuits shutter contacts for test flashes.

BASIC COMMON FEATURES

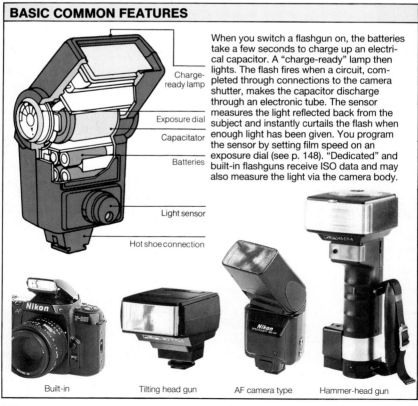

Charge-ready lamp

Exposure dial

Capacitator

Batteries

Light sensor

Hot shoe connection

When you switch a flashgun on, the batteries take a few seconds to charge up an electrical capacitor. A "charge-ready" lamp then lights. The flash fires when a circuit, completed through connections to the camera shutter, makes the capacitor discharge through an electronic tube. The sensor measures the light reflected back from the subject and instantly curtails the flash when enough light has been given. You program the sensor by setting film speed on an exposure dial (see p. 148). "Dedicated" and built-in flashguns receive ISO data and may also measure the light via the camera body.

Built-in   Tilting head gun   AF camera type   Hammer-head gun closes briefly each time the shutter fires. In a compact camera (lens shutter) the circuit is completed and the flash fires at all shutter speeds when the blades are fully open. In an SLR camera (focal plane shutter), the flash normally fires when the first blind is fully open, and so you cannot use flash with fastest shutter speeds (see p. 39). All separate, add-on flashguns have a manual test-firing button. This allows you to discharge the flash independently of the camera, which may be useful during a time exposure, for example.

Power supply

Small flashguns are powered by alkaline-manganese batteries or more expensive nickel-cadmium types, which you can recharge hundreds of times. The most powerful units need a separate power pack. Most guns will also work off domestic power supplies through a transformer.

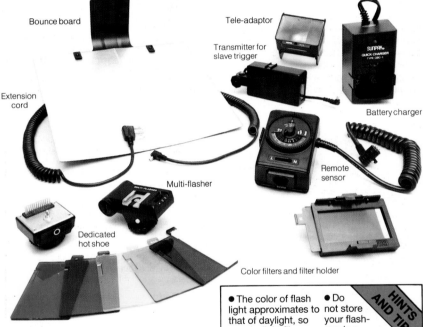

Bounce board

Tele-adaptor

Transmitter for slave trigger

Extension cord

Battery charger

Remote sensor

Multi-flasher

Dedicated hot shoe

Color filters and filter holder

Accessories and special units
A wide range of accessories is available for most flashguns which help to make your flash system more versatile. A *tele-adaptor* narrows the light beam to suit telephoto lenses. (Wide-angle adaptors have the opposite effect.) *Extension cords* allow off-camera use of synchronized flash. *Color filters* are used for special effects, or to match other lighting. A white panel forms a small, portable *bounce board* for softening flash lighting. The *multi-flasher*, fitted between gun and camera, can program 3–5 flashes per frame. A *transmitter* and *slave trigger* will synchronize several flash heads. A *charger* re-energizes Ni-Cad batteries.

HINTS AND TIPS

● The color of flash light approximates to that of daylight, so use daylight film.
● Camera sockets (and shutter settings) are often marked X for electronic flash. On old cameras, FP or M are for flash-bulbs and should not be used.
● Recycling time ranges from 0.5–9 sec. Recycling is quickest with Ni-Cad batteries, and when flash is used at briefest duration.
● Do not store your flash-gun in a humid, hot place. Remove batteries if storing the flash unit for an extended period of time (months, for example).
● Do not try internal repairs – guns work at high voltages.
● Typically, a built-in flashgun will correctly expose subjects only up to about 20 ft (6 m) from the camera.

Calculating flash exposure

Electronic flash has a briefer duration than the fastest shutter speed offered by most cameras. It is usual, therefore, to keep to one shutter setting for flash and use the lens aperture to control exposure. The oldest and most basic system to calculate correct exposure is based purely on subject distance and film speed (see right). This has been largely replaced by self-regulating equipment, in which a sensor, built into the flashgun or camera, shortens or lengthens flash duration to suit the subject as well as the film and aperture set. Autofocusing cameras make exposure simpler still by feeding film ISO, lens aperture, and the subject's distance into the flash system.

Manual calculation

Each flashgun has a guide number (GN) for manual exposure calculations. The GN is the flash-to-subject distance in meters multiplied by the f number necessary for a correct exposure using ISO 100 film. For example, with a GN of 16 you will have to set f8 for subjects 6 ft (2 m) from the flash.

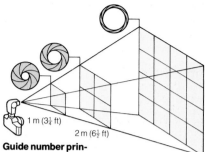

1 m (3¼ ft)
2 m (6½ ft)
4 m (13 ft)

Guide number principle When subject distance doubles, brightness is quartered because light spreads over four times the area. Image brightness increases fourfold with each halving of f number. Multiply distance by f number for a constant GN.

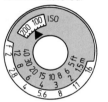

Calculator A manual flashgun has a calculator dial (left). First, set the ISO, then focus and read the scale to find the subject distance. Finally, read off the aperture to set for that distance.

SELF-REGULATING FLASH

A self-regulating flashgun is easier to use because you do not have to change aperture for every change of distance. Most camera-based units have a light-sensor window that views the subject and makes an overall reading, shortening the flash the closer or lighter the subject is. If the flash tube pivots (see p. 152), the sensor must still point directly at the subject for a correct reading.

Some SLR camera meters read the light off the film surface during exposure. They can program flash duration and automatically take the aperture set into account. Measurement through the lens in this way matches the view of any lens, and works whichever way the flash head is pointed.

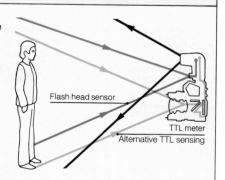

Flash head sensor

TTL meter
Alternative TTL sensing

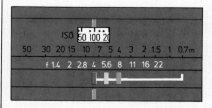

Sensor programmer Basic sensor flashguns have a programming panel (see left). You set the ISO, then select one of the three f numbers signaled, and set it on the lens. This establishes the maximum distance that can be exposed correctly. As shown here, working at f4 the flash will measure and expose correctly at subject distances between 0.7 m and 8 m (2¼ ft and 26 ft).

With ISO 400 film you must work at f16 for this subject distance. GN figures are also useful for comparing the light output of different flashguns (see pp. 208-9).

Autoexposure units

Self-regulating units cut short the flash, under control of a sensor that views the light reflected back from the subject from beside the flashgun, or measures it off the film itself (see opposite page). If the flash is built in or is a "dedicated" attachment, it will pick up information such as ISO speed directly from the camera. The most automated systems are on autofocusing cameras, principally compacts. Some mechanically couple the opening or closing of the aperture with the focusing of the lens, so that whatever is focused on is correctly exposed (although near objects may be too light and far objects too dark).

Many such cameras simply offer three settings – "flash off", "autoflash", and "fill-in". Fill-in gives correct exposure for the existing light present, plus flash. This produces more natural results for portraits indoors where you want to show the general setting (see p. 156), and also for backlit scenes and for subjects with dark foregrounds. Built-in flash units are neither very

Semi-automatic flashgun The LCD panel on the back of this add-on flashgun (right) is first set for the camera's lens aperture and the film ISO speed. By setting the lens focal length, the reflector adjusts to give a suitable spread of light. The central scale now displays the range of subject distances over which the gun will regulate itself to produce correct exposure. The flashgun also offers settings that underexpose the flash by set amounts, which is extremely useful for flash fill-in purposes.

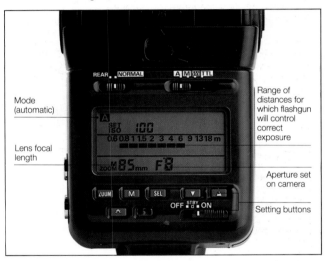

EXPOSURE MEASURING SYSTEMS	
Type of system	**Comments**
Manual (Guide number)	Lowest cost equipment. Takes time to calculate exposure, and assumes "average" subject and surroundings. You must modify f number if you diffuse, bounce, or filter flash, or if you fit a telephoto beam attachment.
Semi-automatic flashgun (Self-regulating)	Uses sensor or TTL camera meter. Ensures correct flash exposure over a range of distances, dependent on aperture and film speed. Takes into account subject and surroundings, also filters and other attachments. Sensor must face subject, so you will need a remote type for some off-camera flash techniques (see pp. 154-5).
Autoexposure flash	"Autoflash" setting computes exposure from AF distance setting and speed of film, and then sets appropriate aperture. "Fill-in" setting sets correct shutter speed/ aperture for existing light, combined with flash aperture for subject distance set by AF. "Flash-off" setting keeps the flash off no matter how dim the light. This is the best choice for subjects beyond flash range, but the camera may need support to prevent blur. (Avoid cameras that do not have a flash-off option.)

powerful nor versatile, however. A semi-automatic, add-on unit will produce a wider range of flash results, provided you are prepared to learn the controls.

Exposure problems

Even through-the-lens (TTL) sensors in the camera can be misled by difficult subjects, just like any other type of overall or center-weighted method of measuring the light from a subject (see p. 43). Be prepared, therefore, to bracket exposures if important foreground objects are composed very off-center, toward the edges of the frame.

You cannot expect a small flashgun to light adequately a large building interior, or exterior, at night. If a scene contains no moving elements, though, you could try increasing the amount of light by firing the flashgun several times. Place the camera on a tripod, lock the shutter open on "B", and fire the flash using its "open flash", or test button. Each doubling of the number of flashes, doubles the exposure given.

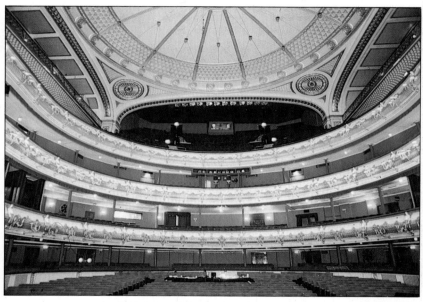

Lighting a large area

When the subject area or distance is beyond the power of your flashgun, repeat the flash several times. The wide-angle shot above was evenly lit by firing one flashgun from five different positions forward of the camera during a 50 sec exposure. Set the f number for the distance of one flash. The smaller version was taken without flash.

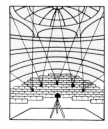

● If flash is pointed direct from the camera, it is impossible for subjects at different distances to all be exposed correctly. Expose for your main element, or compromise between nearest and furthest away.
● Firing a flashgun before the unit has fully recycled gives only a reduced, partial light output.
● To make a self-regulating flash recycle faster and give a briefer flash, use it close up or set it to less than full power.
● When buying a flashgun, check that its light beam covers the whole scene included by your lens. You may need a zoom-head flash to match the coverage of your zoom lens.

HINTS AND TIPS

Identifying flash faults

Electronic flashguns sometimes fail to fire when you take a picture, so it is obvious that a fault has occurred. Other kinds of failure happen even though the flash has fired, and you only discover them when you see the processed results. Some of the faults you can identify from processed films are shown below.

When flash itself fails this is generally because the batteries are weak or exhausted and did not charge up the unit properly (the flashgun's "ready" signal fails to glow). Alternatively, the flash may have failed to fire because of faulty contacts between the flashgun and the camera itself.

IDENTIFYING ERRORS

First, examine your negatives to make sure that the fault is not the result of bad printing technique. If your picture is underexposed, you may have used a manually set flash at the wrong ISO. Perhaps the subject was too distant or your finger was obscuring the flash tube. Even with a semi-automatic flash, a dark-toned subject against a large, reflective background will mislead the sensor. Overexposure is a result of too low an ISO setting – perhaps you read feet when your GN is for meters, or obstructed the sensor. A small, light subject and a dark or distant background may give a faulty reading.

RED EYE

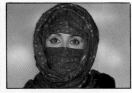

Cause A small flashgun used close to the lens has illuminated the pink retina at the back of the eye.
Avoid by moving nearer the subject, taking the flash off camera (see p. 154), or bouncing it off the wall or ceiling.

UNEVEN COVERAGE

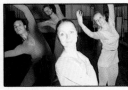

Cause Your gun has a narrower angle of illumination than the camera's angle of view.
Avoid by using a wide-angle light spreader, changing to a longer lens, or using flash off-camera, further from subject.

HOT SPOT

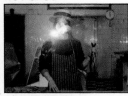

Cause Light was reflected back from a highly reflective surface (glass here). Glare also causes overexposure.
Avoid by looking out for this sort of situation, and pick a viewpoint that is slightly angled.

COLOR CAST

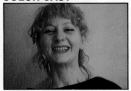

Cause A result of bouncing flash off a colored wall or ceiling. Mild casts can happen with direct flash if strongly colored surfaces surround subject.
Avoid by covering bounce surface with white material.

SECTION MISSING

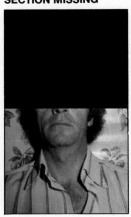

Cause Flash was used with a focal plane shutter set too fast. (If your shutter travels vertically, the lost area will be parallel to film edge instead.)
Avoid by selecting a slower speed – read your camera instructions.

BLANK FRAME

Cause Flash failed. If it went off, the gun may have been plugged into FP or M sockets. You may have left the lens cap on, or the shutter failed.
Check camera by looking through back. Fire flash at a white wall.

Using on-camera flash

Flash gives consistent color, freezes action, and prevents camera shake. And it makes you independent of existing lighting for all but distant subjects. You will find a flashgun on the camera is very convenient, but do not make this your only use of flash. Your shots will be dull if you always use the same lighting effect.

Basic technique

With a manually set camera, start by setting the shutter speed for flash (the one marked "X"). Now you need only set aperture and focus for each shot. With a basic compact, just keep within the distance limits of your flash – usually 3-8 ft (0.9-2.5 m). If subjects are closer they will not be sharp, if they are further away they will be underexposed. If you have a TTL flash-metering camera or a sensor gun that gives you a choice of apertures, pick one that gives the depth of field you want. Note the distance limits for correct exposure with this aperture and work within them.

Direct flash produces harsh lighting. Learn to anticipate results – do not shoot in a smoky atmosphere, and organize your viewpoint so that light will not flare back

---

SOFTENING THE LIGHT

The most effective way to reduce harsh shadows from direct flash is to scatter the light by reflecting it off a matte, colorless (if working in color) surface like a ceiling. "Bounce" flash gives a more natural, even effect over subjects at different distances. You must use a gun with a head which will tilt or swivel upward. Alternatively, use a diffuser – a wide-angle attachment or tracing paper – over the flash head. Leave the sensor uncovered. This has a less softened, more frontal effect than bouncing. Both techniques reduce light output. A sensor will read accurately provided it can still measure the subject directly. When using GNs, open up two stops for bouncing, one for a diffuser.

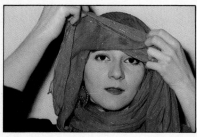

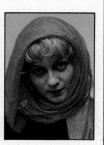

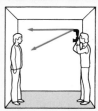

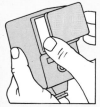

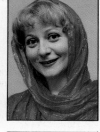

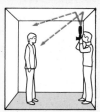

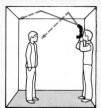

Direct flash Direct flash from the camera (above) provides detail but this lighting has a flattening, unnatural effect. Assertive shadows are cast on the background.

Diffuser attachment A wide-angle attachment or diffuser on your flashgun scatters the light. Its small size cannot soften lighting quality as much as bouncing.

Bounced above camera Here the flash was reflected from the ceiling directly above the camera. This gives more frontal, less toplighting. Results are soft and natural.

Bounced above subject Flash was bounced off the ceiling above the girl. Light is soft, but too overhead, shadowing the eyes. It is made worse by her posture.

from reflective surfaces. Avoid set-ups where one element casts ugly shadows on another, or where subjects are at widely differing distances from the flash. With most add-on guns, you can diffuse the flash to create more natural-looking lighting.

Advanced techniques

As you become more experienced, you will find that flash is a versatile lighting tool. You can use flash on camera to reduce the contrast of daylight – for example when photographing room interiors or portraits against the light (see pp. 156-9).

With specially filtered flash you can take pictures unobserved, in darkness, using infrared film. Tape a No. 87 infrared filter firmly over the flash window. This filter stops any light being seen when the flash goes off. Use black and white IR film, set the gun to manual, and reduce the GN to two-thirds normal.

A flashgun which recycles quickly will allow you to take a brief sequence of shots of a moving subject all on one frame. Working in darkness, place your camera on a tripod. Hold the shutter open and press the test button each time the flash recycles. A multi-flasher accessory (see p. 147) will do this automatically. Some advanced flashguns offer a "strobe" option of up to five flashes per second.

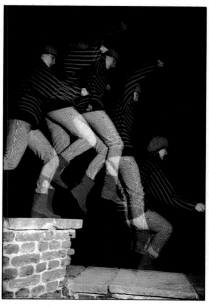

Multi-flash The picture above was shot using a multi-flash unit between the camera and flashgun. The multi-flash triggered a powerful flashgun five times (at reduced output) during a 1 sec exposure. Black backgrounds are essential for this technique. Static elements, such as the wall in this picture, receive five times as much exposure as each image of the moving figure. Very similar results to this are available using a stroboscopic lamp.

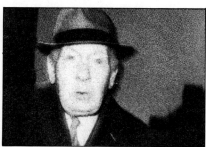

Infrared flash The man in this picture could not see it was being taken. It was shot in the street at dusk on infrared black and white film. A type 87 filter covered the flashgun window.

By using a shutter speed of 1/15 the man's forward movement after the flash fired created a false "shadow" on the sky. The pale complexion and grainy image are usual for IR film.

HINTS AND TIPS

● To preview the lighting effect of bounced flash, shine a flashlight on the ceiling of a darkened room.
● If you cannot bounce flash, because of a high or colored ceiling, or if shooting outside, fit a bounce board to the flash itself (see p. 147).
● You can use speeds slower than the one marked for flash – to record some existing light, for example, if your equipment does not offer "fill-in" mode.
● Dark or light backgrounds often fool the sensor. Compensate by setting apertures smaller or larger than shown on a sensor head gun. With a TTL meter, use the exposure-compensation dial.

Using off-camera flash

Taking your flashgun off the camera extends the range of lighting effects available to you. Attach an extension cord and hold the gun at arm's length or place it on a tripod. Your set-up will be still more versatile with additional guns.

Linkage and exposure

You must have a synchronizing cord to connect your flashgun to the camera when positioning them separately. For arm's length use, buy an extendable spiral type which plugs into the coaxial socket or hot shoe of the camera and gun. To obtain an accurate exposure with a built-in flash sensor make sure that it has a direct view of the subject. With a manual unit, calculate the f number from the guide number using flash-to-subject distance (see p. 148). If you have a "dedicated" gun, attaching it to a camera with an appropriate lead will allow normal, through-the-lens (TTL) flash

SINGLE SOURCE AT ARM'S LENGTH

Think carefully about where you place the flash in relation to the subject and camera viewpoint. The basic flashgun acts like a spotlight used in darkened surroundings. Start by using it from above and well to one side of the camera, at full stretch. Shadows will be quite strong on the opposite side of your subject. To give softer, more natural lighting, you should either diffuse or bounce the flash as shown below right and center.

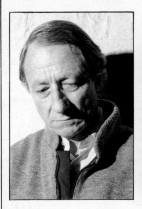

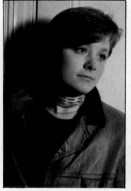

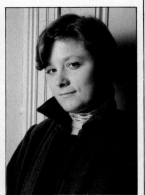

Direct flash For the portrait above, one flashgun was held at arm's length, tilted down 45° toward the subject. Some light reflected back from a nearby wall. Avoid using a long focus lens – you will be too far back to allow much lighting variety.

Bounced flash Lighting quality here was softened by directing the flashgun sideways at a white wall. Flash off-camera allows you to use a wider range of bounce surfaces. The gun was set to manual, exposure calculated by guide number then increased two stops.

Diffused flash You can vary lighting direction easily with off-camera flash. For this version the photographer changed hands. Curved tracing paper over the gun softened the light. Exposure was calculated as left, but increased by one stop only.

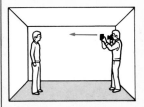

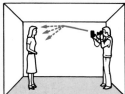

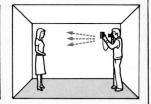

exposure control. With this set-up you should always get a correct exposure in all off-camera situations.

Using two or more flashguns

If you want to use more than one flash head, the simplest arrangement is to have extra guns with slave triggers. Although separate, each of these heads will fire in unison provided one flashgun is mounted or wired directly to the camera. You can set the heads to manual, then calculate exposure from the flash-to-subject distance of your main flashgun. Guns that are dedicated to in-camera metering will each need a cable connection to the camera.

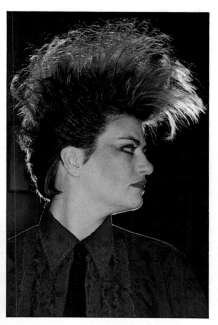

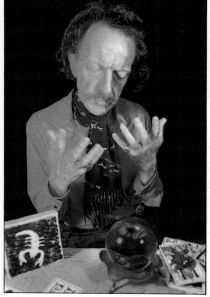

Off-camera filtered flash If you have more than one flash head and a set of color filters you can use them off-camera to produce colorfully lit images. The final effect depends on the number and position of guns used. Here, the photographer placed one head either side of the subject, and filtered one in magenta, the other in green. Parts which received light from both flash heads appear yellow. Working this way can be very versatile – you can position guns for sidelighting, backlighting or fill-in, and you can light from above or below.

Combining on- and off-camera flash

Taking your flash off-camera gives more depth to your shots, especially if you add a second gun to provide fill-in. For this shot, one gun was wired to the camera and placed behind the subject to give a backlit effect. The other gun was camera mounted.

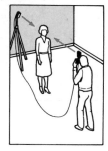

● If you have one flash on the camera and one off, make the off-camera head your main light. Diffuse the on-camera head.
● Avoid having two flash heads on the same side of the lens.
● Learn to visualize shadow-fall and flashgun placing. Practice with a still life and household lamps. Work in a darkened room.
● Support extra heads taped to a chair or curtain rail or on a tripod.
● Use off-camera flash to simulate sunlight (see p. 156) or paint with light (see p. 188). You can use two heads for copying (see p. 111).

HINTS AND TIPS

Flash with other light sources

Flash can be combined with existing lighting so that the natural conditions in the scene you wish to photograph are improved without destroying their effect. For example, you can use flash on the camera to lighten just the shadows. It will dilute excessive contrast when your subject is side- or backlit by harsh sunlight, but be careful not to overwhelm the subject with flash light. You can also use flash off-camera to give "pseudo-sunlight" in overcast conditions, provided that your subject is reasonably close to the flash.

Basic principles

An autofocus camera with "fill-flash" will lighten shadowy scenes up to a distance limited by the power of the flash unit. For a wider range of effects, however, work with a camera that offers a range of aperture

FLASH AS A SHADOW-FILLER

When the existing light on the subject is too contrasty from the viewpoint that you want to use, try filling in the shadows with flash. As long as the flash is positioned close to the lens it will add light to all the shadows seen without adding any new ones. The usual error is to overfill, so that shadows look unnaturally bright. Aim to make the shadows about one-quarter the strength of the highlights. Measure exposure from lit parts of the subject, ignoring shadows, then set the f number that this reading suggests for your flash shutter speed. Attach a gray filter or diffuser over your gun, or turn down its power to suit an aperture 2-3 stops wider than the one set on the camera. Bracket exposures, taking versions with the flash set both slightly dimmer and slightly brighter.

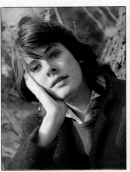 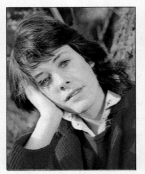 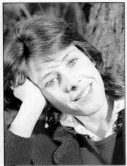

No flash Lit by harsh winter afternoon sunlight alone. 1/60 at f 8.

Fill-in On-camera flash lightens shadows, highlights eyes. Gun was set to quarter power.

Overfilled Here the flash was set to full power for f 8. Lighting is unnatural.

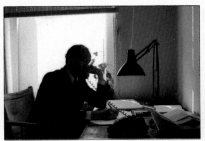 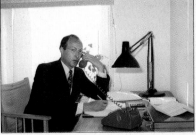

Without flash Taken from the only available viewpoint. Contrast is extreme, but additional exposure would just burn out the figure.

Fill-flash Using the same exposure settings as for the picture left, flash on-camera was fired at half the correct power.

and shutter settings, and set it to manual. And if your flash has a sensor for exposure control, set this to manual, too. You will have more control if you work with GNs, rather than a sensor that varies the flash output. First, measure the existing light using the camera's meter. Find the aperture to give correct exposure when the shutter is set to the speed for flash. (On compacts with a lens shutter you can use any setting.)

Now divide the subject distance into the guide number. If this gives the same f number, both flash and existing light will be equal. To make the flash stronger, move closer. To make existing light predominate, diffuse the flash or reduce it to half power.

Flash as sunlight

In dull, flat light you can use flash to give your subject – provided it is not too large – a

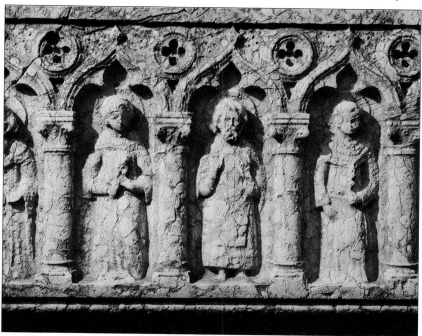

Flash as "sunlight" The smaller picture of stone detail (right) was taken in dim, overcast conditions. Exposure was 1/60 at f 5.6. The general detail is good, but to bring out the depth of relief hard side-lighting was necessary. For the version above, a flashgun (GN of 33) was set up off-camera, high and well to one side, 10 ft (3 m) from the center of the stone figures. This picture was taken at 1/60 at f 11, making the existing daylight only one-quarter as strong as the flash "sunlight".

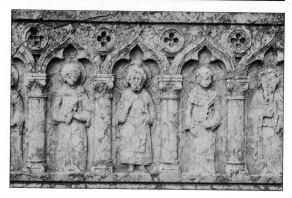

FLASH WITH ARTIFICIAL LIGHTING

Flash can improve your results when photographing artificially lit situations – from candlelit suppers to stage-lit rock concerts. Often you can combine techniques – for example you can fill in a lit interior with bounced flash. All these improvements should be as subtle as possible – the idea is to compensate for differences between the subject as you see it, and the more contrast way it records on film.

If you are working in color, avoid mixing different color sources. If your flash gives bluish, daylight-color illumination and you are filling in a subject lit by domestic lamps, you must fit an orange filter (see p. 174) over the flash window. However, you can use mixed lighting for effect. Off-camera flash will "spotlight" a figure or feature in correct color on daylight film while tungsten-lit surroundings record with a warm color cast.

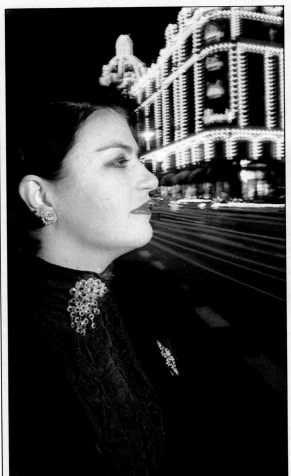

Flash with tungsten light
The street scene (left) was shot on daylight film. Flash records correct colors and freezes details on the foreground figure. Tungsten lighting on the store and cars has a yellower cast. Exposure was 10 sec, handheld. Traffic movement and camera shake separate figure from surroundings.

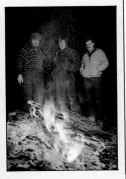

Matching the color of the flash In the picture above flash was used to reduce contrast between bonfire and figures. An orange filter over the flash matched flash color to the fire. Aperture was chosen to underexpose figures by one stop, and an exposure time of 2 sec selected to "burn in" flames. The camera was supported on a tripod.

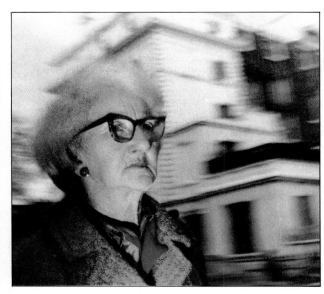

Flash and slow shutter This picture was taken at dusk using on-camera flash and a shutter speed of 1/8. The camera was panned to follow the woman during the exposure. Brief flash duration has frozen detail in the otherwise shadowy foreground figure. Existing light has caused back-ground street detail to blur during the remaining exposure. To increase the strange effect the flash was held below the level of the camera lens. This makes the light cast upward shadows, giving an unnatural stage-like appearance.

directional, "sunlit" appearance. This is useful for subjects like a small, fixed, still-life or a head-and-shoulders portrait. Use a powerful flashgun on an extension cord, held well off the camera high and to one side – positioning is very important to give a natural-looking effect.

The flash should be up to four times as strong as existing lighting. For example, if you are shooting in lighting which requires f 8 at 1/125, position a flash unit with a 32 guide number $6\frac{1}{2}$ ft (2 m) from the subject. Set the camera to 1/125 at f 11 – midway between the correct apertures for flash (f 16) and existing light (f 8). Make sure that the flashgun will illuminate the whole subject included in your picture. Unlike real sunlight, the relative closeness of the flash means that its illumination will fall off rapidly with distance.

Blur plus detail

Mixed flash and daylight can sometimes produce strange effects when you photograph a moving subject using a slow shutter speed. Results have a surreal mixture of blur and detail, flatness and depth.

Shoot in fairly dim light – for example outdoors at dusk. Conditions that read 1/2

sec or 1 sec at about f 5.6 are ideal. Choose a subject that is darker in tone than the background, and make it the nearest element in your picture. Work with the flashgun on the camera, using settings which make flash and existing light equally bright. You can either move the camera during exposure (perhaps panning on a moving subject), or lock it on a tripod. Panning results in a mass of blur, but the main foreground subject will have sharp detail overlaid too. If the camera was fixed, surroundings and main subject will appear sharp, but the subject movement that occurred while the shutter was open will give a blurred "shadow". This may even appear cast against the sky.

● On-camera flash can "fill-in" only one subject distance at a time. Closer subjects will be overfilled, and more distant ones unaffected.
● For pseudo-sunlight and mixed light techniques, buy a gun that gives three or four choices of output.
● A camera with a wide range of speeds suitable for flash is ideal for mixed lighting. Use the shutter to dim or brighten existing light without altering the flash.

HINTS AND TIPS

Studio flash

Some flash equipment is designed for studio use – situations where you control and set up the lighting and backgrounds. These units work from the household electricity supply. Each head incorporates a tungsten lamp close to the flash tube which enables you to preview where shadows will fall. Studio flash units are more powerful than portable types – guide numbers are usually between 30 and 150, yet they still recycle quickly.

Using studio flash

To soften harsh shadows flash heads are usually faced into a white or silver-lined umbrella reflector. Umbrellas give soft, even, bounce lighting, and they fold and store easily. You can tilt and swivel the head with umbrella in any direction. A basic kit – a single umbrella flash and separate reflector board – can give excellent lighting, resembling diffused daylight (see right). Extra flash units are useful to light the background, backlight hair, or to group together for lighting a large area. The best way to measure exposure for studio flash is with a hand-held meter.

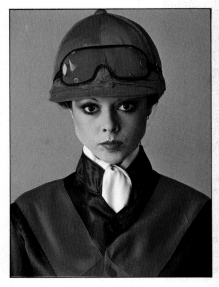

Using basic studio flash This portrait was lit from low left by a flash head pointed into a white-lined umbrella.

A white reflector board on the right returns some light to the shadowed side of the subject's face.

TYPICAL TWO-HEAD KIT

You can create a simple home studio with this type of inexpensive kit. The two flash heads here are identical – one head is bounced into a silver-lined umbrella, the other is used as a direct source with a conical snoot to give spotlighting. A white reflector board fills in shadows. The translucent umbrella can act as a diffuser in front of direct flash. The camera fires one head via a synchronizing cord, the other uses a slave trigger. The paper roll has its own support. Flash is measured from the direction of the subject by flash meter.

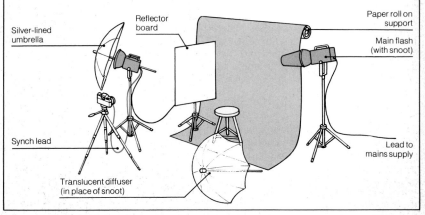

Silver-lined umbrella

Reflector board

Paper roll on support

Main flash (with snoot)

Synch lead

Translucent diffuser (in place of snoot)

Lead to mains supply

ACCESSORIES

Camera accessories expand and "personalize" your photographic kit, matching it to your chosen subject interests and ways of working. But do not overload yourself with unnecessary items – they easily get in the way of the actual picture taking.

In this section, the various types of interchangeable lenses – telephoto, wide-angle, zoom, and close-up – are discussed and compared. You will probably find this a strong argument in favor of the SLR over fixed-lens compact cameras. You will also find advice on building up different kinds of camera outfits, using various combinations of lenses and camera bodies.

Other accessories, such as filters and camera supports, are no less important, but you can save money by identifying the most practicable types for your particular photography. This then leads on to more specialized items – bulk film backs, ring flash, and data backs. Some of these items can be more expensive than the basic camera itself, but they are invaluable for particular tasks. The section ends by discussing ways of storing film originals and presenting finished prints or slides so that the images can be seen in the most effective possible way. Overall, this is the section you should read before making a final choice about buying a new camera. You may find that the range of useful accessories available is a deciding factor.

Lens focal length

Your opportunities for interesting photographs will be much greater if you can change the focal length of your camera lens. Change from a standard to a longer (telephoto) lens to fill the frame with a distant subject, and to a shorter (wide-angle) lens in order to include more of the area around your subject.

Standard lens

The normal, or "standard", lens for an SLR camera generally has a focal length of 50 mm. This gives an angle of view of about 45°. A longer focal length lens has a narrower angle of view, and a shorter lens a wider angle. With a 50 mm lens, the image seen through your SLR will match the size of your subject seen direct. Fixed focal length lenses used in compact cameras are mostly wide-angle 28 mm or 35 mm focal lengths. Working at a maximum aperture of f4, these produce a generous depth of field and so help to avoid focusing errors.

Focal length range

Some compacts have a dual focal length lens. Typically, this allows you to select either 35 mm or 70 mm, or 28 mm or 45 mm. Most advanced compacts, though, have a zoom lens – 38-60 mm, for example, or 35-105 mm. Unlike dual types, a zoom allows you to set any focal length within the range

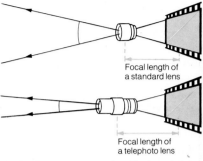

Focal length of a standard lens

Focal length of a telephoto lens

Angle of view A 50 mm standard lens has a focal length similar to the picture diagonal, giving a 46° angle of view. The barrel of a telephoto sets the lens further from the film, giving it a narrower angle.

offered. Optics in the camera viewfinder adjust to show you the changed angle of view of the selected focal length.

On SLRs you can remove the lens and replace it with a different focal length lens, or a zoom lens. A wide range of focal lengths is available, from extreme wide-angles to telephotos of more than 1000 mm (see below). Zooms for SLRs include 21-35 mm, 28-70 mm, and 70-210 mm. Both fixed focal length and zoom lenses are made in AF and manual-focus forms, and some AF bodies will accept some brands of non-AF lenses for manual focusing only.

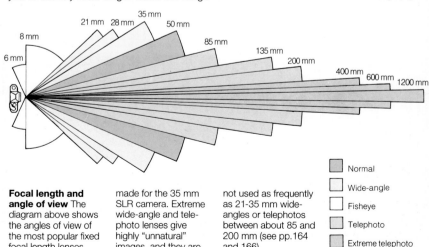

Focal length and angle of view The diagram above shows the angles of view of the most popular fixed focal length lenses made for the 35 mm SLR camera. Extreme wide-angle and telephoto lenses give highly "unnatural" images, and they are not used as frequently as 21-35 mm wide-angles or telephotos between about 85 and 200 mm (see pp.164 and 166).

Normal
Wide-angle
Fisheye
Telephoto
Extreme telephoto

THE EFFECTS OF CHANGING FOCAL LENGTH

When you change to a different lens focal length, you alter image magnification. Details enlarge in direct proportion – for example, subjects in a 135 mm lens image appear nearly five times larger than in a 28 mm lens shot. In cramped conditions, use a wide-angle to include more of the subject; when the subject is far away, change to a telephoto to fill the frame. Telephotos give less depth of field than wide-angles at the same aperture.

You can change the perspective in your pictures by changing camera distance along with lens focal length. Using a wide-angle lens close to foreground elements exaggerates their size relative to elements farther away, giving a strong sense of depth and distance. Move farther back and change to telephoto for the opposite perspective effect.

CHANGE IN IMAGE SIZE

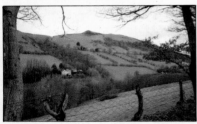

28 mm A wide-angle takes in plenty of foreground. But the distant main subject is very small and insignificant at this size.

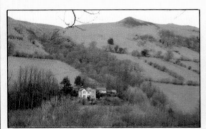

50 mm Shooting with a standard lens from the same camera position as above will enlarge the house, but lose foreground and surroundings.

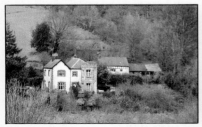

135 mm This telephoto shot is from the same viewpoint as above. It gives still greater magnification, filling the frame with the subject.

PERSPECTIVE CHANGE

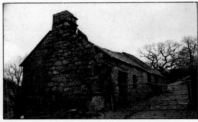

28 mm The picture above was taken close to the cottage, using a wide-angle lens. Note the steep front-to-back perspective.

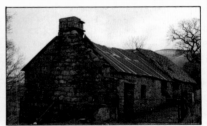

50 mm A standard lens was fitted and the camera moved back until the chimney matched. Compare near and far ends of the cottage.

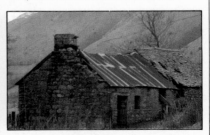

135 mm A telephoto, used from more than double the distance, gives flattened perspective. The background appears to be closer.

Telephoto lenses

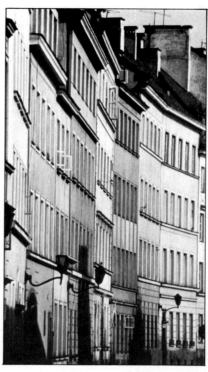

Telephoto lenses range from about 85 mm to 1000 mm and beyond. Size and weight increase with focal length, although this is minimized in mirror designs. Telephoto images have enlarged detail and shallow depth of field – you can exploit this by using differential focus to isolate subjects at different distances.

Using medium telephotos

The most versatile telephoto lenses have focal lengths between 85 mm and 200 mm. A 100 mm lens allows you to fill the frame with a head when shooting from 5 ft (1.5 m), and gives a slightly flattened perspective that is usually flattering for portraits. Lenses in this range are also useful for sports photography, distant landscapes, and natural history subjects. Medium-range telephoto lenses are fairly compact and they usually offer maximum apertures of f 2.8 or f 3.5, making them suitable for hand-held candid photography.

Using extreme telephotos

Telephotos with a focal length of 300 mm or beyond tend to be specialist types – for picking out subjects such as distant sports, wildlife, or architectural details. Images show

Lens size The SLR telephoto lenses shown right, range in focal length from 135 mm to 600 mm. A 135 mm lens is approximately twice the physical size of a standard 50 mm lens. The two longest lenses in this range have tripod threads, since extra support is essential to prevent shake. Also, the weight of these long lenses may put undue strain on the lens mount.

Compressed perspective This picture (above) was taken with a 400 mm lens. It shows the unnaturally flattened perspective typical of extreme telephotos. Differences in scale between nearest and furthest buildings are minimized. Use a telephoto for "stacked-up" patterns.

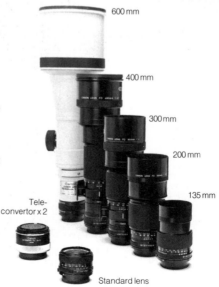

600 mm

400 mm

300 mm

200 mm

135 mm

Tele-convertor x 2

Standard lens

MIRROR DESIGNS

A mirror design telephoto lens (right) has "folded-up" optics. Circular mirrors front and back reduce the lens to about one-third the length and one-half the weight of a regular telephoto. However, you cannot alter aperture or depth of field – to reduce light you have to add a neutral density filter (see p. 173). Out-of-focus highlights take on a "donut" shape (below) due to the rear-facing mirror blocking the center of the front lens element.

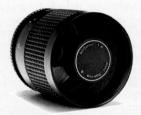

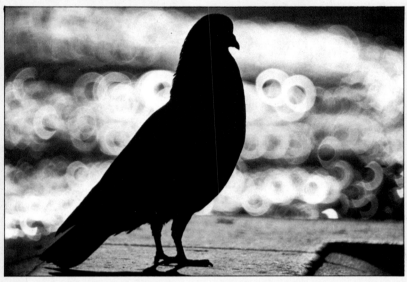

an acute flattening of perspective (see facing page). You will have to support most extreme telephotos on a tripod – their size and very narrow angle of view exaggerates camera shake. It is advisable to keep to briefest shutter speeds, so you may need to use fast film. Good-quality extreme telephotos are very expensive.

Teleconvertors

A teleconvertor attachment for an SLR is a worthwhile alternative to buying a telephoto lens. It fits between the camera body and any standard or telephoto lens. A x2 convertor will double the lens focal length, but it will also reduce the maximum aperture available by two f numbers.

HINTS AND TIPS

● To avoid camera shake with a hand-held telephoto, make your minimum safe speed match focal length – for example, 1/250 for 200 mm.
● Avoid photographing through window glass with long focal length lenses.
●.The longer the focal length, the greater the closest subject focusing distance. Typical closest distance for a 300 mm non-mirror lens is 12 ft (3.6 m), compared to 20 ft (6 m) for a 600 mm.
● Most telephotos with a focal length of over 200 mm do not allow split screen focusing aids to function properly.
● For accurate follow-focus with a telephoto and a moving subject, use an autofocus type and set the camera program to "focus priority" (see p. 30).

Wide-angle lenses

Lenses with focal lengths of 35 mm and less give an increasingly wide angle of view. Beyond 16 mm, shortening produces a "bowing-out" of image shapes, and even shorter lenses may give a "fisheye" effect (see p.169). Wide-angle lenses miniaturize image detail – they include far more of the scene, especially the foreground. Small shifts of camera position create large changes in the relationships between foreground and background. And depth of field is greater than with a standard lens set at the same aperture.

Using medium wide-angles

The most versatile wide-angle lenses are in the 35 mm to 21 mm range with a maximum aperture of f 2.8. These lenses "pull in" more of your subject without excessive distortion. They allow you to photograph cramped interiors, landscapes with important foregrounds, and candid half-length shots at close range. Because wide-angles exaggerate the size difference between near and far elements, pictures have a strong sense of depth and distance. Close-up portraits are unflattering as parts of the face closest to the lens (forehead and nose) appear much too large.

Short wide-angles

Wide-angles of 21 mm down to current limits of about 16 mm betray their extreme optics. Straight lines still appear straight,

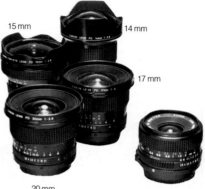

15 mm 14 mm 17 mm

20 mm

Lens size The medium wide-angle lens (right) has a focal length of 35 mm. Extreme wide-angle lenses increase in bulk. 20 mm and 17 mm lenses will accept special shallow lens hoods. The 14 mm and the 15 mm fisheye lenses have built-in shaped flanges.

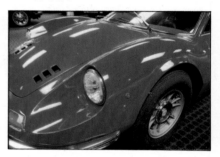

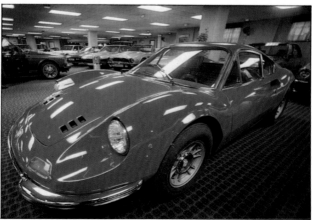

Image size These two photographs were taken from the same camera position. The picture above was taken with a 28 mm wide-angle, the photograph on the left with a 14 mm extreme wide-angle. The 28 mm includes nearly twice as much of the scene as a 50 mm lens does. The 14 mm almost doubles this again, but natural perspective begins to distort. Distortion is greatest in the corners of the picture area.

PERSPECTIVE CONTROL LENS

Some SLR wide-angles – 28 or 35 mm – have a perspective control feature that allows the lens to shift downward, upward (see right), or sideways. This is particularly useful in architectural photography. To include the tops of tall buildings when shooting with a normal lens, you have to tilt the camera, producing converging verticals (below right); but with a PC lens, you keep the camera back vertical and slide the lens upward, giving an undistorted result (below).

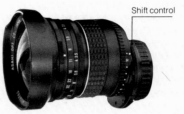

Shift control

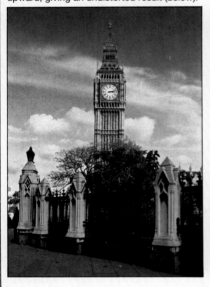

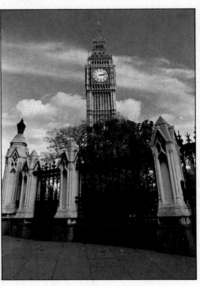

unlike a fisheye result, but shapes of elements in the picture corners are elongated. Use these ultra-wide-angle lenses to give your images dramatic perspective or to make faces seem nightmarish. You seldom need to adjust focus because of the extreme depth of field these lenses have. The maximum aperture is usually about f 4.

Wide-angle adaptors
You can fit an adaptor over the front of a standard SLR lens to convert it to a wide-angle. A typical attachment converts a 50 mm lens into a 30 mm, and a 35 mm into a 21 mm without altering the f number. Because the image quality is usually poor, avoid using apertures wider than f 5.6.

● Make sure that any filter, attachment or lens hood you fit is designed for wide-angle use and does not intrude into picture corners.
● If you are using flash, fit it with a wide-angle adaptor or bounce it, otherwise only the center of your picture will be illuminated.
● With wide-angles of 21mm or less, avoid including recognizable shapes

HINTS AND TIPS

near picture corners. Distortion is less obvious if you have sky, grass or plain surfaces here.
● Beware of accidentally including your fingertips, hair, or part of the camera case when using extreme wide-angle lenses. Make it a rule always to look carefully at all the four corners of the viewfinder.

Zoom and special lenses

Zoom lenses are common to most advanced compacts, and they are a viable alternative to fixed focal length lenses for an SLR, although they offer a smaller maximum aperture. The advantages of a zoom include continuous changes of image size (within the limitations of the lens design) and the ability to create unusual effects during exposure. One or two anamorphic attachments and SLR fisheye lenses also allow special effects, but these should not be over-used.

Zoom lens features
Each zoom lens spans a range of focal lengths – the typical shortest to longest ratio is about 1 to 3. Lenses offering higher ratios may sacrifice image quality at each extreme. Whereas zooms for compacts tend to be mid-range (either side of standard focal length), zooms for SLRs include wholly wide-angle and wholly telephoto types. Often a zoom lens will change its f number, becoming a higher f number as the focal length becomes longer. The camera's exposure system will take this into account if necessary. Most

SLR zooms offer a "macro" mode. When set to macro, the lens may focus on a subject only an inch (25 mm) from the lens.

Applications of zooms
A zoom lens allows you to keep pictures tightly composed, which is especially useful with slides, but you should not ignore the

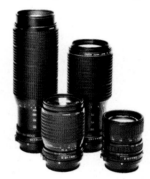

Zoom lenses This group of zooms includes a wide-angle, moderate wide angle to short telephoto, and two telephotos. Most zooms are one-touch – slide the focus ring along the lens barrel to zoom, rotate it to focus.

Filling the frame A zoom lens will help you to fill the frame when you cannot change your distance from the subject. Both shots (right) were taken from the same position with a zoom lens. The zoom was set at 85 mm (near right) and 200 mm (far right). Depth of field is much shallower at the longest setting.

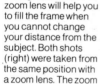
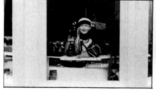

How to zoom during exposure This shot of a brightly lit store (right) was taken with an 80–200 mm zoom. The camera was supported on a tripod, and a 1 sec exposure given. While the shutter was open, the photographer shifted the one-touch control from its longest to shortest setting.

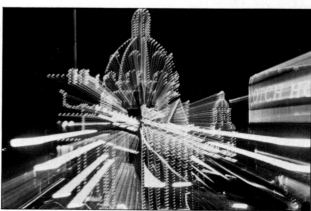

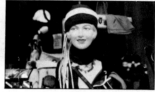

creative possibilities of viewpoint on perspective (see p. 163). With an SLR, a zoom means you do not have to carry around several lenses, perhaps missing shots as you swap one lens for another. In dim light, however, a zoom's smaller maximum aperture makes it less useful than a wider-aperture, fixed focal length lens.

A unique feature of using a zoom lens is that you can set a slow shutter speed and then shift focal length while the shutter is open to create blurs and streaks radiating out from the picture center. For dynamic, semi-abstract effects, try combining this zoom-movement technique with panning (see p. 95 and p. 98).

DISTORTING LENSES

An anamorphic lens attachment has a front face that is flat in one dimension and curved in another. This "squeezes" the image either horizontally or vertically, depending on how you rotate the lens. When using the attachment you set your main lens to its smallest aperture to avoid poor image definition. "Fisheyes" are extreme wide-angle lenses,

uncorrected for linear distortion. They give a perspective similar to a convex mirror reflection. Fisheye lenses and attachments provide angles of view of between 170° and 220°, according to focal length. Extreme types form a circular image which can confuse the camera's TTL meter unless it is strongly center weighted.

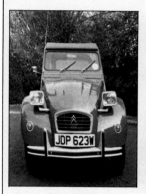

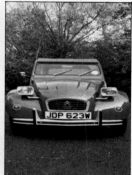

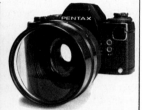

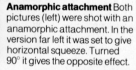

Anamorphic attachment Both pictures (left) were shot with an anamorphic attachment. In the version far left it was set to give horizontal squeeze. Turned 90° it gives the opposite effect.

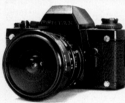

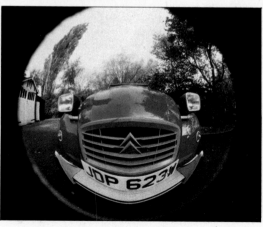

Fisheye lens Here, the photographer used a 180° 8 mm fisheye lens, $2\frac{1}{2}$ ins (64 mm) from the front grill. Although shot at f 22, the depth of field is extraordinarily large. With a fisheye, you must hold the camera well forward to avoid including your feet.

Close-up equipment

Close-up photography offers you a rewarding new source of picture material. Simple, natural objects provide dramatic forms, colors and patterns. You can also make a record of small objects – for insurance or valuation purposes, for example. Close-up accessories are mostly designed for SLRs, but limited close-up work is possible on a compact.

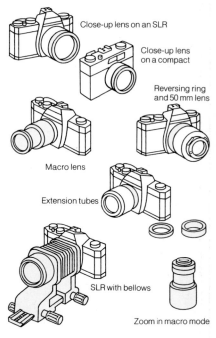

Close-up lens on an SLR

Close-up lens on a compact

Reversing ring and 50 mm lens

Macro lens

Extension tubes

SLR with bellows

Zoom in macro mode

Choosing equipment

You cannot get a sharp image of subjects closer than your camera's nearest focusing distance with a normal lens. One solution is to fit a filter-size supplementary lens which acts like a reading glass. When your main lens is set for infinity you get sharp pictures of objects the same distance as the focal length of the supplementary. At other lens focus settings you can work closer still.

Some close-up accessories – extension tubes and bellows – work by spacing the camera lens further from the film. Because they require removing the lens from the body, you can only use them on SLR cameras. Extension rings are tubes of different lengths which fit singly or in combinations. The longer the tube (and the shorter your lens focal length) the closer you can photograph. This principle also applies to a bellows attachment (see right) which allows continuous rather than stepped changes in length.

Good general-purpose lenses give poorer results when you are working so close that the image is larger than the subject. To overcome this problem, either use a lens reversing ring (see right) or change to a macro lens.

Solving technical problems

The main problem in close-up work is the extremely shallow depth of field. Focusing must be accurate, and it is best to arrange your subject so that it is all at one distance from the lens. Camera shake is greatly magnified, so work on a tripod and use flash for subjects like flowers, which move in the slightest air currents. If your camera casts shadows on subjects that are very close, change to a longer focal length lens. This will allow you to work further back

Types of equipment
Supplementary or *close-up lenses* come in various focal lengths and diameters, and fit over existing lenses. A *macro lens*, built for close work, has extended focusing. A low-cost *reversing ring* increases standard lens extension, improving its close-up image quality. Sets of *extension tubes* and a *bellows unit* all increase lens-film distance. Most zooms have a *macro mode* setting. This allows the lens to focus close up.

from the subject, although you will need a longer lens-to-body extension in order to get the image sharp.

Applications and aids

The easiest close-up subjects are stamps, coins, copies of slides, and other flat-surfaced materials. You will find subjects such as live insects or large close-ups of parts of plants difficult unless you can shoot them under controlled conditions indoors. Aids available range from simple devices to set distance and framing with a compact (right) to ring flash (see p. 179) for a single lens reflex.

IMAGE MAGNIFICATION

In close-up work "magnification" means the height of the subject divided into the height of its image on the film or focusing screen. When your image is the same size as the subject, magnification is x1. When it is half subject size, this is a magnification of 0.5x. In general, close-up photography greater than x1 is known as macrophotography. A standard 50 mm lens will focus down to a subject distance of about 15½ ins (39 cm), giving a magnification of 0.15x. You can reduce subject distance further and extend magnification using close-up attachments, tubes or bellows (see below). For magnifications above x1 reverse mount your standard lens (see facing page) to improve its sharpness. For best results change to a macro lens. Close-up lenses are often marked in "diopters". Each diopter is the number of times the focal length of the lens will divide into one meter.

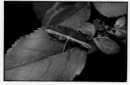
Half life-size

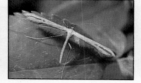
Life-size

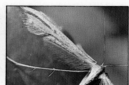
Twice life-size

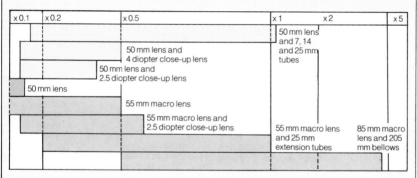

x 0.1	x 0.2	x 0.5	x 1	x 2	x 5
			50 mm lens and 7, 14 and 25 mm tubes		
		50 mm lens and 4 diopter close-up lens			
	50 mm lens and 2.5 diopter close-up lens				
50 mm lens					
	55 mm macro lens				
	55 mm macro lens and 2.5 diopter close-up lens		55 mm macro lens and 25 mm extension tubes	85 mm macro lens and 205 mm bellows	

Copying stand The unit centers camera looking downward. Extending legs have settings in diopters to indicate magnification.

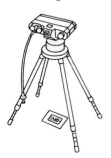

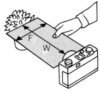

Simple spacer A cardboard spacer gives you accurate framing and focusing with a compact camera and close-up lens. Make dimension W the focusing distance, and F the width of field, as given for your close-up lens.

● The shortest in a set of extension tubes is often the most versatile. Three rings plus a lens give seven permutations.
● When shooting very close-up with an SLR, first approximate the image size you require using the focusing control. Then shift the whole camera nearer or further from the subject until it is sharp.
● You do not need to adjust exposure for close-up lenses. All other close-up devices reduce image brightness, but your TTL meter will take this into account.
● To check close-up magnification, focus on a ruler. If your lens has a magnification of 0.5x, for example, the amount that fills the 36 mm wide focusing screen should be 72 mm.

Choosing an SLR outfit

Unlike an all-in-one compact, when buying an SLR you are potentially "buying into" a complete system. Check which lenses and accessories the camera will accept, then plan your purchases so that eventually you build up a versatile kit. (You can buy bodies independently of lenses.) Your priorities will depend on the type of photography you are interested in. Most people start with a wide-aperture 50 mm lens or mid-range zoom. A sports or portrait photographer might next need a telephoto, while for architectural or journalistic pictures you might choose a wide-angle. Fisheyes and other special optics are best rented when needed.

BUILDING AN OUTFIT

The outfits shown below are a few of the alternatives that you can consider when building up a range of different lenses. Avoid overlap or duplication, and do not purchase more than you need – you can miss vital shots while changing lenses. Accessories can be important too – for example, a tele-adaptor (see pp.164-5) doubles any focal length, and extension tubes (see p. 170) improve your close focusing range.

OUTFITS

One lens kit

50 mm standard lens

SUGGESTIONS

Your first decision will probably be whether to get an economical f 1.4 or f 2 standard 50 mm lens with your camera and add to this later, or to buy a body and a wide-ranging 28–135 mm zoom. The zoom forms a one-lens kit, and for general photography you could manage without further purchases. However, it is bulky and expensive, and only offers f 4.5

Two lens kit

50 mm standard lens

28 mm wide-angle lens

To make a two lens kit, you might add a fixed focal length wide-angle or telephoto to an existing standard lens. If your choice of second lens is a telephoto, this might be a moderately priced 80–200 mm zoom which offers high quality. If you are starting from scratch, you could pair two lenses – say, a 28–50 mm and 50–250 mm f 4 zooms. However, this would be a more expensive choice.

Three lens kit

135 mm telephoto lens

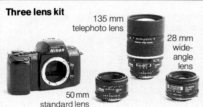

28 mm wide-angle lens

50 mm standard lens

A three lens kit developed from an initial standard lens might contain 28 mm, 50 mm and 135 mm lenses. Or if you bought an 80–200 mm zoom as your second lens, you could add a 28 mm to get three lenses of similar quality. Another approach is to build up from your standard lens with 28–45 mm and 80–200 mm zooms. This gives an almost continuous range from 28 mm to 200 mm, and a good quality image.

Two body kit

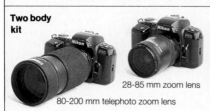

28-85 mm zoom lens

80-200 mm telephoto zoom lens

When you have three or more lenses you can waste a lot of time changing from one to another. One answer to this problem is to buy another body, and fit each camera with a zoom giving a complementary range of focal lengths. Using two bodies also enables you to duplicate shots on different types of film. And you are less likely to miss a picture because your film has finished.

Filters

Filters are tinted or colorless transparent lens attachments which "take out" some of the light. They range from types which just dim the image as an alternative to reducing the aperture, to others designed to let you expose color film in different kinds of artificial light. Most filters are inexpensive and very useful aids.

Colorless filters

Filters which are colorless are equally useful for color and black and white work. "Neutral density" gray filters are made in various strengths, see right. In brilliant lighting or with fast film an ND filter allows

NEUTRAL DENSITY FILTERS

A selection from the Kodak ND filter (No 96) range

Filter	N.D.	Factor	Exposure increase in stops
	0.3	x2	1
	0.5	x3	1.5
	0.6	x4	2
	0.7	x5	2.3
	0.8	x6	2.6
	0.9	x8	3
	1.0	x10	3.3
	2.0	x100	6.6

COLOR FILTERS FOR BLACK AND WHITE PHOTOGRAPHY

With regular panchromatic black and white films color filters will lighten or darken the tone that one color records relative to another. A red automobile against green vegetation, for example, photographs as two similar tones of gray when the lens is unfiltered. But if you shoot through a red filter, red records paler and green darker, clearly separating each element. Deep orange or yellow filters darken a strong blue sky, and make white clouds stand out. And if you shoot a document or drawing which has a colored stain, this may disappear through a filter that closely matches the stain. Use filters designed for black and white work, or the strong filters you may already have for color photography.

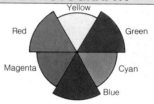

The effects of color filters A filter always lightens its own color, and darkens colors opposite to it in the spectrum. The diagram above shows the primary colors of light against their opposite "complementary" colors. These are cyan (greenish-blue), magenta (purplish-red), and yellow. A green filter lightens green but darkens magenta, blue and red. A cyan filter lightens cyan, darkens red, magenta and yellow.

Darkening skies The scene (left) contained white clouds against a blue sky. When photographed without a filter (left half), there is little tonal difference between clouds and sky. To darken blue and emphasize cloud shapes shoot through a deep orange filter (right half). The original exposure of 1/250 at f 11 had to change to 1/125 at between f 8 and f 11.

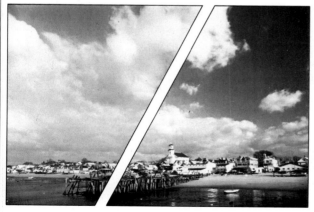

you to set a slow shutter speed for blur or a wide aperture for shallow depth of field without overexposing.

An ultraviolet (UV) absorbing filter looks like clear glass. It helps reduce haze that is too blue (or too pale on black and white film) in distant landscapes or seascapes.

A polarizing filter looks like a neutral density type and given the right conditions it will act as one, but it can also suppress polarized light (see p. 207). This includes reflections from shiny surfaces (other than bare metal) at about 45°, and light from a blue north sky. You rotate the filter to discover the best position to make reflections disappear, or to darken a blue sky without changing other colors (see p. 206). The light-stopping power of the polarizing filter

also changes as it is rotated but meters should take this into account.

Colored filters

You can buy a wide range of pale colored filters, like the Kodak CC series, which very slightly "warm up" or "cool down" color results. For example, when you shoot in the late afternoon on Kodachrome, results can be too orange unless you use a pale blue or cyan filter to correct the color cast. You can use pale tinted filters to intensify a mood or color scheme. Each CC filter is made in a variety of strengths (see pp. 206–7).

Strong color filters balance either daylight color film for tungsten lighting (blue 80A) or tungsten film for daylight or flash (orange 85A). For a monochromatic color

---

FILTER CONSTRUCTION

Filters for camera lenses are made of optical glass or thin sheet gelatin. Circular glass filters screw directly on the lens, but it is also possible to fit a filter holder which takes standard size square or circular slide-in filters. (A circular shape is essential for filters which you have to rotate.) You can simply hold gelatin filters over the lens, but it is best to mount each one in a frame to fit in a holder. Handle and clean filters like lenses.

UV filter • Type 8 filter

Polarizer • Type 11 filter

Neutral density filters

Type 80A filter

Type 2C filter

Type 1A filter

Type 85B filter

Screw-on filters Glass filters usually screw directly on the front of your lens. In general, each manufacturer uses the same front diameter for most of its lens range.

"Cool-down" gelatins

Type 24 filter

Gelatin holder This hood accepts gelatins mounted in a plastic frame. Screw clamps attach it to lens.

Flash head filters These plastic filters have the same effect as a lens filter if light is solely flash.

"Warm-up" gelatins

Choosing filters Some of the most useful filter types are shown here. They include UV, polarizing and other colorless types, strong filters for black and white work, and color balancing filters. Bluish and pink CC gelatins each come in a range of strengths (see p. 206).

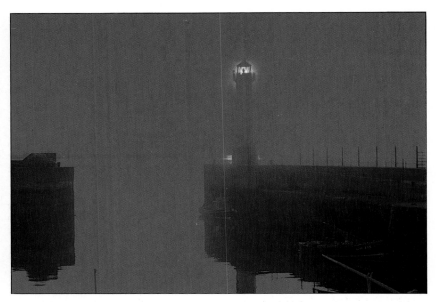

Filtering for effect
Strong filtration gives interesting color results with extremely contrasty scenes. The picture above was shot through a deep red filter, with the sun directly behind the lighthouse. The filter destroys all subject colors, but the overexposed sun "burns through" the red.

picture try shooting a scene that includes low sun straight into the light. The sun will overexpose to white, and everything else will simplify to a single color or black. (For uses with black and white, see p. 173.)

Effects on exposure

Most filters reduce the amount of light reaching the film. (Exceptions are UV and palest CC types, which have a minimal effect.) The amount by which exposure is affected is often marked on the filter mount or container. A filter with a factor of x3 requires three times the unfiltered exposure. But calculations are unnecessary if you have either a TTL meter or a meter on the front of the lens barrel of your compact. Both types read through the filter itself. (Some older models give incorrect readings through strong color filters.) When you use filters over a flashgun make sure that they do not cover the sensor.

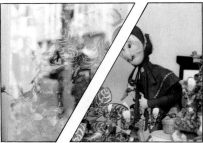

How to suppress reflections Shooting through angled glass creates ugly reflections (left). Add a polarizing filter (right), and rotate it until you get the best result.

HINTS AND TIPS

● To preview the effect of a color filter when shooting in black and white, look through it and note which colors look darker or lighter.
● You can test the accuracy of your camera meter when using a filter. Take readings with and without the filter in place, then compare the difference between the two readings with the marked filter factor.
● When ordering prints from color negatives shot using strong filters, warn the laboratory which filter you used so that they do not compensate.

Supports and general items

Accessories such as camera supports, motors, and meters are useful for a wide range of photographic situations. You can also use most of these items with many types of cameras, or interchange them between several camera bodies. Choose each accessory to suit your types of subject and the way you prefer to work. There is no point, for example, in buying a tripod that is very stable if it is too heavy for you to carry comfortably.

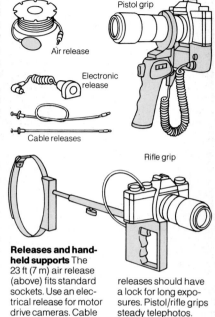

Pistol grip

Air release

Electronic release

Cable releases

Supports and releases

There are many aids available to help you avoid the problems associated with camera shake. Some, such as tripods and spikes, also fix camera position for picture sequences or remote control shots. Rifle or pistol-type hand supports improve steadiness with long-focus lenses, especially when panning action shots where a tripod may get in the way. Similarly, a monopod is easier to carry and quicker to set up than a tripod. It allows exposures down to about 1/8, provided that you brace the camera against your body so that your legs form

Rifle grip

Releases and hand-held supports The 23 ft (7 m) air release (above) fits standard sockets. Use an electrical release for motor drive cameras. Cable releases should have a lock for long exposures. Pistol/rifle grips steady telephotos.

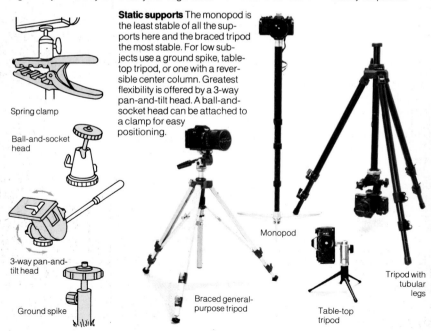

Static supports The monopod is the least stable of all the supports here and the braced tripod the most stable. For low subjects use a ground spike, table-top tripod, or one with a reversible center column. Greatest flexibility is offered by a 3-way pan-and-tilt head. A ball-and-socket head can be attached to a clamp for easy positioning.

Spring clamp

Ball-and-socket head

3-way pan-and-tilt head

Ground spike

Monopod

Braced general-purpose tripod

Table-top tripod

Tripod with tubular legs

Camera and accessory cases

The ever-ready case (right) stays on the camera, and a flap folds down for instant use. The fishing-type bag is the best choice for working on the move. Rigid cases are more protective – you can even use metal types to stand on. One case (below) includes a changing bag.

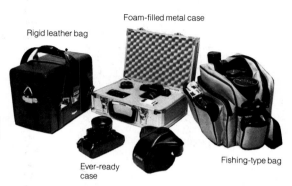

Foam-filled metal case

Rigid leather bag

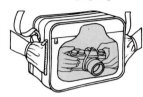

Ever-ready case

Fishing-type bag

part of the support. When comparing tripods, models with shortest legs when closed may not extend to heights above waist level. Taller, braced types which have fewer extensions are less compact.

Motors

If your camera does not have a built-in motor, you may be able to fit a matching power winder or motor drive accessory. A motor drive offers a choice of continuous shooting speeds – typically up to 5 or 6 frames per second against a power winder's 2 fps. In practice, shooting rate is restricted

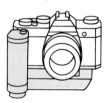

Motor drive This unit allows you to take single shots, or gives up to 3.5 frames per sec at speeds of 1/125 and faster. Gears and contacts connect through camera base.

Compact winder The clip-on winder (right) gives single frame operation and also forms a camera grip.

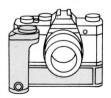

Linked drive The film winder (left) connects to the in-focus signaling circuit of this SLR. It shoots single frames or 2.5 pictures per sec, provided the lens is focused.

by your shutter speed or flash recycling rate. Both accessories allow single frame shooting with fast wind-on so that you can keep the camera up to your eye. You attach these units via contacts on the baseplate of your camera. Each has either a screw-on or slide-out battery pack, and you can buy different packs for penlight disposable or rechargeable Ni-Cad batteries. And you can replace battery packs without removing the motor unit. If your camera has "in-focus" signaling you can link either type of motor to this circuit. For panning, keep the release depressed and pictures are then automatically taken when the image is sharp.

Bags and cases

If you have just one camera protect it with an ever-ready case (usually purchased with the camera). One catch releases the front section for quick use. If, however, you have several items of equipment some form of gadget bag becomes essential. A waterproof fisherman's bag is ideal. The top flaps must allow you quick access to lenses and accessories while the bag is on your shoulder. Rigid bags offer greater protection, particularly those types that are filled with solid foam surrounding equipment.

Meters

Hand meters allow you to measure exposure independently of camera and flashgun. Several measure continuous light only.

177

This is essential for cameras that lack built-in meters. Most hand meters take an overall or an incident light reading, and a few have a facility for spot metering (see right). Flash meters measure either flash only or read continuous existing light, too.

Viewfinders and focusing screens

With some advanced SLRs you can remove the pentaprism and attach an alternative viewfinder over the focusing screen. For example, a fold-out light shield forms a waist-level view, ideal for shots near ground level or for vertical copying. A magnifying finder is another alternative. If you wear glasses, an action finder allows you to view the whole screen from several inches away. It is also excellent for sports photography. Many SLRs, even types with fixed pentaprisms, allow you to change the focusing screen. This can be of advantage simply for ease of focusing, or for more specialist use – a gridded screen for architectural photography, for example. You change screens through the front of the body.

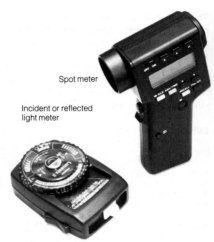

Spot meter

Incident or reflected light meter

Hand-held exposure meters This photograph shows two types of meter for measuring continuous light. The large spot meter has a reflex viewfinder system. It reads exposure over 1° angle of view, and shows settings on a side display. The smaller meter takes a 40° view (reflected) but can also make readings toward the light (incident).

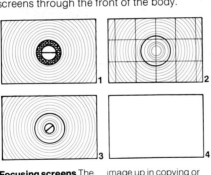

1 2 3 4

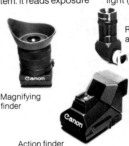

Right-angle attachment

Magnifying finder

Action finder

Waist-level finder

Focusing screens The standard screen (1) has split image center zone and microprism ring focusing aids. A screen with a split image area set at 45° (3) makes focusing easier when shooting horizontal as well as vertical lines. A screen without a split image (2) is more suitable for small aperture telephoto or shift lenses. The grid is helpful for squaring an image up in copying or architectural work. A plain etched screen (4) gives the minimum distraction when composing pictures.

Alternative viewfinder fittings The two waist-level finders and the action finder above right replace the normal SLR pentaprism. The right-angle eyepiece fits behind a regular pentaprism.

178

Specialized items

The extreme limits of a camera system may cover many specialized technical and scientific applications. Data backs, for example, print standard or preset information within each picture frame. Used in conjunction with a 250-exposure film back, a regular SLR can become a surveillance recording unit. You can also use cameras with unusual light sources such as ring flash or infrared-filtered flash units for "invisible light" photography. An image intensifier or an endoscope attachment allows you to shoot in near darkness and inaccessible places. And adaptors enable your camera to become part of a telescope or microscope.

Data back Cameras designed with removable backs can also accept a data back (see below). A data back contains a quartz clock and will automatically record time and date, even camera settings, exposed on the frame by a tiny internal flash. This information is recorded at the bottom of the frame each time you take a picture. Most types also feature a keyboard, allowing you to program up to 30 additional words or figures.

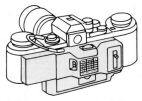

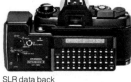

SLR data back

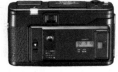

Compact data back

250-frame exposure back The recording camera above combines a special data back with 250-exposure capacity film compartments and motor drive. The heart of the unit is a slightly modified SLR body and lens. The data recording kit imprints hand-written information and exposure settings at the side of each exposed frame and the motor unit can shoot pictures at the rate of one per second for over four minutes. Coupled to an extended interval timer you can easily increase this time to several weeks by taking pictures at intervals of minutes or even hours. The special, enlarged cassettes are reusable and loaded with bulk film in the darkroom (see p. 64).

Ring flash This unit is a combined light source and macro lens, and is used for medical and dental close-up work or any photography where there is no room to position lighting units. The flash tube surrounds the lens and so gives absolutely even frontal lighting. You can also buy independent ring flash.

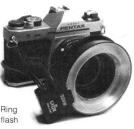

Ring flash

Endoscope An endoscope is a special lens system forming a thin rod or long flexible tube. It is designed for close-up photography in inaccessible locations – such as inside the human body. A lens at the tip of the endoscope relays the image to the film through thousands of fiber optic strands. Other fiber optics, surrounding the tube, duct light from a lamp to the tip to illuminate the subject.

Image intensifier With an image intensifier you can take hand-held pictures under extremely dim, even starlit, conditions. The unit is the size of a large telephoto lens. A lens at the front forms an image on the face of a tiny electronic tube. The tube intensifies brightness several thousand times and displays the picture at the rear, where it is exposed on film. Image resolution is poor.

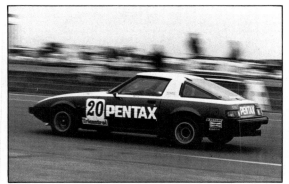

Data back in date mode

Presentation and storage

You can make good use of different forms of presentation to enhance your pictures. Successful photographs look even better if they are displayed in a frame, album or folio. Slide presentation does not stop at hand viewing and conventional projection today – you can create audio-visual shows in conjunction with your hi-fi, or show color pictures through the domestic television. You can even buy a special projector for prints.

Slide protection and storage

Slides are returned from processing in glassless cardboard or plastic mounts (unless you ask for the film uncut). These are cheap, but give little protection to the emulsion surface, and they often bow during projection, stopping you from sharply focusing the whole image. To protect slides, use glass and plastic mounts, and store them in a dry place away from heat and light, either in boxes or slide magazines. Transparent sheets that have pockets for 36 slides and hang in a filing cabinet are ideal for large quantities.

Print presentation

If you display enlargements in frames, do not keep them in parts of the room which receive direct sunlight. Colors in prints fade like dyes in fabrics, and sometimes the plastic print base becomes crazed.

A simple but effective type of print album has cling-film page overlays which hold the

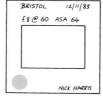

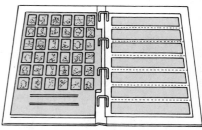

Mounting slides Glass mounts protect your film and hold it flat. Avoid thick types – they jam in projector magazines. Some mounts are dark on one side, and light on the other. Position the emulsion (dull) surface toward the dark half. The light half faces the lamp during projection.

Marking up slides
Write data on an adhesive label or directly on the mount. Hold the picture as it should appear on the screen and mark a spot bottom left. Spots must be top right when loaded.

Storing negatives
You can buy a ring binder with looseleaf transparent sheets which hold the film in strips. If possible, file contact prints facing film. Give negatives and prints the same reference number.

Framing prints The simplest way to frame a print is to sandwich it between glass and cardboard. Carefully cut out a cardboard matte to set off your picture. Avoid strong matte colors – usually a white or neutral tone is best. If you use a matte, mount the print on cardboard to ensure that it stays flat. It is essential to back up the cardboard with hardboard. Use a frame to clamp print and matte together.

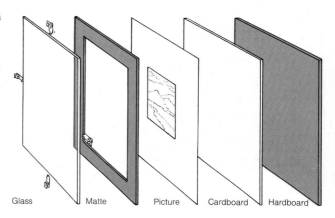

Glass   Matte   Picture   Cardboard   Hardboard

PROJECTORS AND VIEWERS

The best way to show slides is to use a projector in a well blacked-out room. A magazine system feeds slides into the projector. Most have a straight-run magazine holding 36 or 50 slides, others accept 80 slides in a circular tray which works either horizontally or vertically, depending on the model. You can store slides in magazines ready for use.

For small group viewing in a lighted room, you might use a back projection unit. These come in box or suitcase form, and contain a projector which shows slides on the rear of a translucent screen. Some have a cassette player with speaker to provide music and commentary. The tape allows you to preprogram picture changes too. Often back projection units have an adjustable optical system which also allows you to project on a separate screen.

Projectors are also available for showing prints, but they are much dimmer than slide types and so limited to a smaller screen.

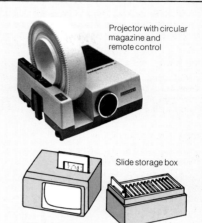

Projector with circular magazine and remote control

Slide storage box

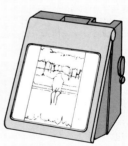

Battery hand viewer

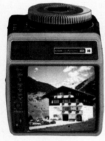

Audio-visual back projection unit

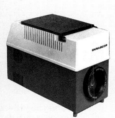

Epidiascope – projects from prints

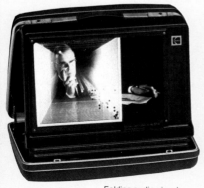

Simple back projection unit

Folding audio-visual presentation unit

Slide presentation aids For home shows a magazine projector gives excellent results. Slides and focus are changed by remote control. A hand viewer is useful for immediate viewing of slides as it can be used anywhere, in any lighting. The epidiascope projects enprints. Place them face down on glass under the top flap of the unit, and provide a good black-out. The two audio-visual units have audio cassette and loudspeaker systems and an 80-slide rotary magazine projector. The squarer unit can also project on an external screen through a sliding door above the built-in screen. The folding AV unit looks like a normal traveling case when closed. The simplest, cheapest back projection units have no audio components.

USING MIXED MEDIA

You can synchronize your stereo sound equipment with dual slide projectors for elaborate audio-visual sequences. Paired projectors registered on one screen allow image dissolves at various speeds, snap changes, and superimposition. To show pictures on an ordinary TV or computer screen, Photo CD is available. With this, you shoot color negatives or slides in the usual way but the processing laboratory supplies the images on a compact disk. Replaying the disk through a special CD player gives high-quality color positives on screen. You can change pictures using a remote control, and paper prints can be produced by thermal or ink-jet printers.

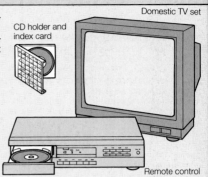

Domestic TV set

CD holder and index card

Photo CD player

Remote control

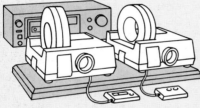

Automatic fade system for audio-visual displays

Photo CD
A photo master compact disk (CD) will hold up to 100 high-resolution color images in a "read only memory" (ROM) form. You can display pictures in any order, or enlarge any chosen part of a picture to double its normal size on the screen. Each disk container has a set of miniature prints held on the disk (top left) for reference and filing purposes.

print in place. If you glue prints to cardboard for framing or putting in a portfolio, use double-sided adhesive sheeting or some form of specialized photo spray adhesive. Avoid domestic glues – they may eventually cause chemical stains to appear on the print.

Albums and frames
There is a very wide range of storage and display aids for prints. You can choose from simple slip-in folders, frames, and cling-film albums, to a weatherproof professional-type portfolio for exhibition-size enlargements.

HINTS AND TIPS

● Try mounting prints on composite board, trimming it flush and painting the edge. And look out for unusual antique frames.
● Avoid projecting slides for long periods. Dyes in most color films start fading after about 30 min continuous screening.
● Never remove the heat filter located in front of your projector lamp. Focused heat burns a hole in slides.
● Make sure that you pick a frame that suits your print. An over-assertive surround may "kill" a picture.

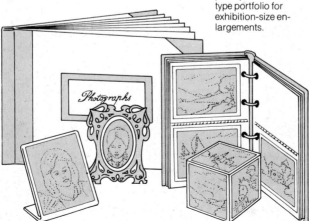

Photographs

SPECIAL EFFECTS

The special effects in this section are all concerned with manipulating the camera image. A wide range of results is now possible, especially if you are prepared to experiment. Most require equipment and techniques that are neither costly nor complicated. In fact, you will find it possible to improvise several effects using materials that readily come to hand.

The section starts by showing some of the lens attachments that are designed to alter the camera image. Extreme types give very dramatic results, but often the subtle ones, such as diffusers, are the most useful. This is followed by effects produced by merging or combining one image with another.

Other topics include false color and tone effects created by shooting on unusual film or with special lighting. Similarly, the use of mirrors or strobes to form multiple images of your subject leads on to some specialized cameras, giving 3D or panoramic effects with normal film.

When reading this section, remember the techniques found in the other sections of the book, such as subject movement during slow exposure, panning, zooming, and mixed lighting. These can also be thought of as special effects. When used together, they give you the means of creating unusual and often outrageous pictures.

Lens attachments

If you want to create unusual or exciting images, consider buying or making some special effects attachments. These can be either faceted or semi-diffusing plastic, colored filters or shaped opaque masks. For the best effect, use them on simple, uncluttered types of subject. Results will vary, however, according to the aperture of your lens as well as the lens focal length. For these reasons, special effects attachments are best used with an SLR, through which you can see the lens image before shooting, preferably using the depth of field preview button.

Fitting attachments to your lens

You can buy a holder which fits on your lens and firmly grips standard-size square or circular special effects attachments. It allows you to shift and rotate attachments in front of the lens to get the exact effect that you want. The holder has several slots, enabling you to combine several attachments and filters. Most attachments are designed for use close to the camera lens, so that their structure is not apparent. But for "shape-out" masks and vignettes you will need an additional holder on the front of a deep lens hood in order to place the mask several inches in front of the lens.

Conditions will influence results

The type of result you get from most attachments will alter with camera settings. Always consider which alternative will suit your subject best. If you set a small aperture when using a device which affects only half the image or splits it up, the division becomes more distinct the greater your depth of field (see pp. 34–6). And if you rotate a diffractor or prism during a slow exposure, you will get blurred circles of light in your picture. For best results, choose subjects that have simple backgrounds.

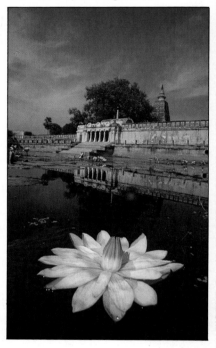

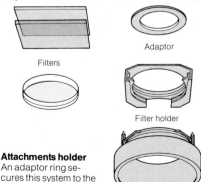

Filters

Adaptor

Filter holder

Attachments holder
An adaptor ring secures this system to the front of your lens. Slots accept square or circular attachments.

Lens hood

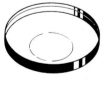

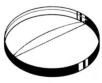

Bi-focals The split field attachment above right is part flat glass, part close-up lens. It focuses half your frame at 3 ft (1 m), half for infinity. The attachment shown left gives a distance-focused patch. Use them to fake extreme depth of field.

ATTACHMENTS FOR COLOR EFFECTS

Colored or color-inducing attachments give you a wide range of special effects possibilities. Further permutations are possible by shooting on the wrong film for your lighting, then using a part-colored filter to correct some areas of the picture. Take care over TTL exposure readings – in most cases set your camera to manual and measure without the attachment in place. Warn your laboratory when you send films containing color effects.

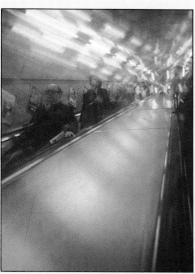

Diffractor This attachment carries an etched micro pattern of lines. Use it with an intense, compact light source, to give a burst of rainbow-colored radial lines. It is also effective for night shots featuring street lamps – try turning the disk during a time exposure.

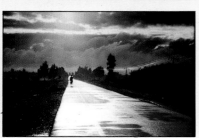

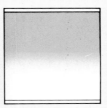

Graduate This half-colored filter is graduated off to clear glass. It is helpful for landscapes, darkening or tinting bright sky when you are exposing for dark ground detail. For the sharpest division select a small aperture. Use pairs to make the image change tint.

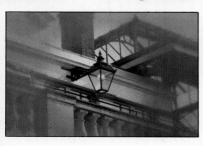

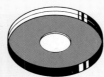

Color spot A spot filter is a color filter with a clear hole, giving normal image color in the center of the frame, and increasing tint, density or diffusion toward the edges. Use the attachment oversize, so that you can shift the unfiltered part anywhere in the frame.

ATTACHMENTS FOR BLACK AND WHITE OR COLOR

The attachments shown here can be used for black and white and color photography. Some work by spreading, reflecting, or repeating parts of the image, rather like looking through cut glass. Others change focus over a local part of the image. Use these attachments to create dramatic patterns, to give an illusory effect, or to add a touch of glitter and romance to your image. Most reduce image contrast, so choose subjects with contrasty lighting.

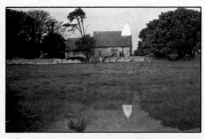

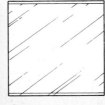

Mirage This mirror attachment projects at an angle in front of the lens. It gives a repeat, upside-down image of part of the scene – for example, adding sky into the foreground. Focus on distant subjects and shoot at a wide aperture.

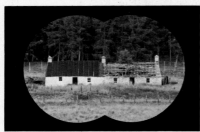

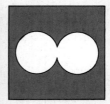

Masks When you use a mask next to the lens on a telephoto at wide aperture, all brilliant unsharp highlights take on the mask shape. Masks used in front of the lens hood form black vignettes around images. Stop down for the clearest outline.

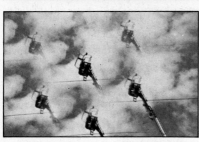

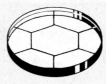

Multifacet This attachment produces 3, 5 or 6 overlapping duplicate images in a circular or parallel pattern, according to design. Grouping is tightest with a wide-angle. Choose a simple subject with a plain background.

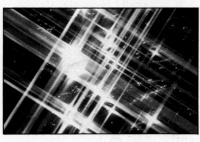

Starburst This etched glass grid spreads highlights into star-shaped flares. The number of "rays" varies with design – typically 4, 6 or 8. Pick brilliant points of light against a dark background.

Sandwiching

Sandwiching two slides in the same mount is a simple way of creating a sur- real effect. You can combine subjects which differ dramatically in size, time or place. And you can use black and white images with color, negatives with posi- tives. You can either project sandwiches or make them into prints.

Ways of working

Each image must be much lighter than normal, or the two will look too dark when combined. (Always keep your overexposed slides for this purpose.) Sometimes you can use an existing slide and shoot another image to fit with it. Or you can copy draw- ings to combine with slides for an artwork effect (see p. 111).

Another option is to copy an existing slide on different kinds of black and white instant film, and then sandwich the results. Or try binding up a slide with some thin, grained material or etched glass. In general, it is best to choose simple subjects to sandwich, and mix a strong shape with an overall pattern.

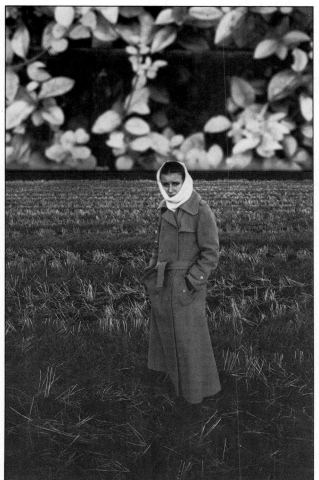

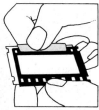

Combining the films
Carefully register the two films, preferably with emulsion (duller) surfaces together. To make one image pro- ject unsharp, place slides back-to-back, or space them with clear film. For a result like the image left, tape the sandwich together as shown above.

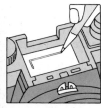

Marking up size
If your camera allows access to its focusing screen, trace the first image with grease pencil. This helps you in sizing and placing. With a fixed top cam- era, change to a fine gridded screen (see p. 178) and count lines.

Creating false colors

It is possible to show familiar objects in strange, unnatural colors by using special lighting, false-color film, or sending your film for mismatched processing. It is best to take some experimental shots first, keeping notes. From these results you can then choose subjects knowledgeably that, although possibly mundane for straight photography, form striking designs when colors are changed.

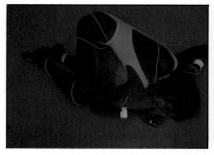

Ultraviolet fluorescence

When some materials are lit solely by ultraviolet light they fluoresce bluish-white or other bright colors. Man-made fabrics, plastics, display cardboard, and chalk solutions all work well. Illuminate objects in a darkened room with a UV lamp. You can see the fluorescence effects immediately, but in order to photograph them attach a clear ultraviolet lens filter and expose on daylight-balanced film.

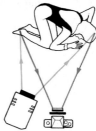

Fluorescent colors
The picture above was lit by a UV display lamp in a darkened room. Plastics and synthetic fibers fluoresce giving visible light, but the girl's skin appears dark. A clear UV-absorbing lens filter was used – without this, results look like bluish tungsten lighting.

Infrared

Any object that reflects infrared records in false colors on Ektachrome IR slide film. Healthy vegetation turns magenta, most red paint records as yellow, and faces appear wax-like. Direct sunlight is the best light source. You must, however, use a deep yellow filter to avoid an overall blue cast. Red and green filter types also give unexpected results (see p. 56).

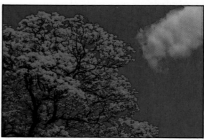

Misprocessing

You can shoot on color slide film and send it, clearly marked, for color negative processing. The result will be slides with bright complementary colors and reversed tones. Unlike regular color negatives, the film has no pink tint. Expose at normal ISO rating. Successful prints from this material are, however, difficult to obtain. Results tend to be harsh and colors degraded, although this may help some subjects.

Infrared effects
Spring foliage on a chestnut tree (above) was shot on IR Ektachrome film through a deep green filter. A deep yellow filter would give whiter cloud but less intense magenta foliage.

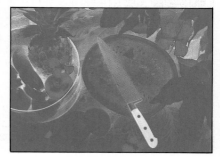

Wrong processing
For the false-color result (right) a bowl of fruit was shot on infrared slide film and processed in chemicals used for color negative film. Most shapes appear as either negative or incorrect tones.

Double exposure

Making two or more exposures on one frame of film allows you to superimpose complete pictures, or make the same subject appear more than once in the same frame. Double exposure in the camera is more difficult to control than copying slide images superimposed by projection (see pp. 192–3), but image quality is much improved. Also you require very little additional equipment. You need opaque cardboard shapes (called masks) and a lens attachment holder to position them in front of the lens. For the technique to work you must have a method of retensioning the shutter more than once without winding the film on.

Camera superimpositions

Taking two exposures on top of each other makes the details of one record most strongly in the shadow areas of the other. Night shots of neon signs, portraits with dark backgrounds, and silhouetted landscapes are all suitable subjects. Try superimposing crowds and traffic or different expressions on a single face to create a

EXPOSING THE FILM TWICE

The easiest way to double expose is by using a camera with a superimpose button. This holds the film still while the wind-on works, so only the shutter resets. With older SLR cameras, use the rewind button or catch to disengage the film transport while you wind once. Take up any slack film in the cassette, since the exposed film sometimes shifts slightly. Another method is to shoot a bracketed series of exposures of your first image, rewind to the original film start position, and then expose the second images.

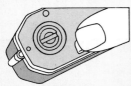

Disengaging the film After making your first exposure take up any slack in the cassette by gently turning the rewind knob in the direction of the arrow. Next, press in the rewind button and hold the knob while you advance the film carefully. Then take your next shot.

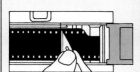

Rerunning the film Mark alignment of film to camera when loading. Take your first exposures of image, then rewind. Align film before shooting your next images.

Double exposure For the result right, two shots were taken on the same frame, each given half correct exposure.

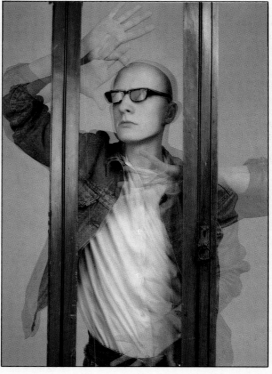

sense of animation. For correct exposure, divide normal exposure for each shot by the number of pictures, if their details overlap. If possible, bracket your combinations of exposures. Take a set of bracketed exposures of an image. Then rerun the film and expose your next image in a different bracketed series.

Using masks

Masks allow you to block out part of one exposure during shooting and then take another shot that exactly fills in the unexposed space. Either buy or make two opaque cardboard masks in matching shapes – one a negative of the other (see below). Use these in turn for your two expo-

sures. Make sure they are slotted accurately into the front of your lens attachment holder. With this technique it is easy to make a figure, for example, appear twice in the same scene. First, mount your camera on a tripod and mask off the right-hand side of your picture area while your figure stands in the left half. Take your exposure and then reverse the mask, and reposition the figure.

Vignettes

Using a similar technique you can vignette a face into the center of a single bloom, or make half a figure fade away into thin air. Correctly expose each component and use an aperture (f 4, for example) that records the mask shape with a soft edge.

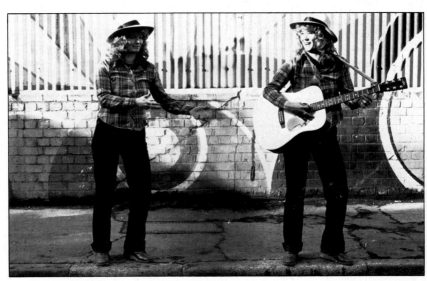

Double mask effect
With the camera on a tripod, first expose one half of the frame with the half mask (right) covering the other part. Then re-pose the figure, reset the shutter using the super-impose button, and turn the mask 180° before making the second exposure.

- Superimpose sharp and unsharp film images, or use a zoom lens to change the relative sizes of the different image components you want to combine.
- Measure exposure before attaching any masks. Try to maintain the same light quality and direction for each part.
- Superimpose the most important part of one image on a dark area of the other. Choose mask shapes that relate to the subject.

HINTS AND TIPS

Using line film

High-contrast "line" films produce photographs in solid black and solid white only. They are designed for copying lettering and ink drawings, but they also give you simplified graphic images from general subjects and make possible effects such as posterization. Use "lith" film if you do your own processing.

Converting an image to line

It is possible to ink-print a line image, like a drawn design, even on cheap paper. Line film is also ideal for turning lettering or diagrams into slides. Take the initial shot on normal film first as line film needs critical exposure and is usually insensitive to red, and then copy the resulting slide or print on line film. Coarse-grain images are especially effective when converted to line – the black specks of the original produce shading and suggest form.

Simple posterization

You can also use line film for "posterization". Copy a normal picture on instant picture line film, giving a bracketed series of exposures. Register your three results on a light box and tape each frame along a different edge. With your camera, expose one line image after the other on a frame of normal-contrast film, giving one-third correct exposure to each. The tape hinges will ensure images register. If shooting in color, change filters between each exposure.

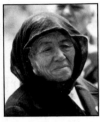 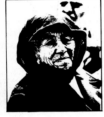

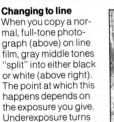

Changing to line
When you copy a normal, full-tone photograph (above) on line film, gray middle tones "split" into either black or white (above right). The point at which this happens depends on the exposure you give. Underexposure turns more grays black.

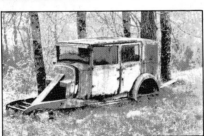

Posterized results
For the effect left, make three images by underexposing, correctly exposing and overexposing a continuous tone original on line film. Copy these in turn on one frame of ordinary film. The result resembles a flat-toned poster print.

COPYING A LINE ORIGINAL

It is difficult to decide correct exposure when you first copy a line subject, such as a drawing, on high-contrast film. Measure the light off a mid-gray card. Overexposure gives results with pale gray lettering, and underexposure produces a patchy gray background. Both errors can also give a slightly unsharp image, due to the spread of light into dark or dark into light, respectively. You can finish off line slides by binding in a pale acetate tint.

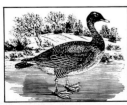 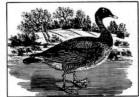 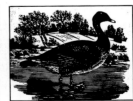

Overexposure Blacks have recorded only as gray. There is some expansion of whites.

Correct exposure All fine detail is present, yet blacks are rich and whites clean.

Underexposure The black lines of engraving have spread; white paper looks blotchy.

Projected images

If you have one slide projector or, preferably, access to two, you have the means of producing fascinating combined-image effects. You can, for example, project slides on three-dimensional light colored objects to create strange visual mixtures. And by directing two projectors on one flat screen, you can montage with complete control. In each case, work in a darkened room and rephotograph your result using color or black and white film. For color, always shoot on tungsten-balanced stock to match the color temperature of the projectors.

Superimposing images
To combine slide images, direct two projectors on to a matte white cardboard screen. If the projectors have zoom lenses this will help you to adjust finely one image size in relation to the other. Project the images so that they superimpose, enlarging or shifting each until a promising composite forms. Unlike sandwiching (see p. 187) details of one image will appear in the darker parts of the other. Set up black cardboard near the projector lenses to shade parts of either image you want to exclude. Then photograph the screen, preferably with a long

lens so that the camera is far enough back not to block the projectors' light. Shoot at a small aperture to allow a long exposure time. During exposure, keep the cardboard moving to soften the edges of the shaded areas. Shift or zoom a projector if you want to form streaks.

Projections on solid objects
Collect a range of objects with simple, recognizable shapes. They should preferably have a matte white (not gloss) surface. Eggs, a paneled door, hands or a face, cups or jugs are all suitable. You can first spray items such as fruit and vegetables and other colored or patterned objects with matte white paint. Set up your objects

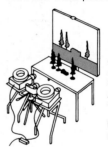

Shadow plus slide For the result below, the shadows of the model train and trees were cast on a screen, using a projector as light source. Another projector containing a slide of foliage was directed on the screen. Finally, the scene was photographed.

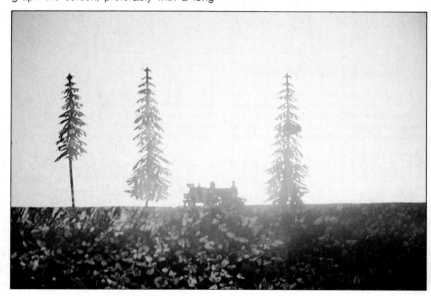

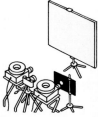

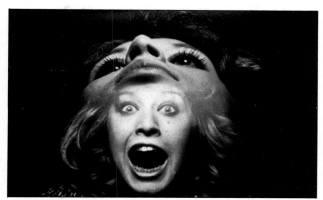

Two projected slides
This montage uses two slides projected separately. The lower half of one beam and the top half of the other were shaded.

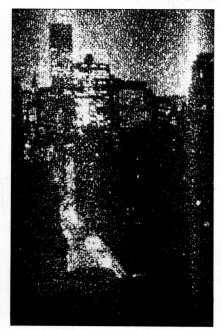

some way in front of a dark background. For the slide image, use a shot with an even, overall pattern. This might be foliage, printed lettering, cracked mud, or a crowd of distant faces.

Where you position the projector has a direct effect on the type of result you will achieve. For a straight effect you can project the slide flat on to the object from near the camera position. Oblique projection, on the other hand, makes the object look more three dimensional, but you may have to reflect some light back on the shadow side to avoid losing the full outline. Photograph your results with the camera on a tripod, and use a cable release. When measuring exposure move close enough for the projector-lit object to fill your picture.

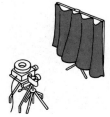

Projecting on coarse material For this picture, a slide of a city skyline at dusk was projected on silvery, draped curtain material. The camera was set up close to the projector to minimize shadows.

● Make sure that your camera, projectors, and screen are all firmly supported.
● Avoid combining a slide and object (or slide and slide) so that one image confuses the other. Keep one element very simple.
● Pick slides that are exposed correctly but contain plenty of shadow areas – dark rather than light backgrounds.

● Try projecting black and white and color negatives, and open-weave or perforated materials mounted as slides.
● You can keep adding projectors to contribute to your result. Eventually, light spill from each projector builds up in the room, turning black parts of the image gray.

HINTS AND TIPS

Multi-image techniques

Both the kaleidoscope and the strobo-scope produce several repeat, or near-repeat images on the same frame. A kaleidoscope uses a pair of mirrors, similar to a child's toy. A stroboscopic light gives regular flashes, and "chops up" movement into frozen, overlapping images. Both techniques can give results similar to images shot with multifacet attachments (see p. 186).

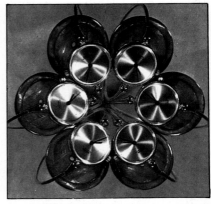

Making a kaleidoscope

For a kaleidoscope you need two flat nar-row mirrors set at an angle of 50°–60° to each other. Avoid glass-fronted mirrors as they produce blurred double reflections. Instead, use mirror foil mounted on flat sur-faces, or metal mirrors. Photograph ob-liquely along the mirrors toward a close, softly lit object. See if the joins in the pattern look best sharp or unsharp by viewing it at different apertures.

Symmetrical pattern
A flower-like repeat pattern was created from a watch and but-ton, using a kaleido-scope. Long mirrors and a wide lens aperture hide joins.

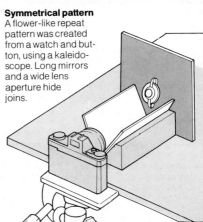

Using stroboscopic flash

For maximum multi-image effects, photo-graph a moving light-toned subject well forward of a dark background (outdoors at night, for example). Use a purpose-built strobing lamp, a flashgun with a multi-flash attachment (see p. 147), or studio flash set to stroboscopic mode. Place your camera on a tripod and set the correct aperture for one flash. Keep the shutter open long enough to take in a complete action.

Sequence shots For this effect a flashgun was fired several times from the far right of the figure, with the shutter locked open. It was taken in a darkened room with the camera on a tripod. The flash-gun, shielded from the background, was fired by the test button each time it recycled. The figure changed pose after each flash. For multi-images of con-tinuous action use a stroboscopic lamp or flash.

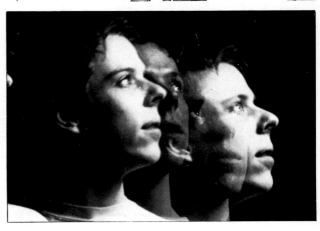

3D devices

It is possible to adapt a regular camera to make pictures which look three-dimensional. You will have to take a pair of photographs from different viewpoints to match the separation of human eyes. For a 3D effect, only the left-hand shot is viewed with the left eye, and the right-hand one with the right eye.

Shooting and viewing in 3D
Scenes that have elements at different distances showing strong perspective are most suitable for 3D, but avoid having anything extremely close to the lens. If your subject is static you can take one picture, then shift the camera about $2\frac{1}{2}$ ins (6 cm) sideways and take another. But for most subjects it is best to fit your standard lens with a simple stereo mirror attachment, or fire two cameras at once.

For individual viewing, mount prints in an old stereoscope. Or buy a special hand viewer to look at results from a stereo attachment (below). For group viewing of 3D slides you will need to use two separ-

ately filtered projectors. Focus the images on the screen, offset slightly. Filter one lens in red, the other in green. Or use polarizing filters set at different angles on each projector lens, and project the two transparencies on a metallic-type screen. Give your audience eyeglasses filtered in exactly the same way, so that each eye sees the light from one image only.

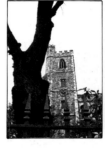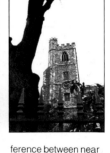

Stereo pair These pictures were taken from viewpoints several inches apart. Notice the parallax difference between near and far objects. When combined, your eyes see them as one three-dimensional image.

Paired cameras Tape two regular cameras baseplate to baseplate, with lenses about $2\frac{1}{2}$ ins (6 cm) apart. Focus both lenses, match exposure settings, then press both shutter releases at once.

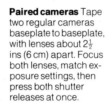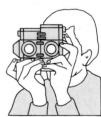

STEREO ATTACHMENT

This mirror box fits on the front of a standard lens. It records a pair of pictures from viewpoints $2\frac{1}{2}$ ins (6 cm) apart as vertical half-frame adjacent images on slide film. Slip your processed stereo slides into a similarly designed viewer. Each eye sees one half frame only and your brain fuses these into a single, three-dimensional picture.

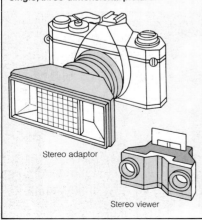

Stereo adaptor

Stereo viewer

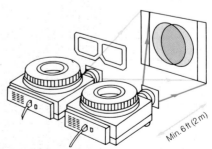

Stereo projection For a 3D slide show, project each slide from a stereo pair overlapped on the screen. Fit red and green color filters over each lens, and give the audience matching viewing glasses.

Min. 6 ft (2 m)

Unusual camera types

Certain non-standard 35 mm cameras will create unusual images. This is either a result of their special optics (panoramic cameras, for example), or because they are designed to take pictures in strange shooting conditions, such as from mid-air or underwater. Some specialized types are expensive and it is best to rent rather than buy them.

Unusual format cameras

Some so-called "panoramic-format" cameras are, in fact, no more than a conventional 35 mm compact with a wide-angle lens and the picture area masked down to form a long, narrow shape. You can achieve an identical effect with any print from a wide-angle shot trimmed top and bottom. True panoramic cameras, however, have a pivoting lens system that is combined with a slit that moves across the front of the film. Results resemble a long, horizontal section across a fisheye image (see p. 169), but they are not distorted in the vertical plane. A straight wall in the foreground will photograph as a curve, while a group of people curved around the camera will come out in a straight line. This panoramic distortion will disappear if you view the result on a long screen or with the print bowed into a deep, concave shape.

Cameras for special conditions

In some conditions, a regular 35 mm camera will not be operable. You will either have to purchase a special camera, or adapt your regular one for specialized use.

Underwater cameras are waterproof as far as a given depth and have lenses that are specially computed for use with water

TYPES OF PANORAMIC CAMERAS

There are two types of 35 mm panoramic cameras. One gives a 180° horizontal field of view, the other a full 360°. To minimize distortion, keep the camera top horizontal (a spirit level is built in). Avoid having objects very close to the camera, and omit any obvious straight lines. A special enlarger and projector are necessary (24 mm by either 65 mm or 152 mm), and results are viewed on a concave surface.

Panoramic pictures are mostly views or architectural record photography. But you can also use panoramic cameras to create strange images. Try shifting the camera or subject while the lens pivots and scans the scene. Or point the camera upward to give a dipped horizon, downward for a hill-shaped one. And for a lozenge-shaped subject, shoot a vertical format close-up of a standing figure from waist height.

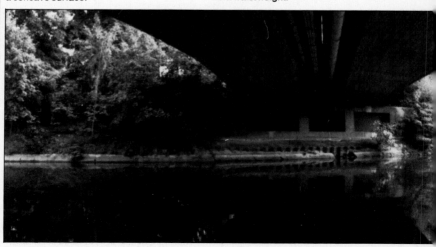

Telephone line transmitter

Video monitor

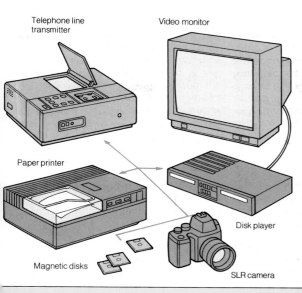

Paper printer

Disk player

Magnetic disks

SLR camera

Still video These cameras (or special backs for regular 35 mm SLR cameras) don't use conventional chemical photographic film, instead they record pictures electronically. A CCD chip forms the light-sensitive surface, and picture signals from this chip record onto a 47 mm diameter magnetic disk housed in the camera back. Each disk records 50 images which can be played back immediately through a TV, printed by ink or photography onto paper, or transmitted over distances by telephone line. Any picture can be erased and its place on the disk reused. At present, the final image quality is poorer than the coarsest-grained conventional film, and the equipment is very expensive.

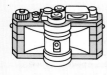

180° Widelux The lens and its rear slit pivot to scan the subject during exposure (left). Keep your fingers out of the marked areas either side of the lens. It is most useful for landscape photography (below).

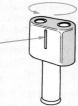

360° Globuscope This spring-wound camera (left) makes one complete rotation on its handle support during each exposure. The film is driven behind a slit. Take special care not to appear in every photograph.

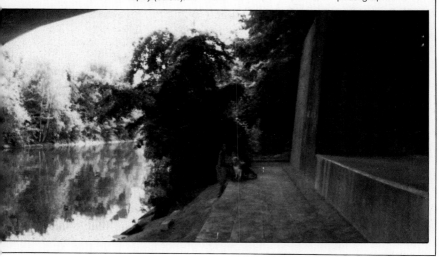

on one side and air on the other. On land they have a wider angle of view, and often poorer definition, than a normal lens. In general, you should use these cameras with a special underwater flashgun (held as far to one side as possible, to minimize reflections from particles in the water). Underwater housings for regular 35 mm cameras are also available. The controls on these underwater cameras are especially enlarged to allow easier operation when submerged. All read-outs tend to be large also for easy visibility.

Cameras for 35 mm aerial and sports-participant photography should have re-mote control facilities. Often the unit has an electrical firing system and is adapted to allow use of a more convenient, separate viewfinder system.

A few cameras are specially designed for scientific analysis of high-speed events. They shoot at rates of up to 1000 pictures per second on continuously-moving film loaded in bulk lengths. The results that they produce isolate sights we do not see normally – frozen sequences of missiles in flight, explosions, and other violent chemical changes. Often, these cameras utilize a rapidly rotating mirror to "flash" the image on to the film.

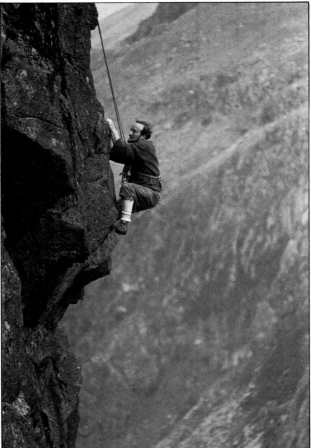

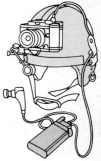

Helmet camera This adapted SLR (above) has an optical sight to replace the viewfinder. Use it for active sports shots (left).

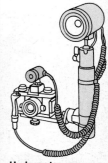

Underwater camera The camera unit and flashgun above have special lens optics and body seals for use down to 164 ft (50 m).

REFERENCE CHARTS

This final section contains tables and charts concerning some of the main sections of the book. Here you will find condensed advice on choosing new or secondhand equipment and the possible markets for selling photographs if you wish to try and make your photography pay for itself.

Brands of 35 mm film are listed in more detail in this section and there are also suggested exposure settings for unusual subject and lighting conditions. And if you want to use your camera for instant pictures the necessary film types and user-processing techniques are included. Similarly, anyone contemplating the purchase of a zoom lens should look at the relevant comparative chart to see the range of focal lengths and maximum apertures typically on offer. This is also where you will find manufacturers' reference numbers for a wide range of filters for color and black and white.

Flash data compares the technical performance of flashguns of different sizes and power. It includes a chart of how automatic and dedicated units program their light output to ensure correct exposure.

Finally, there is a glossary that concentrates on the practical and colloquial terms used in everyday photography.

Camera information

CHOOSING A CAMERA

New cameras

General Is it comfortable to handle and carry? Scope of system – has it a good range of lenses and accessories?

Degree of automation Choose from totally automatic to full range of manual options. Does exposure metering system offer mode or modes you need?

Controls Has it a good range of shutter speeds, apertures, ISO ratings? Can controls be accidentally mis-set or altered?

Viewing Look at size and clarity of image in viewfinder. Is subject area recorded on film shown accurately? Does it have an aperture preview button?

Other features Has it built-in flash? A tripod bush? Is there a battery check facility?

Secondhand (additional features)

General Look out for body dents or deep scratches, damaged or loose screwheads, peeling leathercloth or signs of poor repairs.

Mechanical Assess smoothness of all functions. Is SLR lens mounting damaged? Are strap lugs bent or thin? Fire at all shutter speeds, looking through camera back.

Controls Compare meter with another TTL or hand meter. Are ISO shutter speed and f number settings firm? Lens diaphragm should form aperture of same shape and size each time, at a given setting.

Lens Examine state of barrel, body coupling, filter thread. Look for abrasion. Dirt within lens indicates amateur repairs.

Other features Look inside battery compartment for corrosion. Are spares available?

SLR FOCUSING SCREENS

(See also general-purpose types on p. 178)

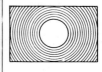

Matte screen Fresnel rings (for improving evenness) absent in central zone. Use zone for fine focusing all lenses at any aperture.

All-matte surface with grid lines For vertical and horizontal picture alignment. Useful for architectural work (shift lens), copying, and close-ups. Suitable for focusing all lens types.

All-matte screen with central engraved cross-hairs Transparency helps compensate for dim images in close-up and macrophotography. Focus on cross-hairs first.

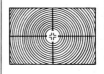

Matte screen with Fresnel rings, clear center zone and cross lines For copying – easy to center originals. Suits all lenses.

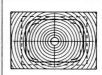

Standard screen, less microprism ring Marked out for TV and movie formats. Used to take still shots to fit these media.

Clear glass, with microprism center Gives extremely bright finder image – useful for dimly-lit conditions, but cannot show depth of field effects. Causes some meters to give false reading.

SHUTTER SPEEDS

Longest exposure time to prevent blurred movement

Subject speed	Typical subject	Distance from camera (feet/meters)		Toward lens	45° to lens	90° to lens
		50 mm lens	150 mm lens			
Under 5 mph	Flowers, grasses, pedestrians, babies, children, walkers, crowds	4/1.25	12½/3.75	1/250	1/500	1/1000
		8¼/2.5	25/7.5	1/125	1/250	1/500
		16½/5	49/15	1/60*	1/125	1/250
		33/10	98½/30	1/30*	1/60*	1/125
		66/20	197/60	1/15*	1/30*	1/60*
5-20 mph	Runners, cyclists, cars in traffic, medium pace sports	16½/5	49/15	1/500	1/1000	1/2000
		33/10	98½/30	1/250	1/500	1/1000
		66/20	197/60	1/125	1/250	1/500
		98½/30	295/90	1/60*	1/125	1/250

*Not advisable for 150 mm – gives camera shake.

The figures above are an approximate guide, and assume that pictures are not enlarged beyond enprint size. They show how blur depends upon focal length as well as subject speed and direction. A 150 mm lens gives an image three times as large as a 50 mm lens and produces the equivalent blur at three times the distance.

HOW ELECTRONIC FOCUSING AIDS WORK

Infrared autofocus This self-activating device works even in darkness. A motor (or first pressure on the release) shifts lens focus and scans the scene with an IR beam. When a narrow-angle sensor on the camera receives maximum reflected signal from the scene focusing and scanning stop and the shutter fires automatically.

Passive rangefinder autofocus This system requires some ambient light to operate. The shutter release or a motor alters lens focus and pivots one of two rangefinder mirrors. Electronic cells compare contrast patterns given by the mirrored views, halting the focusing movement of the lens when they match.

Phase detection SLR autofocus With this system, part of the center of the image is projected under the mirror and split in two onto a multi-segment CCD sensor. Relative locations of the two images change with the lens position (see below). The CCD strip "phase detects" this separation and calculates the lens focusing movement necessary for a sharp image. A fully focusing single lens reflex camera may have an in-body motor to change lens position, or motors in each interchangeable lens. A green light alongside the focusing screen signals when the image is in sharp focus. In dim light conditions, a dedicated flashgun gives a pre-flash pulse of IR light so that the IR-sensitive CCD can still auto-focus before the shot is taken.

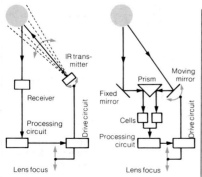

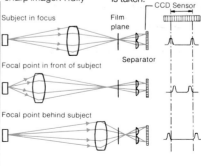

Film and exposure data

There are several systems in use for numbering film speed. IS0 (International Standards Organization) figures are now the most common speed figures given on film bought in the West. ISO figures combine the older ASA (American Standards Association) and DIN (Deutsche Industrie Norm) figures (as shown in the table right). Sometimes the first ISO figure only (i.e. the old ASA number) is shown on film boxes. In the former USSR and Eastern bloc countries, the Russian standardizing authority speed rating – GOST figures – are often given instead.

Amateur and professional film types
Films described as professional types are manufactured to meet exacting tolerances. They are designed to give the best results under professional working conditions.

EQUIVALENT SPEED RATINGS			
ASA	DIN	ISO	GOST
12	12	12/12°	11
25	15	25/15°	22
32	16	32/16°	28
64	19	64/19°	56
100	21	100/21°	90
125	22	125/22°	110
160	23	160/23°	140
200	24	200/24°	180
400	27	400/27°	360
650	29	650/29°	560
800	30	800/30°	720
1000	31	1000/31°	900
1250	32	1250/32°	1125
3200	36	3200/36°	2880

PROGRAMMED EXPOSURE SETTINGS

Automatic-only cameras and multimode cameras set on "Program" (P) work through a sequence of shutter and aperture changes to suit different subject and lighting conditions. Sequences differ in detail with brand. Semi-automatic cameras offering multimode often use the following codes. Set A on the lens aperture ring to get a shutter-priority exposure system, and set A on the shutter speed dial for an aperture-priority exposure. Selecting both A settings gives "Program" – the camera's completely automatic exposure system. When neither A is in use, the camera will be in manual and you decide settings.

Program design
These graphs show two programs. Adjustments (right to left) occur as the meter reads progressively dimmer light. One program (solid line) alternates speed and f numbers. Another (broken line) uses faster speeds more, to suit a telephoto lens.

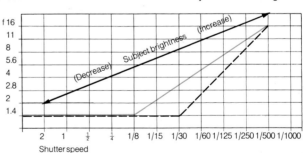

EXPOSURES FOR DIFFICULT LIGHTING (ISO 100 FILM)					
	Shutter	Aperture		Shutter	Aperture
Domestic interior, night (average)	1/15	f 1.4	Lightning at night, aerial fireworks (hold open shutter)	Duration of event	f 8–16
Store window at night	1/15	f 4	Floodlit buildings, fountains	½ sec	f 2.8
Brightly-lit street at night	1/15	f 2.8			
Scene with full moon, late dusk	1/30	f 8	Theater – fully lit stage	1/30	f 2.8
Landscape lit by full moon	2–10 min	f 4	spotlit acts	1/60	f 2.8

This assumes refrigerated storage, controlled lighting contrast, and prompt processing for precise results. With some brands, different versions are made for best performance under slow or fast shutter speed exposure conditions. The performance of all amateur films is less precise, but they are better at handling wide-ranging subjects and lighting conditions on the same roll. And they are more resistant to changes when stored for long periods. Retail laboratories have printing equipment geared to amateur color negative films. So unless you do your own printing or use professional laboratories, results from professional films may be less satisfactory.

Reciprocity compensation

Halving exposure time and doubling the brightness (opening up one f stop) should

FILM TYPES					
Brand name	**ISO**	**Comments**	**Brand name**	**ISO**	**Comments**
Color negative			Kodak HIE Infrared	50	Infrared sensitive
Kodak Gold 100	100	Wide exposure latitude	Agfapan 100	100	Wide exposure latitude
Agfacolor Optima 200	200	Modern high resolution emulsion	Ilford FP4	125	
Kodak Gold 400	400		Ilford HP5	400	Can be push-processed to 1000
Fujicolor 400	400	Good push-processing characteristics	Kodak T-Max P3200	3200	Grainy. Will push process to 50,000
Ektar 1000	1000	High speed, minimal grain structure	Ilford XP2	400	Dye image film (process in color negative solutions)
Fujicolor 1600	1600		Agfa Dia-Direct	32	Slide film
Color slide			Kodalith Ortho Type 3	12	Line image (Lith developer)
Kodachrome 25	25	Finest resolution slide film	**Instant picture**		
Fujichrome 50D	50	Extremely fine grain	Polaroid Polachrome	40	Color slide, micro grid structure
Kodachrome 64	64	More contrasty than 25 type	Polaroid Polapan	125	B/W slide, normal contrast
Agfachrome RS100	100		Polaroid Polagraph	400	B/W slide, line image
Ektachrome 160T	160	Tungsten light balanced	**Professional color negatives**		
Fujichrome 200	200		Vericolor Type L	160	For long exposures, tungsten
Ektachrome 400HC	400	Good in mixed lighting	Vericolor Type S	160	For short exposures
Agfachrome 1000RS	1000	Can be push-processed to 3200	**Professional color slides**		
Ektachrome Infrared	100	False color film. Special E-4 processing	Ektachrome 400X	400	Fine grain
Black and white			Fuji Velvia	50	Strong colors, high resolution
Kodak Technical Pan	25	Extreme fine grain. Also usable for high contrast	Ektachrome P800/1600	1600	Designed for pushed processing
Ilford Pan F	50	Can be processed as slides			

give film the same exposure. In practice, this reciprocal relationship between shutter speed and lens aperture settings holds good until you set a speed longer than about 1 second. Then films behave as if slower in speed. It is best to compensate for this by opening the aperture – setting a longer time compounds reciprocity failure. Color response may also change slightly, so use a pale compensation filter. The exact effect varies according to film brand (see below). With subjects like night shots or landscapes at dusk a slight shift of color will often go unnoticed, and you will probably bracket exposures anyway. Bracket in the direction of more exposure rather than less. But for critical work, look at the reciprocity data for your film. Black and white films tend to increase slightly in contrast at long exposure times, as well as losing speed. To compensate for this, you should reduce the development time.

EXAMPLES OF RECIPROCITY FAILURE

Color slide film			Color negative film			Black and white negative film		
Shutter speed (sec)	Aperture increase	Filter	Shutter speed (sec)	Aperture increase	Filter	Shutter speed (sec)	Aperture increase	Reduce dev. time
Kodachrome 25			**Gold 400**			**Tri-X 400**		
1	½	—	1	½	—	1	1	10%
10	1½	CC10M	10	1	—	10	2	20%
100	Not recommended		100	Not recommended		100	3	30%
Ektachrome 400			**VR 1000**					
1	½	—	1	1	CC10G			
10	1½	CC10C	10	2	CC20G			
100	2½	CC10C	100	3	CC30G +10B			
Fuji Velvia								
1	—	—						
10	½	CC10M						
100	Not recommended							

POLAROID AUTOPROCESSING

You have to process instant 35 mm films yourself. To do this you need an autoprocessor unit. These are similar in size to a bulk film loader. Each instant film is sold with its own processing pack – a box containing processing fluid and a film-wide roll of plastic strip sheet. In the machine, the chemically-coated strip sheet is laminated to the sensitive face of the exposed film, and they are wound together onto a large take-up spool. After about 60 seconds film movement is reversed, rewinding the processed film into its cassette and the strip sheet into its disposable box. The strip sheet takes with it the wetted top layer of the film. Now you can open the unit, remove the cassette and pull from it a dry completely processed slide film, ready to cut up and mount for projection.

Processing procedure The pack and cassette fit into autoprocessor (right). Attach protruding ends of strip sheet and film to a clip on take-up spool, which hinges open for loading. Close take-up spool and light-tight lid, then wind film and strip sheet on to spool. After 60 sec reverse transport, and open unit.

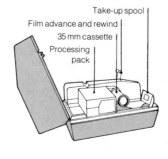

Take-up spool

Film advance and rewind

35 mm cassette

Processing pack

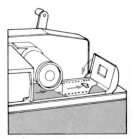

Lens charts

DEPTH OF FIELD LIMITS

The chart below shows changes in the limits of depth of field when you change either aperture or lens focal length. Figures are computed for one focus setting only – with closer subjects you get less depth of field, and more distant settings give you greater depth. Assume infinity (∞) is the distant horizon. These figures hold good provided you do not make enlargements beyond about 8 x 10 ins (20 x 25 cm). Larger prints demand higher standards of negative sharpness, and this means a reduction in depth of field.

DEPTH OF FIELD (LENS FOCUSED AT 10 FT/3 M)

Lens	Aperture settings		
	f 2.8	**f 4**	**f 5.6**
28 mm	$7\frac{1}{4}$-$13\frac{1}{2}$ ft (2.3-4.1 m)	$6\frac{1}{2}$-19 ft (2-5.8 m)	6-$31\frac{1}{4}$ ft (1.8-9.5 m)
50 mm	9-11 ft (2.7-3.4 m)	$8\frac{1}{2}$-$11\frac{1}{2}$ ft (2.6-3.5 m)	$8\frac{1}{4}$-$12\frac{1}{4}$ ft (2.5-3.7 m)
85 mm	$9\frac{1}{2}$-$10\frac{1}{2}$ ft (2.9-3.2 m)	$9\frac{1}{4}$-$10\frac{3}{4}$ ft (2.8-3.3 m)	9-11 ft (2.7-3.4 m)
135 mm	10-$10\frac{1}{4}$ ft (3-3.1 m)	10-$10\frac{1}{2}$ ft (3-3.2 m)	9-$10\frac{3}{4}$ ft (2.7-3.3 m)
200 mm	—	$9\frac{1}{2}$-$10\frac{1}{4}$ ft (2.9-3.1 m)	$9\frac{1}{4}$-$10\frac{1}{2}$ ft (2.8-3.2 m)
Lens	**Aperture settings**		
	f 8	**f 11**	**f 16**
28 mm	5 ft (1.5 m)-∞	4 ft (1.3 m)-∞	$3\frac{1}{4}$ ft (1 m)-∞
50 mm	$7\frac{1}{4}$-$13\frac{1}{2}$ ft (2.3-4.1 m)	$7\frac{1}{2}$-$16\frac{1}{2}$ ft (2.2-5 m)	$6\frac{1}{2}$-23 ft (2-7 m)
85 mm	$8\frac{1}{2}$-12 ft (2.6-3.6 m)	$8\frac{1}{4}$-13 ft (2.5-4 m)	8-18 ft (2.4-5.5 m)
135 mm	9-11 ft (2.7-3.4 m)	$8\frac{1}{2}$-12 ft (2.6-3.6 m)	$8\frac{1}{4}$-13 ft (2.5-4 m)
200 mm	$9\frac{1}{4}$-$10\frac{3}{4}$ ft (2.8-3.3 m)	9-11 ft (2.7-3.4 m)	$8\frac{1}{2}$-$11\frac{1}{2}$ ft (2.6-3.5 m)

ZOOM LENS LIMITS

The main design challenges for zoom lens makers are to offer wide-ranging focal lengths, give an image quality as good as regular lenses, allow a wide maximum aperture, and also maintain focus and f number settings over the full zoom range. Most manufacturers sacrifice f number to avoid a bulky, expensive lens. Typically, you lose up to two f numbers at the longest focal length setting (see below). This is taken into account by the camera's exposure measuring system. Zoom lenses fitted into compact cameras are coupled to zoom viewfinders, and this forms another limiting factor.

TYPICAL ZOOM LENS RANGE

Focal length (mm)

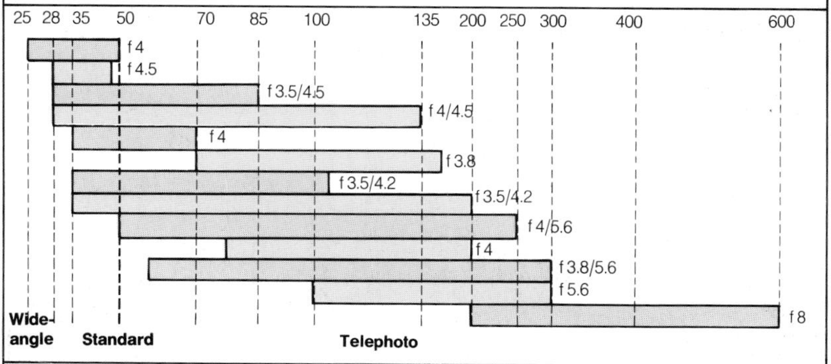

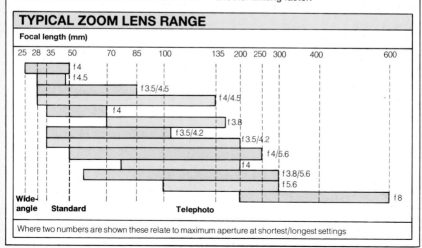

Where two numbers are shown these relate to maximum aperture at shortest/longest settings

Filter choices and uses

The Kodak color balancing filters in the table below are mainly intended for color slide photography. Always try to use film balanced as closely as possible to the color of your lighting. The more filters necessary, the more likely it is that colors will not be fully corrected. And multiple use of filters can often upset lens definition. Color balancing filters are still desirable, but not essential, with color negative materials.

All filters absorb some light, so you must give extra exposure. The increase necessary is expressed in filter factors (not shown for the filters below). The difference is automatically taken into account by the camera meter if it reads through the filter. However, you must act on these factors when using a hand meter.

Strong special effects filters

These filters are intended for use with black and white film to increase contrast between colors which otherwise reproduce as similar tones of gray. In color photography they give strong overall casts for dramatic effects. Split (dual color) filters combine

KODAK COLOR BALANCING FILTERS

Light source	Filters for accurate colors on Daylight film	Tungsten film
Daylight	—	85B
Daylight (overcast)	81A	85B+81A
Flash (electronic)	—	85B
Flashbulb (blue)	—	85B
3200 K lamps	80A	—
3400 K photolamps	80B	81A
Fluorescent tubes*		
"Daylight"	40M+30Y	85B+30M
"White"	20C+30M	40M+40Y
"Cool white"	30M	50M+60Y
"Cool white deluxe"	30C+20M	10M+30Y

*Suggested starting point for tests – color often alters with age

FILTERS FOR BLACK AND WHITE AND COLOR

Function	Appearance	Kodak refs	Hoya refs	Factor	Uses
Absorbs UV only	Clear		UV (0)	—	Reduces blueness of distant haze
Absorbs UV (haze)	Pale pink	1A	Skylight 1B	—	As above, stronger
Neutral density	Pale gray	ND .03	ND x 2	x 2	To reduce light and allow slow shutter or wide aperture without overexposure
	Mid-gray	ND .06	ND x 4	x 4	
	Dark gray	ND .09	ND x 8	x 8	
	Very dark gray	ND .2		x 100	
Polarizer	Mid-gray	POLA	PL	x 3	Controls reflections, darkens skies
Passes UV only	Black	18A	Variable		Fluorescent photography
Passes IR only	Black	87	Variable		IR shots, flash

two contrasting strong colors, matched so that each half has the same exposure increase factor. Factors of strong filters can vary with the light source you use. Blue or green filters have a higher factor in tungsten light but red filters may need more exposure in daylight.

Pale filters

The pale color-compensating filters below are all made as small gelatin sheets. They are designed to "warm up" or "cool down" color schemes, or to correct small variations in lighting or film batches. CC filters are particularly useful for color slides. For example, if you find that your first results are too blue, view them through a yellow or pink filter. Find the filter strength which makes the mid-tones in the slide look neutral gray. Then reshoot using a filter half this strength over the camera lens. In general, you can ignore filter factors – the highest exposure increase with a CC 50B filter is only x1.3. With color negative materials these filters can be used to make adjustments at the printing stage.

DEEP COLOR FILTERS

Filter color	Kodak ref	Hoya ref	Approximate filter factor (daylight)	(tungsten)
Yellow	8	K2	x 2	x 2
Deeper yellow	12		x 2	x 2
Yellow/green	11	X1	x 4	x 4
Deeper green	58	Green	x 7	x 5
Blue	47	Blue	x 9	x 20
Orange	16	Orange	x 2.5	x 2
Red	25	25A	x 8	x 4
Deeper red	29		x 20	x 8

KODAK CC FILTERS

Tint	Strengths
Magenta (reduces green)	CC 05M 10M 20M 30M 40M 50M
Yellow (reduces blue)	CC 05Y 10Y 20Y 30Y 40Y 50Y
Cyan (reduces red)	CC 05C 10C 20C 30C 40C 50C
Greenish (reduces blue, red)	CC 05G 10G 20G 30G 40G 50G
Bluish (reduces green, red)	CC 05B 10B 20B 30B 40B 50B
Pink (reduces blue, green)	CC 05R 10R 20R 30R 40R 50R

POLARIZED LIGHT

Rays of light vibrate in all directions at right angles to their direction of travel – as in the unpolarized ray shown below. Light reflected from a polished, non-metallic surface suppresses – "polarizes" – these vibrations in all but one plane. The angles at which light is most polarized are fairly narrow, and vary with the material – for glass it is 33°, for water 37°. Air molecules in clear sky will also partly polarize light. This effect is strongest in blue sky areas at 90° to the direction of the sunlight. A polarizing filter acts like a slatted gate – orientate it in parallel with the remaining plane in polarized light to allow illumination to pass. If you turn it at right angles, it dims this light relative to unpolarized illumination.

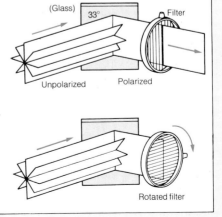

(Glass) 33° Filter

Unpolarized   Polarized

Rotated filter

Flash data

The distance of the light source is important when exposing for flash. The chart (right) shows how illumination from undiffused flash falls off quite abruptly. In a scene that contains objects at different distances, if flash exposure is correct at $2\frac{3}{4}$ ft (0.8 m), anything 2 ft (0.6 m) from the flash will be overexposed, and anything beyond $4\frac{1}{4}$ ft (1.3 m) underexposed.

Sunlight is quite different – on a clear day nearby rocks give the same exposure reading as similar rocks on a distant mountain. Although the light is hard and direct in each case, the difference in brightness fall-off is a result of the relative distance of the source.

Flashgun performance data
The comparative chart (facing page) shows the performance of a typical range of flash-guns. Size and price decrease from left to

EXPOSURE WITH FLASH

GN = 14 (m)	Flash to subject distance in meters (ISO 100 film)		
Lens aperture	Over-exposed 1 stop at	Correctly exposed at	Under-exposed 1 stop at
f 2	5	7	9.8
f 2.8	3.5	5	7
f 4	2.5	3.5	5
f 5.6	1.8	2.5	3.5
f 8	1.3	1.8	2.5
f 11	0.8	1.3	1.8
f 16	0.6	0.8	1.3
GN = 30 (m)			
f 2	10.6	15	21
f 2.8	7.5	10.6	15
f 4	5.3	7.5	10.6
f 5.6	3.7	5.3	7.5
f 8	2.7	3.7	5.3
f 11	1.9	2.7	3.7
f 16	1.3	1.9	2.7

FLASH PROGRAMS

Self-regulating gun
The chart below shows settings offered by a clip-on, self-regulating flashgun with a guide number of 32 (m). Each ISO rating you set offers three f number settings. Choose an f number to adjust the sensor response and then select one of three

programs. Each alters the flash duration between 1/1000 and 1/30,000 over a different set of distances. If you change the flashgun to the manual setting, you must keep to the distance the chart shows for 1/1000 sec flash to ensure the correct exposure.

Dedicated flash This chart shows the settings made when you use a dedicated flashgun with a GN of 32 on a TTL meter camera that reads exposure off the film. Setting the film ISO adjusts the relationship of f number settings to meter sensitivity. You can select any lens

f number and the meter will adjust flash duration to give consistent exposure within the range of subject distances shown below, right.

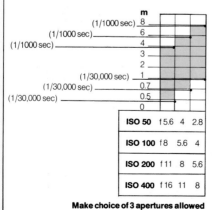

Make choice of 3 apertures allowed

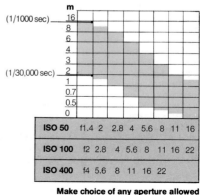

Make choice of any aperture allowed

right, together with light output. Mains-operated studio flash units offer much higher guide numbers (typically 120–160). Guide numbers and calculating data are usually given in metric measurements only. The smaller the gun, the more limited the range of self-regulated flash duration it provides, and the slower the recycling time. However, the shortest recycling times are only possible when a fraction of full power is used per flash (for example, when working close-up).

Fill-in flash

The sequence below shows some of the ways you can use a separate, self-regulating flashgun to give flash fill-in exposures in contrasty existing light. Flash is either mounted on the camera or used frontally close to the lens. In general, a 4:1 ratio (four times more existing light than flash) will give the most naturalistic result. This guide doesn't apply to cameras that read flash exposure off the film surface. If you want to find out the percentage of light absorbed by any diffusing material, compare exposure readings with and without the diffuser over the meter cell.

Sometimes it is useful to group flash heads together and use them as a single, powerful light source – for example, if filling shadows in a large room when bright daylight is entering through windows. With two heads, multiply guide number for one unit by 1.4. When you group three heads, multiply guide number by 2.

COMPARATIVE FLASHGUN RANGE

Guide number: (m) ISO 100	48	38	30	24	20	16	14	12
Auto f number range	2.8-8	2.8-11	2.8-5.6	2.8-4	4	4	4	4
Flash duration	1/30,000-1/300	1/30,000-1/800	1/30,000-1/1000	1/30,000-1/2000	1/30,000-1/2000	1/30,000-1/2000	1/30,000-1/2000	1/2000-1/500
Recycling time (sec), alkaline batteries	0.2-10	0.2-8	0.2-10	0.5-8.5	0.5-8	7	7	10
Number of flashes per battery set	250-3500	140-800	120-700	140-800	130-740	200	200	150

FILL-IN FLASH GUIDE

For a non-dedicated, self-regulating flashgun

	For 4:1 ratio	For 2:1 ratio	For 1:1 ratio
First **Camera meter** By measuring the existing lighting on subject find f number for correct exposure when shutter set to maximum sync speed (or slower). If using compact with lens shutter, choose any speed.	**Then** **Flash unit (set manual)** Use at quarter power, or at twice the distance, or diffuse with material that absorbs 75 per cent of the light necessary for correct flash exposure at f number shown left.	Use at half power, or at 1.3x distance, or diffuse with material that absorbs 50 per cent of light necessary for correct flash exposure at f number, far left.	Use at full power, and at correct distance for correct flash exposure at f number shown far left.
	Flash unit (set auto) Set to four times correct ISO, or set auto for f number two stops smaller than f number shown left.	Set to double correct ISO, or set auto for f number one stop smaller than f number shown far left.	Set correct ISO and auto for f number shown far left.

Selling your photographs

Photography is such a universal medium that markets exist for all kinds of good pictures – taken by amateurs as well as by professionals. Newspaper "scoops", advertising campaign shots and various other glamorous, highly-paid assignments are well-known. But more sales are made of less publicized, wide-ranging types of image – pictures which inform, educate, decorate and record.

Different markets

Markets range from portrait and wedding photography for friends, to pictures for magazines, newspapers, books, and every kind of printed material. Some photographs sell in galleries and print shops as fine art. Television, video tape and disk production is becoming a major picture consumer too.

Annuals for photographers and writers are available in most countries. They list publications and agencies, and outline the kind of work they will buy. You will find that there is a potential market for almost every picture you take. However, it is better to specialize if you have interests and knowledge of particular subjects which you can combine with your photography. Often the best sports, natural history, mountaineering and underwater pictures are produced by individuals who know these subjects and situations well.

Slides or prints

The vast majority of published color pictures are reproduced from slides, not prints. This is partly because sophisticated electronic equipment for turning photographs into ink printing plates was originally developed for slides. And the detail and color quality of the original film exposed in the camera is difficult to match. Black and white pictures are reproduced from glossy-faced prints.

You will need some means of carrying around and presenting slides – preferably in multi-pocket transparent film sheets which are easy to hold up to the light. Duplicate slides are suitable for reference, but the original is essential for actual reproduction. In order to allow you to offer it to two places at once, make "original dupes" at the time of shooting, taking several identical shots. And consider shooting both horizontal and vertical versions. Often a sale is lost because the picture must fit a vertical space, and you can only offer a horizontal format.

Selling your work

It is far better to visit potential buyers of your work than to send it in by post. You may not make a sale, but you may get a great deal of constructive comment from an art editor. Do your homework first – make sure that you have seen the sort of material that the client produces, and know the kind of market they serve. Then select and make up an appropriate portfolio of your work.

Some photographers prefer to sell work through picture agencies. The agency can hold a volume of your work and place it with customers you would not find yourself. Agencies take over all the selling side, giving you more time to take pictures. But for this service they take 50–60 per cent of the proceeds. Most agencies only take on photographers with a reasonable volume of good-quality pictures. Some agencies specialize – in sports, personalities, or the arts, for example. Others are much more general, and you should show a good selection of timeless subjects.

Copyright and model release

Copyright law varies from country to country. In general, copyright of a photograph belongs to the photographer. The exception is when you are commissioned to take the pictures. Then you may be asked to agree that copyright belongs to the client, even though you retain the originals.

When you sell a picture for publication, you usually agree a single reproduction right. Then you can sell the picture again to someone else, or use it for some other purpose. Only very occasionally is copyright sold outright, and this commands a much larger fee. (Always avoid photography competitions that take the copyright from the winners, unless, of course, the prizes offered are exceptionally large.)

If you have used amateur or professional models in any picture, ask them to sign a suitable model release form, below. This is unnecessary if people in the picture are clearly "part of the general scene", as in a candid street photograph, for example.

also have the responsibility of taking care of these picture masters, and locating them speedily when required. A good filing system is important for all of your work. Make sure that negatives, contact prints, and slides are identifiable.

Assignments

When photographs are commissioned, rather than bought "off the file", payment is usually agreed on a daily basis, or as a fee for the overall job. In addition, general expenses are paid. Always obtain an agreement in writing before starting. Even when the client owns the copyright, you should expect to supply all reprints from negatives, or duplicates from slides. You

Scaling pictures

Sometimes you may be asked to take photographs to fill an area of different proportions to the usual 2:3 ratio of a full 35 mm frame. If your camera allows access to the focusing screen, you can mark out new picture limits with a grease pencil. Some focusing screens (see p. 200) are made with limits ready marked out for movie-frame and television-format pictures.

Model release form

Photographer _____ **Date** _____

Description of photographs _____
_____
_____

Neg/Slide Refs: _____

For consideration received, I agree that the whole copyright (including all rights of reproduction) in the photograph(s) above belongs to ....
I also agree that all licensees and assignees are entitled to use the photograph(s) described above in any manner or form whatsoever, either wholly or in part, in any medium, and in conjunction with any working or other photographs or drawings, for any purpose worldwide. I understand that unless I agree that my name is published, used or referred to in connection with the photograph(s), the photographs or words published with them will not be attributed to me personally.

* I am over the age of majority

* I am the parent or guardian of....................
and I consent to these conditions.

* Delete which ever does not apply

Name _____ **Date** _____
Signature _____
Address _____

Model release form
It is always a good idea to ask portrait sitters to sign a form, such as the one on the left, either in return for a fee or prints. Sometime later you may have the chance to sell the picture. A release is then required, but it may be difficult to contact your original model. The form can also include some protection for the model against the picture's misuse.

Glossary

Ambient light See Available light.

Angle of view The amount of subject included in the picture. Expressed as the angle made between lines drawn to the camera from the two extremities (opposite corners) of picture contents. Alters with change of focal length. Wide-angle lenses have a wider angle of view than telephoto lenses.

Aperture Circular hole in front of or within a lens that restricts the amount of light passing through the lens to the photographic material. On the majority of lenses the size of the aperture can be varied, and controlled by an iris diaphragm. This can be set to a series of "stops" calibrated in f numbers by rotating an external ring.

Aperture preview Looking at the image with the aperture stopped down to the setting you intend to use when taking the picture. Allows visual assessment of depth of field.

Aperture-priority mode Semi-automatic camera exposure system in which the user selects the aperture, and the camera meter then automatically sets the shutter speed.

ASA American Standards Association. Denotes a speed system with which manufacturers may "rate" their film in terms of its sensitivity to light. Now superseded by ISO.

Available light General term applying to light normally occurring in a scene, not supplemented by illumination intended specifically for photography.

Backlighting Artificial or natural lighting coming toward the camera from behind the subject.

Bellows Concertina-type folding fabric tube that fits between lens and SLR camera body. Allows continuous forward extension of the lens when focusing very close subjects.

Bracketing The technique of shooting a number of pictures of the same subject and viewpoint at different exposure levels in order to obtain the most accurate result.

B setting Shutter setting at which the shutter will remain open for as long as the release is kept depressed.

Cable release Flexible cable used for firing the shutter. Particularly useful for slow shutter speeds and time exposures, when touching the camera may cause shake.

Cassette Cylindrical metal or plastic film spool container. A light trap allows handling and film threading in the camera in daylight.

Cast Overall bias toward one color in a color photograph.

CC filters Pale color conversion filters, used in various hues and degrees of saturation for correcting or inducing color casts when shooting.

Color balance Adjustment in color photographic processes ensuring the accuracy of subject color rendering under lighting of a particular color temperature.

Color temperature Convenient way of expressing the color content of a white light source. Typically, sunlight is 5,400K. Redder household lamps are about 2,800K.

Complementary color The hue most opposite to a given color. For blue, green, and red light complementaries are yellow, magenta, and cyan, respectively.

Contact print Negative-sized photograph made by exposing the printing paper in direct contact with the negative.

Continuous-tone image Pictures that have a continuous range of graduated tones.

Contrast The range of tones in a photograph and their graduation. Extremely bright highlights and dark shadows with few intermediate tones give high contrast. Opposite features produce low contrast.

Correction filter Filter used in front of the camera lens to correct differences between the color temperature of the subject lighting and the color balance of the film.

Cropping Removing unwanted areas of an image by trimming a print or masking a slide.

Cyan Blue-green subtractive color, complementary to red.

Dedicated flash Flashgun designed for use with a specific camera or group of cameras. It links directly into the internal camera circuitry, for example reprogramming the shutter, using the TTL meter, receiving ISO data.

Delayed action Operation of the shutter some time after the release is depressed. Most shutters have a delayed action timer built in.

Density The darkness of a photographic image. A "dense" image is excessively dark. A "thin" image is too pale.

Depth of field The distance between the nearest and furthest point from the camera within which subject details record with acceptable sharpness at any one focus and aperture setting.

Development Key stage in processing, by which the exposed parts of the image become different in appearance to unexposed parts.

Diaphragm See Aperture

Diffuser Any substance that can cause light to diffuse and scatter.

DIN Deutsche Industrie Norm. The German system of rating film sensitivity to light.

Diopter Unit sometimes used to denote the light-bending power of a close-up lens. The diopter value is the number of times its focal length will divide into one meter.

Directional lighting Illumination that creates a shadowed area one side of the subject and lit surfaces on the other, as seen by the camera.

Direct vision viewfinder Sighting device with which the subject is viewed directly, without the aid of a prism or mirror.

Distance symbols Symbols used on the focusing control of some old, simple compacts.

Downrating Exposing a film at a reduced ISO rating. This is usually followed by held-back processing.

Dry mounting Method of attaching prints to flat surfaces by heating a shellac layer, under pressure, between the print and the mount.

DX-code System using electrical contacts in the camera's film chamber to sense checkerboard pattern printed on film cassette. Automatically sets camera for film speed and length.

Electronic flash Equipment that produce a brief pulse of light by electrical discharge through a flash tube.

Emulsion The light-sensitive layers (basically silver halides in gelatin) forming the pale side of the film. After processing, the emulsion carries a permanent, visible image.

Enlargement Print that is larger than the negative used to produce it.

Enprint Small enlarged print, with dimensions of a fixed ratio, produced commercially in an automatic printer.

Ever-ready case Camera case that need not be completely removed to operate the camera controls.

Expiry date Numbers printed on most film boxes indicating the date before which the material should be processed if it is to maintain its stated speed, contrast, and (if color) color balance.

Existing light See Available light.

Exposure The product of the intensity of light reaching the film (controlled by lens aperture) and the length of time this intensity of light is allowed to act (controlled by shutter speed or flash duration).

Exposure latitude The amount by which you can under- or overexpose film and still produce an acceptable result.

Exposure meter Instrument for measuring the amount of light falling on or being reflected by a subject. Generally taken to mean hand meter.

Extension tube (or ring) Metal tube that fits between the lens and the camera body to extend the range of focusing for close-up photography.

Fast film Film which has an emulsion that is very sensitive to light. Such films have high ISO ratings.

Fast lens Lens with a wide maximum aperture (low f number).

Fill-in light Light used to illuminate the subject's shadow side.

Film Photographic material consisting of a thin, transparent plastic base coated with light-sensitive emulsion. After exposure and processing film is left carrying a visible image in black silver or dye.

Film speed The sensitivity of a film emulsion to light. This is expressed as a speed rating number such as ISO.

Film winder Term generally used for a simplified motor drive. Gives automatic wind-on after single exposure. Many also allow continuous rate firing of 2 fps.

Filter Transparent material, such as glass, acetate, or gelatin, which modifies light passing through it.

Filter factor Amount by which unfiltered exposure must be multiplied to give the same exposure effect when the filter is used. Taken into account automatically by most meters reading light through the filter.

Fisheye lens Extreme wide-angle lens uncorrected for linear distortion.

Fixed focus Camera lens offering no method of focus setting adjustment.

Flare Scattered light, often due to reflections within the lens, lens hood, or camera interior. Sometimes used to describe glare from illumination reflected from shiny backgrounds. Gives reduced contrast and degraded shadow areas.

Flash See Electronic flash.

Flash synchronization Arrangement by which the flash fires when the camera shutter is completely open.

Flat lighting Low contrast. Can also mean frontal, flat-on lighting.

F number Number sequence – f2, 2.8, 4, 5.6, 8, etc. – that is equivalent to the focal length divided by the effective diameter of the aperture.

Focal length Basically the distance between the lens and the film, when focused for a subject at infinity.

Focal plane shutter Shutter consisting of blinds or blades positioned just in front of the film surface.

Focus The point at which light rays passing through a lens converge to form a clear and sharply defined image.

Focusing scale Scale of camera-to-subject distances marked on a lens focusing ring.

Focusing screen Plastic or glass screen built into SLR cameras at the same distance from the lens as the film. Allows both viewfinding and focusing.

Fogging Allowing sensitive film to receive generalized, non-image-forming light. Has a darkening effect on negatives, gives a pale, washed-out result on slides. Can also be caused chemically.

Format Size or shape of negative, slide, printing paper, or camera viewing area.

Fresnel Moulded plastic sheet used beneath many focusing screens to improve evenness of illumination. Consists of a series of concentric rings, shaped to direct light toward the viewfinder eyepiece.

Gelatin filters Filters consisting of thin, dyed gelatin sheet.

Graininess Irregular clumps of dye molecules or black metallic silver making up the developed image. Graininess limits the image detail recording ability of the film.

Guide number (GN) Number given by multiplying the flash-to-subject distance by the f number needed to give correct exposure. Often quoted when comparing the light output of different flashguns and, unless otherwise stated, relates to the use of ISO 100 film.

Hard lighting Harsh contrast. Applies to a photograph with an extreme range of tones or colors, perhaps the result of contrasty lighting.

Hide Barrier, hut, or tent used by natural history photographers to conceal themselves.

High key Photograph in which light or pale tones predominate, rather than dark, deeper tones associated with low-key.

Highlights The brightest areas of the subject.

Holding back Shortening the developing time given to a film to help compensate for over-exposure, or reduce image contrast. Also known as "pulling".

Hot shoe Fitting on top of a camera body to hold a flash-gun. It contains electrical connections which automatically make contact between flashgun and shutter synchronization circuit when the shutter release is fired, operating the flash.

Hue The name of a color (for example, red, blue, yellow).

Infinity Focusing setting (often marked ∞ or inf.) at which the lens gives a sharp image of very distant objects, such as the far horizon.

Infrared Band of wavelengths beyond the red end of the spectrum. They are invisible to the human eye, but can be recorded on specially sensitized film.

Inverse square law The intensity of light reaching a surface is quartered each time the distance from a light source is doubled. Does not apply to light sources that are diffused in any way or focused into a beam.

ISO International Standards Organization. Current speed system (embracing ASA and DIN) used to express relative light sensitivity of films.

Key light The principle of a dominant light source illuminating the subject.

Latitude (of exposure) The degree of underexposure and overexposure that a photographic emulsion will tolerate with acceptable results.

Leaf shutter Shutter placed within a compound lens, usually close to the iris diaphragm.

Lens Optical device made of glass or plastic capable of bending light.

Line film High-contrast film that simplifies the final image to two tones only, black and white, for example.

Long-focus lens General term for a 35 mm camera lens having a focal length longer than 50 mm. See also Telephoto lens.

Low key Photograph in which heavy, dark tones predominate, with few highlights. Also applies to lighting that produces such results.

Macro lens A lens – typically 50 or 100 mm – designed to give best image resolution at close subject distances. The lens barrel allows extended focusing movement.

Macrophotography Extreme close-up photography in which images larger than the original subject are recorded without the use of a microscope.

Magenta Purple-red subtractive color, complementary to green.

Magnification Ratio of the height of the image to the height of the subject. When subject and image are the same size magnification is said to be x1.

Matte 1 Cardboard surround for a picture when framed. 2 Term used to describe a non-reflective, non-textured surface.

Mirror lens Telephoto lens using mirrors in its construction to allow an extremely long focal length to be accommodated within a short barrel. The aperture is usually fixed. Such lenses are also known as reflex or catadioptric types.

Mode The programmed operating function of automatic SLR cameras, for example aperture-priority mode or shutter-priority mode.

Monochrome Single colored. Most frequently applied to black and white photographs.

Motor drive Power-driven film wind-on allowing single or continuous firing at a choice of rates, typically up to 5 fps.

Usually an accessory attached to the camera base.

Multimode camera See Mode.

Negative Developed photographic image with subject highlights dark and shadows light. With color materials, each subject color is represented by its complementary hue.

Neutral density filter A gray filter used to reduce the amount of light entering the camera when aperture and speed settings cannot be altered. This filter will not affect the color content of the light.

Normal lens Lens with a focal length approximately equal to the diagonal of the picture format. On 35 mm cameras this is usually 50 mm (SLRs), and 40 mm or 35 mm (compacts). Also known as a standard or prime lens.

Object Generalized term for an element in a scene. Often interchangeable with subject.

Opaque A material or substance that prevents all light from passing through it.

Open flash Technique of firing flash while the shutter remains open on its B setting.

Opening up Increasing the size of the lens aperture to admit more light to the light-sensitive film surface.

Overdevelopment See Push processing.

Overexposure The result of giving a light-sensitive material excessive exposure, either by exposing it to too bright an image or by allowing light to act upon it for too long.

Panning Swinging the camera horizontally in a smooth arc to follow a moving subject. If the shutter is released during panning the subject records sharply against blurred image of static surroundings.

Parallax error Viewpoint difference between the image seen in the viewfinder and the image recorded by the lens. Does not occur with SLR cameras.

Pentaprism Five-sided silvered prism in SLR cameras, used to give an upright left-to-right view of the image on the focusing screen.

Perspective The use of converging lines, differences in scale, or changes of tone with distance, to give an impression of depth in pictures.

Polarized light Rays of light that have been restricted to vibrate in one plane only.

Polarizing filter Colorless filter able to absorb polarized light.

Positive Photographic image in which light and dark areas correspond to the highlights and shadows of the original subject. In a color image, colors are represented truly.

Preview button See Aperture preview.

Primary colors In light, the three primary colors of the spectrum are blue, green, and red. Each contains about one-third of the visible spectrum.

Print An image (normally positive) that has been produced by the action of light (usually passed through a negative or slide) on paper or similar material coated with a light-sensitive emulsion.

Processing General term used to describe the sequence

of steps whereby a latent image is converted into a visible, permanent image.

Pulling See Holding back.

Push processing Extending development, used in conjunction with uprating the ISO speed of the film when exposing. Used to increase speed and contrast.

Reciprocity failure The increasing loss of sensitivity of photographic emulsion when exposures are extremely brief or long.

Red eye Effect where the pupils of a subject's eyes appear red in color photographs taken with certain flash illumination set-ups.

Reflector Any surface from which light can be reflected. In particular white cardboard or similar material, used to reflect light from a main source into shadow areas.

Scale The linear relationship between the size of the subject and the size of its image, or between the size of the negative and the size of the enlargement.

Sharpness Term describing image clarity – the combination of accuracy of focus, freedom from movement blur, and contrast.

Shutter Mechanical system used to control the time that light is allowed to act on a sensitive emulsion.

Shutter-priority mode Semi-automatic exposure system whereby the user selects the shutter speed, and the camera meter then sets the lens aperture.

Shutter speed The time (normally set in fractions of a second) the shutter mechanism effectively allows the film to receive light.

Single lens reflex (SLR) Camera that allows the user to see the exact image formed by the picture-taking lens, by means of a hinged mirror between the lens and film.

Skylight filter Pale pink color correcting filter. Used to eliminate a blue color cast when photographing in dull weather or where light is solely from blue sky.

Slave unit Small electronic relay system that fires one electronic flash in response to light from another. Both flashes are effectively simultaneous.

Slide A positive transparency intended for viewing by projection.

Slow film Film having an emulsion with low sensitivity to light.

Soft focus Purposely diffused image, often a mixture of sharp and unsharp detail.

Spectrum That part of the electro-magnetic spectrum showing the visible colors of red, orange, yellow, green, blue, indigo, and violet, according to wavelength. Mixed together they appear as white light.

Speed See Film speed and Shutter speed.

Split image focusing Focusing system where an area of the subject appears bisected to the viewfinder. The two halves of the bisected image come into alignment when the correct focus is set.

Spotlight Artificial light source that uses a simple focusing system to produce a beam of light of controllable width.

Spot meter Narrow-angle exposure meter used to take accurate light readings from any small area of a subject. Can be used from some distance away.

Standard lens See Normal lens.

Stop See Aperture.

Stopping down Reducing the size of the aperture, by selecting a higher f number, for example.

Strobe General term sometimes used to describe electronic flash equipment generally.

Strobe light Stroboscopic light produced by a special lamp or tube flashing repeatedly at a chosen time frequency.

Subject The person or thing photographed. Often refers to specific, animate things (as opposed to generalized inanimate things referred to as objects).

Telephoto lens Long-focus lens optically designed to be used at less than its focal length from the film – saving length and bulk. (Most long-focus lenses are now of telephoto design and the two terms are used interchangeably.) Forms an enlarged image of distant subjects, has a narrow angle of view, and gives shallow depth of field.

Time exposure General term for an exposure longer than can be set using the camera's fixed shutter speeds.

Tone On a print, slide, or negative, an area that has a uniform density and which can be distinguished from darker or lighter parts.

Translucent Transmits and also scatters light.

Transparency A positive image of any size produced on transparent film.

Transparent Transmits light directly, as with clear glass.

TTL (through the lens) Metering system in which light-sensitive cells within the camera body measure exposure from image-forming light that has passed through the lens.

Tungsten filament lamp Artificial light source using a tungsten filament heated by the passage of electricity, and contained within a glass envelope.

Ultraviolet (UV) Band of wavelengths shorter than the blue end of the spectrum. All films are sensitive to some ultraviolet radiation.

Underdevelopment See Holding back.

Underexposure The result of insufficient exposure – either by exposing it to too dim an image, or giving too short a time.

Uprating Exposing a film at an inflated ISO rating. This is usually followed by push processing.

Viewfinder System for viewing the subject, showing the field of view of the camera lens.

Wide-angle lens 35 mm camera lens having a focal length appreciably shorter than 50 mm. Gives a wide angle of view and considerable depth of field.

X socket Electrical contacts or socket on the camera, marked X. Denotes the connection for an electronic flashgun.

Zoom lens Lens that is constructed to allow continuously variable focal length within a specific range.

Index

A

Action
  conveying 126-7
  impression of 98
Action finder 178
Adaptors
  telephoto 147
  wide-angle 151, 167
Aerial photography 198
Albums, print 180, 182
Anamorphic attachments 168-9
Angle of view 162
Animals 121-3
Aperture 33-8
  position in camera 18
  setting faults 58
  setting ring 24
Aperture-priority exposure system 43, 45
Aquarium
  photographing 142
  reducing glare 123
Architectural photography 138-9
  gridded screen 178, 200
  panoramic cameras 196
  perspective control lens 167
Arctic photography 77
Artificial light
  and color accuracy 82-3
  films for 52-3, 103
  filtering for 82-3, 206
  flash 156-9
Assignments 211
Atmospheric conditions and color 78
Attachments, special effects 184-6
Audio-visual equipment 182
Autobracketing 25
Autofocus 32, 201
  and compacts 22
  – uses 133
Automatic exposure system 43
  advantages 45
Automatic loading/rewind 47
Automatic SLR 23

B

Babies 118-20
Backgrounds 68-71
  exposure problems 44
  losing 72
  suppressing 30
Backlighting 88-9
  for effect 104-5
  exposure problems 44
  and low-key 9

Back projection unit 181
Bags, equipment 177
  for bad conditions 75, 77
  ever-ready case 27
  tips 178
Basic SLR 23
Batteries
  and camera care 27
  for flash 147
  and low temperatures 77
Battery charger 147
Bellows 170-1
  using 143
Birds, photographing 142
Black and white film see Film
Black and white, reproduction of colors in 78
Blank frame 151
Blur
  controlling 40-1
  flash effect 159
  to isolate subject 72
  and movement 98
  zoom effect 168-9
Bounce board 147
Bouncing flash 152, 154
Bracketing exposure 42
  automatic 25
B shutter setting 93
  using 40
Bulk film back 179
Bulk film loader 64

C

Cable release 176
Camera bodies
  buying 172
  using two 48
Camera care 26-7
  in extreme climates 77
  tips 48
Camera movement 93
Cameras 18-48
  automated loading 47
  choosing 200
  compact 20-2
  data 200-1
  handling 26
  and high or low temperatures 77
  holding still 26
  opening safely 46
  panoramic 196-7
  single lens reflex 23-5
  special 196-8
  still video 197
  underwater 196
  using 6-8
Camera settings
  faults 58-9

for flash 147
  shutter 39-43
Camera shake 59
  avoiding 26
Candids 132-3
Capacitor, flash 146
Cases, equipment 177-8
  ever-ready 27
  for extreme conditions 77
Cassettes 46-7, 50
Casts see Color casts
Center-weighted meter 43-4
Charge-ready lamp 146
Chemical reduction 58
Children 118-20
Circular image 169
Circus, photographing at 124
Cleaning lenses 27, 48
Climates, working in extreme 77
Close-up equipment 170-1
Close-ups
  in bad weather 75-6
  and contrast 85
  focusing screen for 200
  lighting for texture 106-7
  shooting into the light 89
Clouds 90-2
  filtration for 81
  and polarizer 173
Co-axial socket 146
Cold conditions 77
Color
  avoiding inaccurate 82-3
  false 188
  intensifying 78-9
  overall 59
  special effects 185-6
Color balance 53
  matching film to light 103
Color casts 151
  green 83
  on negatives 57
  overall 59
  with window light 102
Color correction 102
Color films see Film
Color filters see Filters
Colors
  appearance in black and white 78
  bright 78-9
  complementary 78
  – principle 173
  showing as tones 80-1
Compact cameras 20-2
  aperture 38
  autofocus uses 133
  compared to SLR 18-19
  and flash 147
  focus controls 30-1
  framing errors 28-9

Acknowledgments

Author's acknowledgments
I would firstly like to thank the Dorling Kindersley team – especially Jonathan Hilton and Neville Graham, for editing and design. Thanks also to Tim Whale for his encouragement, Tim Stephens for technical help, and to my wife Pamela for typing her seventeenth book.

I appreciate the co-operation of the many manufacturers and suppliers who loaned products. Thanks also go to photographers Martin Dohrn, Tim Woodcock, John Sims, Robin Bath, Arlene Restaino, Anthea Sieveking, and many others. Their pictures add greatly to the range of approaches shown. Most of all I acknowledge the value of questions from students and amateur photographers, for it is around these questions that most of the contents of this book have been structured.
Michael Langford

Dorling Kindersley would like to extend thanks to Vic Chambers, Tony Wallace, David Mellor (Negs), Brian Retter (Airedale Graphics), Richard Dawes, Carl Zeiss Jena Ltd, Bowens Sales and Service Ltd, CPS Advertising Limited, Tom E. Cooper, and John Walsh (Micrographia) for the grain enlargements on pp. 52–3.

Photographers
Key t=top, c=center, b=bottom, l=left, r=right

Mike Anderson 171
Nic Barlow 188t
Robin Bath 6b, 13, 14, 15b, 44r, 55tl, 75, 80, 87r, 90b, 91b, 106t, 110l, 130t, 131t, 184
Mark Bayley 153bl, 159
Michael Boys 140b
David Bradfield 163
John Chitty 105
John Cleare (Mountain Camera) 57, 198
Amanda Currey 114t
Andrew de Lory 8, 9b, 28c (pair), 30, 32, 36, 37, 40, 42, 44tl, 52tl (pair) and bl (pair), 54b, 66b, 67cl, 68t, 69cr, 70, 71, 72, 73t, 72b, 76, 77, 79b, 85, 86t, 88r, 89b, 90c, 93tr, 96b, 98, 103c, 112tr, 114b, 115, 117t, 120b, 123c and bl and br, 124t, 127bl, 129, 134bl, 136b, 137, 150, 151cl and r, 155b, 156bl and br, 165, 168 c (pair) and b, 173, 175r, 185, 186b, 188b, 190, 191t, 193b, 194t.
Martin Dohrn Title page, 7, 10c, 16, 26, 28r (pair), 29r (pair), 31bl, 33, 34, 46–7, 63, 73b, 82c and b, 83c and t, 100, 101, 102, 104r, 107t, 109, 131c, 142, 143, 144bl and br, 146, 147, 151bl, 152, 153t, 154, 155t, 156tl and tc and tr, 157, 158, 195
Lori Eiseman 141
Calvin Evans 186 (second from bottom)
Franco Fontana 164
Joanna Godfrey Wood 9t, 54t, 87l
Jonathan Hilton 82t, 120t
Michael Langford 11, 15tl and tr, 28l (pair), 29l and c, 31tr and br, 50, 55tr, 56, 68bl and br, 74t, 83b, 90t, 92, 93b, 94b, 95t and b, 96t, 97, 104l, 106b, 107bl and br, 110tr and br, 121r, 127br, 128, 130b, 131b, 134t, 135b, 136tc, 138t, 144t, 169, 175t, 186 (second from top), 188c, 193t
Ian McKinnell 166
Trevor Melton 86l, 108, 151tl
Erik Pelham 10t, 118r, 124b, 126t

Arlene Restaino 66tr and cr, 103b, 116, 117b, 121l, 122, 123t, 125, 135t, 138bl and br, 139
Ken Sharp 132t
Anthea Sieveking 12, 84b, 119
John Sims 6t, 10b, 38, 45, 55br, 69t, 79t, 91t, 103t, 126b, 127t, 132bl and br, 133, 138c, 139, 140t
John Starr 99
Tim Stephens 186t, 187, 189t, 191cb, 192, 194b
Dick Swayne 160
John Wainwright 144c
Tim Woodcock 20, 22, 25, 41, 44bl, 67tl and tr, 69cl, 78, 81, 84t, 88, 89t (pair) and c, 93tl, 118l, 134br, 167l and r, 168t, 172b, 179, 197

Illustrators
Kuo Kang Chen
Les Smith
David Worth
Gary Marsh
Nicholas Harris
Norman Lacey
Jim Robins

Photographic services
Negs
Paulo Colour Processing